The musicsocket.com
Music Industry Directory 2023

The **music**socket.com
Music Industry Directory 2023

EDITOR
J. PAUL DYSON

Published in 2022 by JP&A Dyson
27 Old Gloucester Street, London WC1N 3AX, United Kingdom
Copyright JP&A Dyson

https://www.jpandadyson.com
https://www.musicsocket.com

ISBN 978-1-909935-44-0

All rights reserved. No part of this publication may be reproduced or transmitted in any form or by any means, or stored in any retrieval system without prior written permission. **MusicSocket**, the **MusicSocket** logo, and the **MusicSocket** oval are trademarks of JP&A Dyson trading as **MusicSocket**. Whilst every effort is made to ensure that all information contained within this publication is accurate, no liability can be accepted for any mistakes or omissions, or for losses incurred as a result of actions taken in relation to information provided. Unless otherwise stated, **MusicSocket** is not associated with and does not endorse, recommend, or guarantee any of the organisations or persons listed within this publication. Inclusion does not constitute recommendation.

**Registered with the IP Rights Office
Copyright Registration Service
Ref: 3365373239**

Foreword

This directory includes hundreds of listings of **record labels** and **managers**, updated in MusicSocket's online databases between 2020 and 2022.

It also provides free access to the entire current databases, including over 1,300 record labels, and over 500 managers, with dozens of new and updated listings every month.

For details on how to claim your free access please see the back of this book.

Included in the subscription
A subscription to the full website is not only free with this book, but comes packed with all the following features:

Advanced search features

- Save searches and save time – set up to 15 search parameters specific to your work, save them, and then access the search results with a single click whenever you log in. You can even save multiple different searches if you have different types of work you are looking to place.
- Add personal notes to listings, visible only to you and fully searchable – helping you to organise your actions.
- Set reminders on listings to notify you when to submit your work, when to follow up, when to expect a reply, or any other custom action.
- Track which listings you've viewed and when, to help you organise your search – any listings which have changed since you last viewed them will be highlighted for your attention!

Daily email updates
As a subscriber you will be able to take advantage of our email alert service, meaning you can specify your particular interests and we'll send you automatic email updates when we change or add a listing that matches them. So if you're interested in labels dealing in hard rock in the United States you can have us send you emails with the latest updates about them – keeping you up to date without even having to log in.

User feedback
Our databases include a user feedback feature that allows our subscribers to leave feedback on each listing – giving you not only the chance to have your say about the markets you contact, but giving a unique artist's perspective on the listings.

Claim your free access to www.musicsocket.com: See p.211

Save on copyright protection fees

If you're sending your work away to record labels and managers you should first consider protecting your copyright. As a subscriber to **MusicSocket** you can do this through our site and save 10% on the copyright registration fees normally payable for protecting your work internationally through the Intellectual Property Rights Office (https://www.Copyright RegistrationService.com).

For details on how to claim your free access please see the back of this book.

Contents

Foreword v
Contents vii
Protecting Your Copyright 1

Record Labels
US Record Labels 3
UK Record Labels 39
Canadian Record Labels 79
Record Labels Index 81

Managers
US Managers 105
UK Managers 143
Canadian Managers 189
Managers Index 191

Free Access
Get Free Access to the MusicSocket Website 211

Protecting Your Copyright

Protecting your copyright is by no means a requirement before submitting your work, but you may feel that it is a prudent step that you would like to take before allowing strangers to hear your material.

These days, you can register your work for copyright protection quickly and easily online. The Intellectual Property Rights Office operates a website called the "Copyright Registration Service" which allows you to do this:

- *https://www.CopyrightRegistrationService.com*

This website can be used for material created in any nation signed up to the Berne Convention. This includes the United States, United Kingdom, Canada, Australia, Ireland, New Zealand, and most other countries. There are around 180 countries in the world, and over 160 of them are part of the Berne Convention.

Provided you created your work in one of the Berne Convention nations, your work should be protected by copyright in all other Berne Convention nations. You can therefore protect your copyright around most of the world with a single registration, and because the process is entirely online you can have your work protected in a matter of minutes.

US Record Labels

For the most up-to-date listings of these and hundreds of other record labels, visit https://www.musicsocket.com/recordlabels

*To claim your **free** access to the site, please see the back of this book.*

76Label Music
Email: 76labelmusic@gmail.com
Website: http://www.76label.com
Website: https://myspace.com/76label

Genres: Electronic; Dance; Pop

Contact: Tommy McGinnis

Founded in 1999 as an independent record label and artist marketing company, now also deals in writer management and marketing.

Abet Publishing
Website: https://www.abetpublishing.com
Website: https://twitter.com/AbetPublishing

Genres: Pop; Rock; World; Electronic; Acoustic; Ambient; Chill; Alternative; Classical

A multimedia publishing company offering eclectic variety of genres. From world music, classical to cutting-edge electronica, acoustic, ambient, chill mood, rock, and alternative.

ABKCO Music & Records Inc.
Fax: +1 (212) 582-5090
Email: info@abkco.com
Website: https://www.abkco.com
Website: https://www.facebook.com/abkco/

Genres: Pop; R&B; Rock

Handles pop, R&B, and rock. Does not accept unsolicited mss. Submission policy on website states that by submitting any material you automatically transfer all rights to them over that work.

Acony Records
PO Box 60007
Nashville, TN 37206
Email: information@aconyrecords.com
Website: http://www.aconyrecords.com

Genres: Folk; Roots

Folk and roots label based in Nashville, Tennessee.

Aeronaut Records
PO Box 26621
Los Angeles, CA 90026
Website: http://www.aeronautrecords.com
Website: https://www.facebook.com/AeronautRecords

Genres: Pop; Rock

Pop/rock label based in Los Angeles, California. An independent label that "attempts to release music that doesn't suck".

All Star Music Corporation
9663 Santa Monica Boulevard
Beverly Hills, CA 90210-4303
Email: rnathanfriedman@gmail.com

*Claim your free access to **www.musicsocket.com**: See p.211*

4 US Record Labels

Genres: All types of music

Contact: Jodi White

Record label based in Beverly Hills.

Alpha Pup Records
Email: hello@alphapuprecords.com
Website: http://www.alphapuprecords.com
Website: https://twitter.com/ALPHAPUP

Genres: Indie; Electronic; Hip-Hop; Pop

Spotify-preferred Distributor and Record Label. 100% family-owned. Celebrating diversity and brilliant artistry since 2004.

American Gramaphone
9130 Mormon Bridge Road
Omaha, NE 68152
Email: mailbox@mannheimsteamroller.com
Website: http://www.
mannheimsteamroller.com

Genres: Classical

Contact: Chip Davis

Label based in Omaha, Nebraska.

Amherst Record Sales, Inc.
Email: info@amherstrecords.com
Website: https://www.amherstrecords.com

Genres: R&B; Jazz; Rock; Pop

Label handling R&B, Jazz, Pop, and Rock.

Amulet Records, Inc.
Email: billy@amuletrecords.com
Website: http://www.amuletrecords.com
Website: https://www.facebook.com/Amulet-Records-2071064413172768/

Genres: Experimental; Avant-Garde

Contact: Billy Martin

Experimental record label specialising in percussion and avant-garde.

Aphagia Recordings
San Francisco
Website: https://www.
aphagiarecordings.com

Website: https://aphagiarecordings.bandcamp.com/

Genres: Experimental Electronic Industrial Progressive Glitch Instrumental Rock Soundtracks

A San Francisco based Independent Record Label focusing on odd forms of electronic and rock music.

Arista Nashville
Website: https://www.
sonymusicnashville.com/label/arista-nashville/

Genres: Country

Record label specialising in Country music.

Arkadia Entertainment Corp
PO Box 77
Saugerties, NY 12477
Email: info@arkadiarecords.com
Website: https://arkadiarecords.com
Website: https://www.facebook.com/arkadiarecords

Genres: Jazz; World

Record label based in Saugerties, New York.

Artists' Addiction Records
Fax: +1 (818) 230-9800
Email: info@artistsaddiction.com
Email: services@artistsaddiction.com
Website: http://www.artistsaddiction.com

Genres: Soundtracks

Contact: Jonathan Scott Miller

Record label based in Encino, California, focusing on film and TV soundtracks.

Aspenbeat LLC
Website: https://aspenbeat.com
Website: https://www.facebook.com/aspenbeat

Genres: All types of music

Radio show, record label, and playlist curation.

US Record Labels

Asylum Records
Website: https://www.asylumrecords.com
Website: https://www.facebook.com/asylumrecordsus

Genres: Hip-Hop; Rap

Rap and hip hop label.

Atlan-Dec/Grooveline Records
2529 Green Forest Ct./P.O.Box 1676
Snellville, GA 30078-4183
Fax: +1 (770) 985-1686
Email: Atlandec@Prodigy.net
Website: http://www.atlan-dec.com

Genres: Country; Hip-Hop; Jazz; Pop; R&B; Rap; Rock; Urban; Rhythm and Blues

Record label based in Snellville, Georgia.

AvatarDigi
2029 Hyperion Avenue
Los Angeles, CA 90027
Email: info@avatardigi.com
Website: http://www.avatardigi.com

Genres: All types of music

Digital music distributor allowing you to place your music on iTunes, etc. directly. $50 set-up cost, then royalty on sales.

BackWords Recordings
334 Tonti St.
South Bend, IN 46617-1149
Email: tim@backwordsrecordings.com
Website: https://www.backwordsrecordings.com

Genres: Avant-Garde; Alternative; Electronic; Melodic; Psychedelic; Traditional; Spoken Word; Singer-Songwriter; Rock; Mystical; Instrumental; Indie;; Guitar based; Classical

Contact: Tim Backer

An Independent Culture Production House.

Basin Street Records
5500 Prytania Street, #110
New Orleans, LA 70115
Fax: +1 (504) 483-7877
Email: info@basinstreetrecords.com
Website: http://www.basinstreetrecords.com
Website: https://www.facebook.com/BasinStreetRecords

Genres: Blues; Jazz; Latin; Pop; R&B; Rock

Record label based in New Orleans.

Berman Brothers
Email: info@bermanbrothers.com
Email: carloc@bermanbrothers.com
Website: https://bermanbrothers.com
Website: http://www.facebook.com/bermanbrothers

Genres: Dance; Pop; R&B

Contact: Christian Berman; Frank Berman

A two-brother team. Recipients of more than 90 gold and platinum awards, two BMI awards, a Golden Globe nomination, a Grammy nomination and a Grammy Award.

Better Looking Records
Website: https://betterlookingrecords.com
Website: https://www.facebook.com/betterlookingrecords

Genres: Alternative; Modern Rock

Contact: David Brown; Paul Fischer

An independent record label founded in 2000. Offices are headquartered in the founder's bedrooms in Los Angeles and New York.

Better Looking Records
Website: https://betterlookingrecords.com
Website: https://www.facebook.com/betterlookingrecords

Genres: Indie; Rock

Indie and rock label based in Los Angeles, California.

Bifocal Media
Email: charles@bifocalmedia.com
Website: https://bifocalmedia.com

Genres: Electronic; Hardcore; Punk; Rap; Hip-Hop

Contact: Charles Cardello; Brad Scott

US Record Labels

Media company founded in 1997.

Big3 Records, Inc.
6090 Central Avenue
St. Petersburg, FL 33707
Email: jb@big3entertainment.com
Website: http://www.big3records.com
Website: https://www.facebook.com/Big3Records/

Genres: All types of music

Record label based in St Petersburg, Florida. Embraces the philosophy that whether reinventing an established artist or developing and introducing new talent to the world, the artist and music comes first.

Blue Jackel Entertainment
PO Box 87
Huntington, NY 11743-0087
Email: info@bluejackel.com
Website: http://www.bluejackel.com

Genres: Electronic; Folk; Jazz; Latin; Roots; World

Record label based in Huntington, New York.

Blue Wave Records
3221 Perryville Road
Baldwinsville, NY 13027
Email: info@bluewaverecords.com
Website: https://www.bluewaverecords.com
Website: https://www.facebook.com/Blue-Wave-Records-2387752671363478

Genres: Blues; Non-Commercial;

Describes itself as an "ARTIST ORIENTED, NON-COMMERCIAL, INDEPENDENT MUSIC LABEL". Handles blues and blues-related music.

Boosweet Records
Website: https://boosweet.com

Genres: Jazz; Alternative; Country; Dance; Classical; Rock; Metal; Latin; R&B; Hip-Hop; Rap; Blues; Folk; Acoustic; Pop

Describes itself as "a full-service indie music label with industry critical global connections along with worldwide presence and reach."

Broken Arrow Records
Email: info@brokenarrowmusic.com
Website: https://www.brokenarrowmusic.com
Website: https://www.facebook.com/BrokenArrowMusicMkt

Genres: Rock; Singer-Songwriter

Independent label and artist marketing management featuring melodic singer/songwriters from America, Germany, Switzerland, Iceland and elsewhere.

Broken Bow Records
Email: contactus@bbrmusicgroup.com
Website: https://www.bbrmusicgroup.com
Website: https://www.facebook.com/BBRMusicGroup/

Genres: Country

Founded in 1997, quickly grew from a fledgling independent label into one of the largest independent Country label groups in the US.

Brunswick Record Corporation
157 E. Franklin St., Suite 5
Chapel Hill, NC 27514
Fax: +1 (984) 999-4339
Website: https://brunswickrecords.com

Genres: R&B

Record label based in Chapel Hill, North Carolina.

Capitol Latin
Website: https://www.universalmusica.com/labels/capital-latin
Website: https://www.facebook.com/universalmusica

Genres: Latin

Record label dealing in Latin music.

Casablanca Records
Website: https://www.casablancarecords.com
Website: https://www.facebook.com/casablancarecs

Genres: Electronic; Dance

Record label with a focus on dance and electronic music.

Cexton Records
Email: johncexton@aol.com
Website: https://www.cexton.com

Genres: Jazz; Swing

An Audiophile Jazz, Big Band and Italian Music Record Label started in 1984, featuring live recordings and top quality audio CDs

Chiaroscuro Records
100 WVIA Way
Pittston, PA 18640
Email: info@chiaroscurojazz.org
Website: http://www.chiaroscurojazz.com

Genres: Jazz

Jazz label based in Pittston, Pennsylvania.

Columbia Nashville
Website: https://www.sonymusicnashville.com/label/columbia-nashville/

Genres: Country

Country music focused subdivision of major international label. Based in Nashville, Tennessee.

Craniality Sounds
Email: cranialitysounds@gmail.com
Website: http://www.cranialitysounds.com
Website: https://www.facebook.com/CranialitySounds/

Genres: Underground House; Underground Dance; Funky House

An underground house music label dedicated to bringing out the essence and eclectic of underground dance music while having fun at it. Focus is funky house music, but have been known to drop other styles of house music.

Crosscheck Records
Silver Lake
Los Angeles, CA
Website: http://www.cmhlabelgroup.com/

Genres: Punk; Rap

Rap and punk label based in Silver Lake, Los Angeles.

Dancing Cat Records
Email: jennifer@dancingcat.com
Website: https://www.dancingcat.com
Website: https://www.facebook.com/DancingCatRecords/

Genres: Instrumental; World

This label's dual mission for the past 20 years has been to produce and promote the music of George Winston, as well as Hawaiian slack key guitar. The production wing of the company is the in-house management and concert production company for George Winston and also assists in the coordination of slack key guitar concerts.

Decca Records US
Website: http://www.deccarecordsus.com

Genres: Mainstream

Releases music that appeals to a mainstream, broad audience.

Delicious Vinyl LLC
6607 Sunset Blvd.
Los Angeles, CA 90028
Email: contact@deliciousvinyl.com
Website: https://www.facebook.com/deliciousvinyl
Website: https://twitter.com/DeliciousVinyl

Genres: Hip-Hop; Pop; Rap; Reggae; Rock

Record label based in Los Angeles.

Dim Mak Records
Los Angeles
Email: syncs@dimmak.com

US Record Labels

Email: sponsorships@dimmak.com
Website: https://www.dimmak.com
Website: https://www.facebook.com/dimmak

Genres: Pop; Punk; Rap; Hip-Hop; Rock; Dance; Electronic; Indie

Send links to music online via online demo submission form.

Dischord Records
3819 Beecher St. NW
Washington, DC 20007-1802
Email: orders@dischord.com
Website: http://www.dischord.com

Genres: Punk; Rock

Only releases music by bands in the DC area, through an organic process of getting to know bands active in the area. No formal contracts.

Dorado Music (US)
4770 Biscayne Blvd. Suite 900
Miami, FL 33137
Email: contact@dorado.net
Website: https://dorado.net
Website: https://www.facebook.com/doradorecords/

Genres: Acid Jazz; Drum and Bass; Jazz

Label with offices in London and Miami.

Downtown Music
155 6th Avenue, Floor 15
New York, NY 10013
Website: https://www.downtownmusic.com
Website: https://twitter.com/downtownmusic

Genres: Indie; Pop; Rock; Singer-Songwriter; Urban

Record label based in New York.

East of Sideways Music
Email: ContactEOS@eastofsideways.com
Website: https://www.eastofsideways.com
Website: https://www.youtube.com/user/barrykeenan

Genres: Blues; Country; Electronic; Jazz; Latin; Pop; Rap; Hip-Hop; Rock; Urban

"All of the songs in our catalog are lyrically well-written, with exceptional melodies, and top notch instrumental and production values.

Our music is distinctive, affecting, and thought provoking."

Easy Star Records
PO Box 1069, Cooper Station
New York, NY 10276
Fax: +1 (646) 602-9655
Email: easystar@easystar.com
Website: http://www.easystar.com
Website: https://www.facebook.com/EasyStarRecords/

Genres: Reggae

Reggae label based in New York, not currently accepting submissions as at April 2021. Any demos submitted will not be listened to, or returned.

Ecko Records
485 North Hollywood Street
Memphis, TN 38112
Fax: +1 (901) 320-9251
Website: http://www.eckorecords.com

Genres: Contemporary Blues; R&B; Soul; Gospel

Contact: John Ward; Larry Chambers

Label founded in 1995 in Memphis, Tennessee, describing itself as "home of great contemporary Soul, Blues and Gospel Music".

Eclipse Records, inc.
c/o A&R Submissions
P.O. Box 51
Pompton Plains, NJ 07444-0051
Website: https://www.eclipserecords.com/
Website: https://www.facebook.com/eclipserecords

Genres: Alternative; Rock

Record label based in Pompton Plains, New Jersey. Submit through form on website, or by post. See website for full submission guidelines.

Access more listings online at **www.musicsocket.com**

US Record Labels 9

eenie meenie records
PO Box 691397
Los Angeles, CA 90069
Email: reiko@eeniemeenie.com
Website: https://www.eeniemeenie.com
Website: https://www.facebook.com/eeniemeenierecords

Genres: Electronic; Indie; Pop; Rock; Singer-Songwriter; Dance

Aims to help artists develop and market their music by providing ongoing and extensive press and radio campaigns, tour promotion, festival exposure, street marketing, film and TV licensing, retail marketing and merchandising.

Emperor Jones Records
PO Box 4730
Austin, TX 78765
Email: brutus@emperorjones.com
Website: http://www.emperorjones.com

Genres: Alternative; Folk; Indie

Record label based in Austin, Texas.

ESP-Disk' Ltd
365 West End Ave. #203
New York, NY 10024
Email: shipping@espdisk.com
Website: http://espdisk.com

Genres: All types of music

Record label based in New York.

Fantasy Records
Email: support@fantasyrecordings.com
Website: https://fantasyrecordings.com
Website: https://www.facebook.com/FantasyRecords

Genres: All types of music

Established in San Francisco in 1949. A home for innovative, authentic artists whose music impacts the world.

Fat Wreck Chords
2196 Palou Ave.
San Francisco, CA 94124
Email: mailbag@fatwreck.com
Website: https://fatwreck.com
Website: https://www.facebook.com/fatwrecksf/

Genres: Alternative; Punk; Rock

Contact: Mike

Independent record label based in San Francisco. Send demos by email.

Favored Nations Entertainment
17328 Ventura Boulevard, Suite 165
Encino, CA 91316
Email: info@favorednations.com
Website: https://www.favorednations.com
Website: https://www.facebook.com/Favorednationsentertainment

Genres: Contemporary; Blues; Classical; Jazz; Metal; New Age; Rock; Acoustic

Contact: Steve Vai

Record label based in Encino, California. Approach by email if you'd like to submit music for consideration.

Fedora
106 West 71st Street
New York, NY 10023
Fax: +1 (212) 877-0407
Email: jazzdepo@ix.netcom.com
Website: http://www.jazzdepot.com

Genres: Blues

Blues record label based in New York, dealing with artists whose lineage reaches back to the roots of blues.

5 Points Records
12 West 37th Street, 4th Floor
New York, NY 10018
Fax: +1 (212) 629-0017
Email: demos@5pointsrecords.com
Website: http://www.5pointsrecords.com

Genres: Contemporary; Electronic; Dance; Pop

Aims to release a wide range of music, including electronica, dance and pop. Accepts unsolicited demos, but no items returned and no phone calls regarding

Claim your free access to www.musicsocket.com: See p.211

10   US Record Labels

submissions. Accepts MySpace links by email, but no MP3s.

Freddie Records
5979 S Staples St
Corpus Christi, TX 78413
Fax: +1 (361) 992-8428
Email: martzcommusic@gmail.com
Website: https://www.freddiestore.com
Website: https://www.facebook.com/FreddieRecords/

Genres: Hip-Hop; Latin; Rap; Urban

Record label based in Corpus Christi, Texas.

Gearhead Records
PO Box 2375
Elk Grove, CA 95759
Email: info@gearheadhq.com
Email: michelle@gearheadhq.com
Website: https://www.gearheadhq.com

Genres: Punk; Rock; Rock and Roll; New Wave Power Pop; Melodic Punk

Record label based in Elk Grove, California. Do not send demos. Instead, get involved with the community, and – if you are good enough – you will get noticed.

GNP Crescendo Records
Email: gnp@pacificnet.net
Website: http://store.gnpcrescendo.com
Website: https://www.facebook.com/gnpcrescendo/

Genres: Blues; Country; Dance; Electronic; Folk; Jazz; Latin; Pop; Rock; Soundtracks; World

Label based in Los Angeles, California.

Grim Reality Entertainment, LLC
1209 Northwest Hwy, #143
Garland, TX 75041
Email: grimrealityent@gmail.com
Website: https://grimrealityentertainment.net
Website: https://www.facebook.com/Grimrealityent

Genres: Underground Hip-Hop; Rap

Aan independent hip-hop label based out of California, USA, with regional, national, and international acts.

Harmonized Records
Asheville:

107 McFalls Road
Asheville, NC 28806

Mebane:

6520 Oak Grove Church Rd.
Mebane, NC 27302
Website: https://www.harmonizedrecords.com

Genres: Blues; Electronic; Jazz; Rock

Contact: Brian Asplin; Lee Crumpton

Record label with offices in Asheville and Mebane.

Heads Up International
Website: https://concord.com/labels/heads-up-international/

Genres: Contemporary Instrumental; Contemporary Jazz; Traditional Jazz; World; Contemporary Latin Jazz

Founded in 1990 to release contemporary instrumental music.

Heartland Recordings
337 Dearstone Private Drive
Bristol, TN 37620
Email: heartlandrecordings@btes.tv
Website: http://www.heartlandrecordings.com

Genres: Americana; Acoustic; Christian; Folk; Gospel; Roots; Singer-Songwriter; Country

Founded in 1987. We are dedicated to preserving and promoting Bluegrass, Folk, Americana and other forms of acoustic music.

We are located in the heart of the Appalachian Mountains. In the middle of the richest Bluegrass music scenes in the country.

Heaven's Disciples, LLC
Email: info@heavensdisciples.com
Email: rodney.burutsa@heavensdisciples.com
Website: https://www.heavensdisciples.com
Website: https://twitter.com/HeavensDisciple

Genres: Christian Rap; Christian R&B; Christian Reggae; Christian Reggaeton; Christian Rhythm and Blues; Instrumental

Contact: Rodney Burutsa

A multimedia entertainment company featuring music, books, comics, films, games, merchandise, and clothing.

HighNote Records
106 West 71st Street
New York, NY 10023
Fax: +1 (212) 877-0407
Email: jazzdepo@ix.netcom.com
Website: http://www.jazzdepot.com
Website: https://www.facebook.com/HighNoteRecords

Genres: Jazz

Jazz record label based in New York.

Hydra Head Records
Website: http://www.hydrahead.com
Website: https://www.facebook.com/hydrahead

Genres: Hard Rock; Metal; Experimental; Hardcore

Independent record label specialising in heavy and experimental music.

iHipHop Distribution
8033 West Sunset Boulevard
Suite 1038
Los Angeles, CA 90046
Email: pr@ihiphopdistribution.com
Website: https://distribution.ihiphop.com
Website: https://www.facebook.com/ihiphop

Genres: Hip-Hop

Founded in 2009 in an attempt to provide artists with a new paradigm for distributing their music and building their brand. Has worked successfully with many artists (check out our list of Top Sellers) and continues its partnership with the A3C Hip-Hop Festival for the release of its annual hip-hop compilation.

Also maintains its own innovative worldwide digital distribution platform, providing superior distribution and marketing services to artists worldwide.

Integrity Music
1646 Westgate Circle, Suite 106
Brentwood, TN 37027
Email: CustomerCare@IntegrityMusic.com
Website: https://www.integritymusic.com

Genres: Christian; Gospel

Christian gospel label based in Colorado Springs. Not accepting submissions as at August 2021.

Invisible Records
Chicago
Website: http://www.invisiblerecords.com
Website: https://www.facebook.com/InvisibleRecords

Genres: Gothic; Metal; Rock

Contact: Katie/Jarin

Record label based in Chicago, specialising in goth, metal and rock.

Island Records (US)
1755 Broadway
New york, NY 10018
Website: http://www.islandrecords.com
Website: https://www.facebook.com/IslandRecords

Genres: Contemporary; Indie; Metal; Pop; Punk; R&B; Rap; Hip-Hop; Rock; Urban

Record label based in New York.

Jade Tree
2310 Kennwynn Road
Wilmington, DE 19810
Email: jadetree@jadetree.com
Website: https://jadetree.com
Website: https://soundcloud.com/jadetree/

US Record Labels

Genres: Hardcore; Pop; Punk; Rock

Contact: Tim Owen; Darren Walters

Independent record company based in Wilmington, DE.

K2B2 Records
Email: webmaster@k2b2.com
Website: https://www.k2b2.com
Website: https://www.facebook.com/k2b2records/

Genres: Blues; Classical; Jazz; Avant-Garde Jazz

Record label founded in 1979 as an outlet for the distribution of unorthodox yet locally popular avant-garde jazz that the major jazz labels weren't interested in.

!K7 Records
55 Washington Street
Suite 734, Brooklyn, NY 11201
Website: https://k7.com
Website: https://www.instagram.com/k7.music

Genres: All types of music

Record label based in Berlin, Germany, with offices in Brooklyn, New York, and London.

King Street Sounds
New York, NY
Email: rich@kingstreetsounds.com
Website: https://www.kingstreetsounds.com
Website: https://soundcloud.com/kingstreetsounds

Genres: Electronic; Dance

Record label based in New York. Send demos by email.

Knife Fight Media
Email: alexander@knifefightmedia.com
Website: http://www.knifefightmedia.com
Website: https://www.facebook.com/knifefightmedia

Genres: Electronic; Metal; Punk; Rock

Record label based in Red Bank, New Jersey.

Knitting Factory Records
Email: info@knittingfactoryrecords.com
Website: https://store.partisanrecords.com/knitting-factory-records
Website: https://www.knittingfactory.com

Genres: Contemporary; Blues; Country; Electronic; Folk; Jazz; Metal; Punk; Rock; World

Company including labels, music venue and concert tour promotion.

Kung Fu Records
P.O. Box 3061
Seal Beach CA, 90740
Email: info@kungfurecords.com
Website: http://www.kungfurecords.com
Website: https://www.facebook.com/KungFuRecords/

Genres: Hardcore; Pop; Punk; Rock

Record label based in Seal Beach, California. Send links to music online by email. No CDs.

La Corporación Muzic
Email: info@lacorpamuzic.com
Website: http://www.lacorpamuzic.com
Website: https://www.facebook.com/LACORPAMUZIC
Website: https://myspace.com/lacorpamuzic

Genres: Electronic; Latin; Reggae; Pop; Rock; Alternative; Rap; Latin Urban

Record label based in City of Industry, California.

Light In The Attic
P.O. Box 31970
Seattle, WA 98103
Fax: +1 (206) 706-1008
Email: info@lightintheattic.net
Website: https://lightintheattic.net

Genres: All types of music

Contact: Matt Sullivan; Josh Wright

Record label based in Seattle.

Lookout! Records
Website: https://www.lookoutrecords.com

---

*Access more listings online at **www.musicsocket.com***

US Record Labels 13

Genres: Punk; Rock

Punk/rock label based in Berkely, California.

Loveslap! Recordings
Website: http://www.loveslap.com
Website: https://www.facebook.com/LoveslapRecordings

Genres: Dance; House

Independent record label and publisher founded in San Francisco in 1997.

Lovitt Records
Post Office Box 100248
Arlington, VA 22210-9998
Fax: +1 (703) 824-0511
Website: http://www.lovitt.com
Website: https://www.facebook.com/lovittrecords

Genres: Indie; Punk

Record label based in Arlington, Virginia. Accepts demos by post but has never yet signed a band from a demo – usually this happens by bands being seen at shows, doing shows with bands already on the roster, etc.

Luaka Bop
New York
Email: iwasthinking@luakabop.com
Website: https://www.luakabop.com
Website: https://www.facebook.com/luakabop1989

Genres: World

Contact: David Byrne

Record label based in New York.

Mailboat Records
15250 Ventura Blvd. Suite #400
Sherman Oaks, CA 91403
Fax: +1 (818) 501-1568
Email: info@mailboatrecords.com
Website: https://www.mailboatrecords.com

Genres: Country; Folk; Pop; Rock

Label established in 1999, based in Sherman Oaks, California.

Malaco Music Group
PO Box 9287
Jackson, MS 39286-9287
Fax: +1 (601) 982-4528
Email: demo@malaco.com
Email: malaco@malaco.com
Website: https://www.malaco.com
Website: https://www.facebook.com/malacomusic

Genres: Blues; Gospel; R&B; Soul; Jazz

Record label based in Jackson, Mississippi. Send demos by email.

Manifesto Records, Inc.
1180 South Beverly Drive, Suite 510
Los Angeles, CA 90035-1157
Fax: +1 (310) 556-9801
Email: csc@manifesto.com
Website: https://manifesto.com

Genres: Alternative; Pop; Rock; Punk; Indie

Contact: Evan S. Cohen

Record label based in Los Angeles.

Mega Truth Records
Website: http://www.jonbare.net/jonbaremegatruth.htm

Genres: Blues; Rock

Contact: Jon Bare

Independent record label devoted to "capturing the world's best musicians playing music that makes you feel good".

Megawave Records
Email: info@megawavemusic.com
Website: http://www.megawaverecords.com

Genres: Blues; Electronic; Jazz; Reggae; Rock; World; Gospel

Small label, big sound – based in Michigan but has a global ear. With roots in graphic arts, audio and video production, it is now an independent full-service media company that is home for both developing and legacy artists alike.

US Record Labels

Meloden Nashville
Email: MelodenMusic@gmail.com
Website: https://meloden.com

Genres: Alternative Acoustic Christian Commercial Contemporary Funky Mainstream Melodic Modern New Wave Americana Blues Country Folk Gospel Guitar based Indie MOR Pop Rock Rock and Roll Rockabilly Singer-Songwriter

An independent record label which also owns and operates an in-house music publishing unit (ASCAP affiliate.) We have partnerships with music distributors worldwide. At this time, we are not accepting unsolicited material from artists and songwriters.

Memphis International Records
Email: jeff@memphisinternational.com
Website: https://memphisinternational.com
Website: https://www.facebook.com/MemphisInternationalRecords/

Genres: Roots; Blues; Rockabilly; Swing; Americana; Country; Folk; Jazz; R&B

Record label based in Memphis, Tennessee. Aims, simply, to produce music that the founders like, focusing on the "music" part of the "music business". Check website to see the kind of music produced, and if you think yours fits in send CD by post.

Mercury Nashville
Website: https://www.umgnashville.com
Website: https://www.facebook.com/UMGNashville

Genres: Country

Country label based in Nashville, Tennessee.

Mosley Music Group
Email: gm@mosleymusicgroup.com
Email: Thomas.Leijgraaff@monomusicgroup.com
Website: http://www.mosleymusicgroup.com

Genres: All types of music

Contact: Gary Marella; Thomas Leijgraaff Sr

Music group with over 25 million albums and over 40 million singles sold.

Mountain Apple Company
P.O. Box 22569
Honolulu, HI 96823
Email: info@mountainapplecompany.com
Website: https://www.mountainapplecompany.com
Website: https://www.facebook.com/mountainapplecompany

Genres: Regional; Traditional; Contemporary

Record label releasing traditional and contemporary Hawaiian music.

MRG Recordings
Email: submissions@mrgrecordings.com
Email: info@mrgrecordings.com
Website: https://mrgrecordings.com
Website: https://www.facebook.com/mrgrecordings

Genres: All types of music

Digital-focussed record label. Approach by email with links to music online. No audio file attachments (these will be deleted).

Nacional Records
Email: hearme@nacionalrecords.com
Email: info@nacionalrecords.com
Website: http://www.nacionalrecords.com
Website: https://www.facebook.com/nacionalrecords

Genres: Latin

Send query by email with links to music online. Response not guaranteed.

New Earth Records
3980 N. Broadway Suite 103-223
Boulder, CO 80304

Administrative Offices:
PO Box 3388
Ashland, OR 97520
Website: https://www.newearthrecords.com

Genres: Chill; New Age; Trance; World; Electronic

Independent record label with offices in Boulder, Colorado, and Ashland, Oregon. Specialises in visionary music.

New Heights Entertainment

Email: info@newheightsent.com
Website: http://newheightsent.com

Genres: All types of music

Privately held personal management and consulting firm with its core business focusing on Music Production, Artist Management, Live Entertainment, Music Producers, Songwriters, Record Label Management, Music Publishing, Brand Development and Strategic Guidance for Entertainment Content and IP Creators.

New Pants Publishing

119 N. Wahsatch Ave
Colorado Springs, CO 80903
Fax: +1 (719) 634-2274
Email: rac@crlr.net
Website: http://www.newpants.com

Genres: Country; Folk; R&B; Rap; Pop; Rock

Contact: Robert A. Case

Company based in Colorado Springs, Colorado.

New West Records LLC

Email: info@newwestrecords.com
Website: http://www.newwestrecords.com
Website: https://www.facebook.com/newwestrecords

Genres: Americana; Blues; Country; Folk; Indie; Rock; Roots

Label boasting a number of Grammy-award winning artists.

Newvelle Records

Email: info@newvelle-records.com
Website: https://www.newvelle-records.com
Website: https://www.facebook.com/NewvelleRecords

Genres: Jazz

A premium, subscription-based record label that releases new music exclusively on vinyl.

NexGen Music Group, LLC

Email: demos@nexgenmusicgroup.com
Email: info@nexgenmusicgroup.com
Website: https://www.nexgenmusicgroup.com
Website: https://soundcloud.com/nexgenrecs

Genres: Underground; Downtempo; Chill; Drum and Bass; Dubstep; Garage; House; Electronic; Hip-Hop; Soul; Funk; Experimental; Dance; Pop

Contact: Daniel Clarke

An established worldwide independent record label with more than a decade of history behind its innovative approach to the fusion of live, vocal and electronic music.

The label is dedicated to the creation of groundbreaking musical compositions, as well as introducing new audiences to the depth and diversity within the dance and electronic music genres. The label showcases multiple musical styles including; Downtempo, Drum & Bass, Dubstep, Chill-Out, Nu-Jazz, Future Jazz, Experimental, Deep House, and Electronica.

Represents 30+ pioneering artists and musicians from across the globe, and supplies music for the television, motion picture and interactive entertainment industries. Has completed music projects for organizations like: BBC, Lionsgate, and OTC Films, securing placements in musical compilations and highly-rated major film and television shows in the UK & US.

Includes industry/scene pioneers and legends such as Chris Paul & Mia V (aka Stolen Identity), Earth Leakage Trip, and D.A alongside established and up-and-coming artists: Rob Sparx, Kyro, Qumulus, Undersound, Physical & Crimea, Faible among many others.

An artist-centric brand committed to creating a forward-looking, inclusive and multi-faceted musical community. Its personalized service includes worldwide distribution, promotion and marketing, alongside top-

16 US Record Labels

quality production services and one-on-one industry consultations. The label fosters a philosophy of artistic growth, collaboration and experimentation, uniting promising new talent with established industry musical magicians.

Nine Mile Records (NMR)
Austin, TX
Email: info@ninemilerecords.com
Website: http://www.ninemilerecords.com

Genres: Indie; Pop; Rock

Record label based in Austin, Texas.

Nitro Records
Website: https://nitrorecords.com
Website: https://www.facebook.com/nitrorecords/

Genres: Punk; Rock

Record label synonymous with the Southern California punk scene.

No Quarter
1717 Green Street #5
Philadelphia, PA 19130
Email: noquarter@noquarter.net
Website: https://www.noquarter.net

Genres: All types of music

Record label based in Philadelphia.

No Sleep
Costa Mesa, CA
Email: hello@nosleeprecords.com
Email: info@nosleeprecords.com
Website: https://nosleeprecords.com
Website: https://www.facebook.com/nosleeprecords

Genres: Indie; Hardcore; Experimental; Hip-Hop

Record label based in Costa Mesa, California.

Noisy Poet Records
276 5th Avenue, Suite 704
New York NY 10001
Email: admin@noisypoet.com
Email: booking@noisypoet.com
Website: https://www.noisypoet.com
Website: https://www.facebook.com/noisypoet/

Genres: All types of music, except: Doom Black Metal; Doom

Music arm of a multi-media company with worldwide music distribution. We deliver the sounds of tomorrow through ear-picked, unique, and authentic artists poised to breathe new life into the music industry. Doesn't aspire to reach the pinnacle of today's music landscape; we are driven to transform it.

NorthSide
Website: https://noside.com

Genres: Regional; Roots

A label to bring Nordic roots music to North American audiences.

Not Not Fun
Email: notnotfunrecords@gmail.com
Website: http://www.notnotfun.com
Website: https://soundcloud.com/not-not-fun-1

Genres: All types of music

Send query by email with links to music online.

Nuclear Blast America
5741 Buckingham Parkway Unit C
Culver City, CA 90230
Email: contact@nuclearblastusa.com
Website: https://www.nuclearblast.com
Website: https://www.facebook.com/nuclearblastusa

Genres: Metal; Rock

Record label based in Culver City, California.

NYC Records
Email: info@nycrecords.com
Website: http://www.nycrecords.com

Genres: Folk; Jazz

Contact: Michael Mainieri

Independent label created in 1992 by an award-winning jazz vibraphonist who has also worked as producer, arranger, and composer.

Oglio Entertainment
3540 West Sahara Avenue #308
Las Vegas, NV 89102
Email: getinfo14@oglio.com
Website: https://www.oglio.com

Genres: Alternative; Electronic; Hip-Hop; Rap; Rock

Contact: Carl Caprioglio; Mark Copeland

Management company based in Las Vegas, Nevada.

Oh Boy Records
PO Box 150222
Nashville, TN 37215
Email: info@ohboy.com
Website: https://ohboy.com
Website: https://www.facebook.com/OhBoyRecords/

Genres: Folk; Roots

Folk / roots label based in Nashville, Tennessee.

Om Records
1890 Bryant Street. #305
San Francisco, CA 94110
Email: connect@om-records.com
Email: info@om-records.com
Website: https://www.om-records.com
Website: https://www.facebook.com/omrecords

Genres: Contemporary; Dance; Electronic; Hip-Hop; Rap; Rock; Singer-Songwriter; Urban

Contact: Gunnar Hissam

San Francisco based music and lifestyle company.

Omnium Records
Minneapolis, MN
Website: http://omniumrecords.com

Website: https://www.facebook.com/OmniumRecords

Genres: World Rock

Contact: Drew Miller

Releases world music that rocks.

Omnivore Recordings
4470 W. Sunset Boulevard, Suite 209
Los Angeles, CA 90027
Website: http://omnivorerecordings.com
Website: https://www.facebook.com/omnivorerecordings

Genres: All types of music

Record label based in Los Angeles. Closed to submissions as at February 2020.

One Little Independent Records US
Email: paulj@olirecords.com
Email: samb@olirecords.com
Website: https://www.olirecords.com/
Website: https://www.facebook.com/olirecords

Genres: Electronic; Folk; Indie; Pop; Punk; Rap; Hip-Hop; Rock; Singer-Songwriter; World

Inspired by the DIY principles and anarchistic ideals of independent labels. Since its inception the label has prided itself on giving complete control to artists it feels deserve a shot at a wider audience.

Orange Recordings
Seattle
Email: rons@orangerecordings.com
Website: http://www.orangerecordings.com

Genres: Blues; Folk; Indie; Punk; Rock

Record label based in Seattle. Send query by email in first instance, selling your band, providing details, where you've played and who with, etc. and explaining why you and this particular label would be a good match. Do not send MP3s or MPEGs.

Palm Pictures
1460 Broadway
New York, NY 10036
Website: http://www.palmpictures.com

Genres: Americana; Chill; Dance; Drum and Bass; Electronic; Latin; World; Pop; Reggae; Rock; Soundtracks; Hip-Hop; Indie

Record label based in New York. Home to a diverse music catalogue, spanning genres from world to trip hop to indie rock to electronica.

Palmetto Records
Website: https://www.palmetto-records.com

Genres: Jazz

Has been an independent leading voice in music since it was founded in 1990. Through its choice of innovative artists and careful attention to sonic value, it has emerged as a heavyweight label, as well as being listed as one of the best jazz labels for four years running in the Downbeat Critics Poll. Its original mission of enabling artists to fulfill their creative visions still remains the label's focus.

According to founder and producer, the label has succeeded so well because it makes music that matters to the artist and to the audience.

Also supports artists who are often overlooked or are considered somewhat "left of center". This enables the label to help expand the boundaries and even the vocabulary of jazz, and also gives the artists the freedom they need to make great music. Truly believes the future of jazz is now.

Paper Garden Records
170 Tillary Street, Apt 608
Brooklyn, NY 11201
Email: demos@papergardenrecords.com
Email: info@papergardenrecords.com
Website: http://papergardenrecords.com
Website: https://soundcloud.com/papergardenrecords

Genres: All types of music

Record label based in Brooklyn, New York. Send demos by email.

Parasol
303 West Griggs Street
Urbana, IL 61801
Email: parasol@parasol.com
Email: promo@parasol.com
Website: https://www.parasol.com
Website: https://www.facebook.com/ParasolLG/

Genres: Alternative; Folk; Indie; Pop; Rock; Roots; Singer-Songwriter

Independent record label based in Urbana, Illinois.

Park the Van Records
Email: jeff@parkthevan.com
Website: https://www.parkthevan.com
Website: https://www.facebook.com/parkthevan

Genres: Alternative; Pop; Rock

Record label originally started in New Orleans in 2004.

Parliament Record Group
357 S. Fairfax Ave. #430+1
Los Angeles, CA 90036
Fax: +1 (323) 653-7670
Email: parlirec@aol.com
Website: http://www.parliamentrecords.com

Genres: Blues; Gospel; Hip-Hop; R&B; Soul

Send 3-10 tracks on CD by post, including lyric sheet and SASE.
If you are a producer of tracks we would love to hear your music. We are always looking for new producers to work with our artists.

Partisan Records
281 N 7th Street, #2
Brooklyn, NY 11211
Website: https://partisanrecords.com

Genres: All types of music

US Record Labels   19

Record label with offices in Brooklyn and London. Not accepting demos as at March 2020.

Pavement Music
6348 N Milwaukee Ave., Suite 301
Chicago, IL 60646
Email: info@pavementmusic.com
Website: https://www.pavementmusic.com/
Website: https://www.facebook.com/Pavementent

Genres: Underground Heavy Metal; Rock

Contact: Rob Bolfer (A&R Manager)

Specialises in the development and distribution of underground heavy metal.

Peek-A-Boo Records
5808 Vicstone Ct.
Culver City, CA 90232
Website: http://www.peekaboorecords.com

Genres: Pop; Rock

Record label based in Culver City, California.

pehr
California
Email: pehr@pehrlabel.com
Website: http://www.pehrlabel.com

Genres: All types of music

Record label based in California.

Penalty Entertainment
Website: http://penaltyent.com

Genres: Hip-Hop; Urban

Contact: Neil Levine

A full service entertainment company consisting of a record label, music publisher, label services, merchandise and management.

Pendulum Records
96 Linwood Plaza, #354
Fort Lee, NJ 07024
Email: ruben@rubenrodriguezentertainment.net
Website: http://www.pendulumrecords.biz
Website: http://www.facebook.com/PendulumRecords

Genres: Christian; Gospel; Latin; Pop; R&B; Hip-Hop; Rap; Urban

Record label based in Fort Lee, New Jersey.

Phase One Network
Website: https://www.phaseonenetwork.net

Genres: All types of music

Music asset management company, owning and controlling the assets of over 20 labels.

Photo Finish Records
New York
Email: hello@photofinishrecords.com
Website: https://www.photofinishrecords.com
Website: https://www.facebook.com/photofinishrecords

Genres: All types of music

Record label based in New York.

Phunk Junk Records Inc
Email: phunkjunkinfo@gmail.com
Website: https://www.phunkjunk.com
Website: https://www.facebook.com/phunkjunkmusicgroup

Genres: Electronic Club Dance House IDM Trance

Contact: Lary Saladin

We are all about EDM Music. House, Progressive House, Electro House, Tech House, some Deep House..

No DNB, No Dubstep, No Trap, etc etc.

Submit demos through online form.

Pi Recordings
Brooklyn, NY
Email: info@pirecordings.com
Website: https://pirecordings.com
Website: https://www.facebook.com/PiRecordings/

US Record Labels

Genres: Electronic; Jazz

Contact: Seth Rosner

Record label based in Brooklyn, New York.

Pinch Hit Records
2400 West Carson Street Suite 223 Torrance, CA 90501
Website: http://pinchhit.com

Genres: Alternative; Indie; Pop

Contact: David Lebental

Record label based in Torrance, California, specialising in alternative and pop music.

Playing In Traffic Records
Website: https://playingintrafficrecords.com
Website: https://www.facebook.com/playingintrafficrecords

Genres: All types of music

Record label founded in 2009.

Plug Research
Email: submissions@plugresearch.com
Email: contact@plugresearch.com
Website: http://www.plugresearch.com
Website: https://soundcloud.com/plugresearch-music
Website: https://myspace.com/plugresearchmusic

Genres: Electronic; Indie; Rock

Send a private soundcloud link. A four sentence paragraph about yourself. Include a link to your personal facebook and twitter pages. No mp3 as attachments.

+1 Records
New York
Email: info@plusonemusic.net
Website: http://plusonemusic.net
Website: https://soundcloud.com/plusonemusic

Genres: All types of music

Record label based in New York.

Polo Grounds Music
Email: info@pologroundsmusic.com
Website: https://pologroundsmusic.com
Website: https://www.facebook.com/Polo-Grounds-Music-360463501306366/

Genres: Gospel; Pop; R&B; Rap; Hip-Hop; Reggae; Reggaeton; Urban

New York based record-breaking imprint boasts streaming numbers of nearly 40 billion (and counting) and sales well over 92 million singles and 16 million albums worldwide.

Polyvinyl Record Co.
Champaign, IL
Email: info@polyvinylrecords.com
Website: https://www.polyvinylrecords.com
Website: https://www.facebook.com/polyvinylrecords

Genres: Indie; Rock

Record label based in Champaign, Illinois. Send demos using online form.

Pop Cautious Records
Email: tyler@popcautiousrecords.com
Website: https://www.popcautiousrecords.com
Website: https://soundcloud.com/popcautiousrecords

Genres: Alternative; Folk; Indie; Rock

Contact: Tyler Porterfield

We accept links to music via our website and email. You can also use submission websites.

Please, email us before attempting to mail a CD or Vinyl.

Poptown Records
Po Box 51
Lincolndale, NY 10540
Email: info@PoptownRecords.com
Website: http://www.poptownrecords.com

Genres: Pop; Rock

Record label based in Lincolndale, New York.

US Record Labels

Posi-Tone
PO Box 2848
Los Angeles, CA 90294
Email: info@posi-tone.com
Website: https://www.posi-tone.com
Website: https://soundcloud.com/posi-tone-records

Genres: Jazz

Jazz label based in Los Angeles, California, releasing both contemporary interpretations of classic material and fresh new ideas by innovative players.

PRA Records
Email: pra@prarecords.com
Website: http://www.prarecords.com
Website: https://twitter.com/prarecords

Genres: Jazz

Contact: Patrick Rains; Stephanie Pappas

Record label based in New York with sister management arm.

Pravda Records
4245 N Knox, Suite 7
Chicago, IL 60641
Email: kenn@pravdamusic.com
Website: https://www.pravdamusic.com
Website: https://www.facebook.com/PravdaRecordsUSA/

Genres: Alternative Rock; Alternative Country; Rockabilly; Pop; R&B; Soul; Rock

Contact: Kenn Goodman

Independent record label based in Chicago. Full-service music licensing company with two in-house publishing companies.

Primarily A Cappella
Website: https://www.singers.com
Website: https://twitter.com/newsacappella

Genres: Contemporary; Jazz; Christian; World

Record label based in San Anselmo, California, specialising in a cappella. Releases include Christmas, Contemporary, Barbershop, Choral, Vocal Jazz, Christian, World, Vintage Harmony, Collegiate, Doo Wop, and Children's Choirs.

Prosthetic Records
11664 National Blvd., #413
Los Angeles, CA 90064
Email: info@prostheticrecords.com
Website: https://www.prostheticrecords.com/
Website: https://www.facebook.com/prostheticrecords

Genres: Hard Rock; Heavy Metal

Heavy music label based in LA.

Provident Label Group
Website: https://www.providentlabelgroup.com/
Website: https://www.facebook.com/ProvidentLabelGroupSonyMusic/

Genres: Christian; Gospel

Includes a number of labels and is itself a division of a multinational music company.

PS Classics
Website: http://www.psclassics.com
Website: https://www.facebook.com/psclassics/

Genres: Soundtracks; Pop; Americana

Label celebrating the heritage of Broadway and American popular song.

Psychopathic Records
Website: https://www.psychopathicrecords.com

Genres: Hardcore; Hip-Hop; Rap

Record label founded by rap duo from Detroit.

Pure Noise
Website: http://www.purenoise.net
Website: https://www.facebook.com/PureNoiseRecords

Genres: All types of music

Submit demos using form on website.

US Record Labels

Putumayo World Music
413 Carpenter Road
Charlotte, VT 05445
Fax: +1 (212) 460-0095
Email: submissions@putumayo.com
Email: info@putumayo.com
Website: https://www.putumayo.com

Genres: Blues; Folk; Latin; World

Send demo by email or on CD by post.

Pyramid Records
11077 Biscayne Boulevard, Suite 200
Miami, Florida 33161
Website: http://pyramidrecords.net
Website: https://www.facebook.com/pyramidrecords

Genres: Rock; R&B; Urban; Hip-Hop; Rap; Gospel; Country; Contemporary; Reggae

Combines recording, touring, merchandising and television into a single co-ordinated entity.

Q Division Records
363 Highland Avenue
Somerville, MA 02144
Fax: +1 (617) 625-2224
Email: info@qdivision.com
Website: http://www.qdivisionrecords.com

Genres: Rock; Indie; Pop

Contact: A&R

Send demo by post, via sonicbids, or send a link to your music online by email. Do not email MP3s or other music files. Prefers bands that play regularly in front of people. Unlikely to sign a band without seeing them, and due to travel budget constraints this generally means most bands are based in the North East. See website for detailed FAQs.

Quality Control
Email: QUALITYCONTROL@UMGSTORES.com
Website: https://qualitycontrolmusic.com
Website: https://www.facebook.com/RealQualityControl/

Genres: Hip-Hop; Urban

Independent record label.

Quango Music Group
Los Angeles, CA
Email: info@quango.com
Website: http://www.quango.com
Website: https://www.facebook.com/quangomusic

Genres: Chill; Electronic

Label based in Los Angeles, California, dealing in chilled-out electronica.

Quark Records
Post Office Box 452
Newtown, CT 06470-0452
Email: ar@quarkmusicgroup.com
Email: webmaster@quarkmusicgroup.com
Website: http://www.quarkmusicgroup.com/
Website: https://www.facebook.com/groups/80122004353/

Genres: Electronic

Record label based in Newtown, Connecticut. Send query by email with links to music online. Response not guaranteed.

Quarterback Records
P.O. Box 40465
Nashville, TN 37204
Email: allums@quarterbackrecords.com
Website: http://www.quarterbackrecords.com/

Genres: Country

Country label based in Nashville, Tennessee.

R.O.A.D. (Riding on a Dream) Records
PO Box 68096
Nashville, TN 37206
Email: bluesland@comcast.net
Email: fred@blueslandproductions.com
Website: http://www.blueslandproductions.com

Genres: Blues; Soul; Americana Roots

Contact: Fred James

Blues label based in Nashville, Tennessee. Describes itself as "one of the world's

US Record Labels

foremost independent music companies devoted to Blues, Soul and American Roots music". Send query by email in first instance.

Radical Records
222 Dean Street #1
Brooklyn, NY 11217
Email: bryoonic222@gmail.com
Website: https://www.facebook.com/radicalrecordsnyc/

Genres: Punk Rock

Record label based in New York. Deals almost exclusively in punk rock.

Radikal Records
Website: http://www.radikal.com
Website: https://soundcloud.com/radikalrecords

Genres: Dance; Electronic; Pop

Interested in dance, pop, and electronic music. Must have vocals. Send streaming links through form on website. No CDs or MP3 downloads.

Rainman Records
Website: https://rainmanrecords.com

Genres: Blues; Metal; Pop; Rock; Americana Blues Rockabilly Rock and Roll Classic

Record label based in Beverly Hills, California, we handle classic rock bands and put out DVDs by classic rock bands.

Ramp Records
Email: info@ramprecords.com
Website: http://www.ramprecords.com

Genres: All types of music

Contact: Michael McDonald; Jeff Bridges; Chris Pelonis

Co-founded by a well-known Hollywood actor. Not accepting submissions as at February 2022.

Rampage Records
197 Illinois St
Battle Creek, MI 49014
Email: contact@rampagerecords.net
Email: demos@rampagerecords.net
Website: https://rampagerecords.net
Website: https://www.facebook.com/RampageRecordsWorldwide/

Genres: All types of music

Contact: Chandler Culler

An independent record. Demos accepted by post or by email.

raSa Music
Email: info@rasaliving.com
Website: http://www.rasamusic.com
Website: https://www.facebook.com/donna.dcruz

Genres: Electronic; New Age; Reggae; World

Record label producing music for meditation.

Razor & Tie
Website: http://www.razorandtie.com
Website: https://www.facebook.com/RazorandTie

Genres: Alternative; Folk; Gospel; Indie; Metal; Pop; Rock; Singer-Songwriter; Urban; World

Label which has enjoyed success in a variety of genres, achieving Platinum sales and Grammy awards. Includes a children's division.

Razor Sharp Records South, Inc.
3772 Pleasantdale Road, Suite 200
Atlanta, GA 30340
Email: admin@razorsharprecordssouth.com
Website: https://www.razorsharprecordssouth.com
Website: https://www.facebook.com/razorsharprecordssouth

Genres: All types of music

Contact: Herbert Goodwin Jr

24 US Record Labels

Independent record label. Company specialises in Artist Management and Development services for all genres of music. Send links to your music online via email or contact form on website.

RCA Records
550 Madison Avenue
New York, NY 10022
Website: https://www.rcarecords.com
Website: https://www.facebook.com/rcarecords

Genres: Hip-Hop; Pop; R&B; Rock; Roots; Urban

Record label based in New York.

Reach Out International Records (ROIR)
Website: https://roir-usa.com
Website: https://www.facebook.com/roirusa

Genres: Reggae; Rock; Punk; Indie

New York label begun in 1979 as a cassette-only label. Send demo via song and talent filtering service.

Rebel Records
PO Box 7405
Charlottesville, VA 22906
Email: questions@rebelrecords.com
Website: http://www.rebelrecords.com
Website: https://www.facebook.com/RebelRecordsBluegrass

Genres: Country; Folk; Roots

Record label based in Charlottesville, Virginia. Handles bluegrass, country, folk, and roots.

Red Bull Records
3535 Hayden Avenue #350
Culver City, CA 90232-2412
Email: customercare@redbullrecords.com
Website: http://redbullrecords.com
Website: https://www.facebook.com/RedBullRecords/

Genres: All types of music

Record label based in Culver City, California. Submit demo using form on website (see "Demo Submissions" link at bottom of page).

Red House Records
916 19th Avenue South
Nashville, TN 37212
Fax: +1 (615) 320 7378
Email: info@compassrecords.com
Email: comments@compassrecords.com
Website: http://www.redhouserecords.com
Website: https://www.redhouserecords.com/about/

Genres: Blues; Folk; Roots; Acoustic; Singer-Songwriter; Traditional; Instrumental

Aims to provide a home and environment in which creative artists can make albums in total freedom, without interference from "mogul types" just looking for the next hit single. A&R submissions may be sent by post on CD or by email as an MP3 streaming link.

Red Parlor Records
PO Box 362
Green Farms, CT 06838
Email: office@redparlor.com
Website: http://www.redparlor.com

Genres: Acoustic Soulful Singer-Songwriter Rock Americana Blues

Contact: Steven Goff

Record label with international distribution, based in New York. No unsolicited material, but accepts queries.

Relapse Records
Email: mailorder@relapse.com
Website: http://www.relapse.com
Website: https://www.facebook.com/RelapseRecords

Genres: Indie; Metal; Rock

Independent metal label.

Renaissance Records
20860 N. Tatum Blvd, Suite 300 Unit 304
Phoenix, AZ 85050

Email: john@renaissancerecordsus.com
Email: devon@renaissancerecordsus.com
Website: https://renaissancerecordsus.com/

Genres: All types of music, except: Ambient Black Metal Black Origin Break Beat C-DUB Blue Beat Blues Classical Club Cuban Dance Dancehall Deep Funk Disco Doom Drum and Bass Dub Dubstep Ethnic Emo Fusion Funk Glitch Gospel Gothic Grind Grime Hardcore Hi-NRG Hip-Hop House IDM Jazz Jungle Latin MOR Mystical New Age Noise Core R&B Psychebilly Punk Nostalgia Ragga Rap Reggaeton Reggae Remix Relaxation Rockabilly Rhythm and Blues Roots Shoegaze Ska Skool Soul Spoken Word Surf Swing Techno Trance Trip Hop World

Contact: John Edwards

While we have primarily found ourselves working with classic artists, we are always searching for new artists. We are looking for those new, modern
artists to bring new life to the company as well as bring new life to Vinyl releases. We are moving into the next phase of our history with some great new talent and a worldwide focus on music from around the planet. We are currently looking for rock-centric artists, but have plans in the near-future to broaden our label and become more inclusive of more modern artists. Feel free to reach out to any of the below emails with any interest or any further questions and we will be happy to help!

Rescue Records
3500 West Olive Avenue, Suite 810
Burbank, CA 91505
Fax: +1 (626) 795-2058
Email: terrilynn@rescuerecords.net
Website: http://www.rescuerecords.net

Genres: All types of music

Record label based in Pasadena, California. Make contact by phone or email a streaming link.

Reservoir Music
276 Pearl St.
Kingston, NY 12401
Fax: +1 (845) 338-4266
Email: mfeldmanmd@hvc.rr.com
Website: http://www.reservoirmusic.com

Genres: Jazz

Contact: Mark Feldman

Jazz label based in Kingston, New York.

Reunion Records
Website: https://www.providentlabelgroup.com
Website: https://www.facebook.com/ProvidentLabelGroup/

Genres: Christian; Pop; Rock

Record label specialising in Christian music.

Revelation Records
PO Box 5232
Huntington Beach, CA 92615-5232
Email: webmaster@revhq.com
Website: http://www.revelationrecords.com
Website: https://www.facebook.com/revelationrecords/

Genres: Hardcore; Punk; Rock; Emo

Record label based in Huntington Beach, California.

Rhino
Website: https://www.rhino.com
Website: https://www.facebook.com/RHINO

Genres: All types of music

Record label acting as the catalogue development and marketing division of its parent company.

Rhombus Records
PO Box 7938
Van Nuys, CA 91409
Fax: +1 (818) 709-8480
Email: rhombusrecords@gmail.com
Website: https://rhombus-records.com

Genres: Blues; Jazz; Latin; Reggae; World; Americana; Jazz Fusion; Traditional Jazz; Funky Jazz; Rock; Pop; Progressive Rock; Latin Rock; New Age; Contemporary Folk; Latin Jazz; Avant-Garde Jazz; Ambient Jazz

Label founded in 1986 to release the owner's music, now has an extensive list of clients.

Rhymesayers Entertainment
Minneapolis, MN
Website: https://rhymesayers.com
Website: https://www.facebook.com/Rhymesayers/

Genres: Hip-Hop

Independent hip hop record label based in Minneapolis, Minnesota, founded in 1995.

Righteous Babe Records
Email: steve@righteousbabe.com
Website: https://www.righteousbabe.com/

Genres: Alternative; Folk; Jazz; Latin; Punk; Rock

International record label with offices in Buffalo, NY, and London.

Roadrunner Records, Inc.
902 Broadway, 8th Floor
New York, NY 10010
Website: http://www.roadrunnerrecords.com
Website: https://www.facebook.com/roadrunnerrecords/

Genres: Alternative; Rock; Metal; Black Metal; Thrash

Record label based in New York.

Robbins Entertainment
A&R Dept.
35 Worth St., 4th Floor
New York, NY 10013
Email: info@robbinsent.com
Website: https://www.robbinsent.com
Website: https://www.facebook.com/robbinsentertainment

Genres: Country; Dance; Electronic; Pop

Record label based in New York. Send demos as download links by email (e.g. YouSendIt / Soundcloud, etc.) or by post. No MP3 email attachments. See website for full details.

Rockzion Records
673 Valley Drive
Hermosa Beach, CA 90254
Fax: +1 (310) 379-6477
Email: rockzionrecords@rockzion.com
Website: https://rockzion.com

Genres: Christian; Rock

Record label based in Hermosa Beach, California, specialising in Christian and crossover rock.

Ropeadope Records
203 W. Atlantic Ave
Haddon Heights, NJ 08035
Email: orders@ropeadope.com
Email: publicity@ropeadope.com
Website: https://ropeadope.com
Website: https://www.facebook.com/ropeadope99/

Genres: Electronic; Folk; Indie; Jazz; Rock; Singer-Songwriter; World

Record label based in Haddon Heights, New Jersey.

Rotten Records
Website: https://www.rottenrecords.com
Website: https://soundcloud.com/rottenrecords

Genres: Extreme Metal; Hardcore; Punk

For the last 20 years, we have held an unyielding fist to the mainstream music industry. We've crushed all walls of conventional industry standards, carved our own niche and have always fought hard for our bands. With a staff of industry veterans and the power of major label distribution, we have always been on the cutting edge of extreme music, taking chances that other labels would never think about.

Rough Trade US
64 North 9th
New York, NY 11249
Email: enquiries@roughtrade.com
Website: https://www.roughtrade.com/us
Website: https://soundcloud.com/rough_trade

Genres: Indie; Rock

US Record Labels 27

US arm of UK label.

Rounder Records
Website: https://rounder.com
Website: https://www.facebook.com/RounderRecords/

Genres: Blues; Folk; Jazz; Rock; Roots; Americana

Describes itself as one of the world's most historic Americana and bluegrass record labels.

S-Curve Records
1 Park Avenue, 18th Floor
New York, NY 10016
Email: info@s-curverecords.com
Email: scurverecords@gmail.com
Website: http://s-curverecords.com
Website: https://www.facebook.com/scurverecords

Genres: Contemporary; Americana; Indie; Pop; R&B; Rock; Singer-Songwriter; Alternative; Pop Rock

Record label based in New York.

Saddle Creek
Email: info@saddle-creek.com
Website: https://saddle-creek.com
Website: https://www.facebook.com/SaddleCreekRecords/

Genres: Indie Rock; Rock; Country Rock; Electronic

An independent record label founded in Omaha in 1993 with staff in Omaha, NE, Los Angeles, CA, New York, NY, Seattle, WA and Glasgow, Scotland (UK).

Schoolboy Records
Email: info@scooterbraun.com
Website: http://scooterbraun.com
Website: https://www.facebook.com/SBProjects

Genres: Pop

Part of a diversified entertainment and media company based in New York, with ventures integrating music, film, television, technology, and anthropology.

SCI Fidelity Records
Email: kevin@scifidelity.com
Email: allie@scifidelity.com
Website: https://scifidelity.com
Website: https://www.facebook.com/scifidelity

Genres: Blues; Electronic; Rock; Singer-Songwriter

Contact: Kevin Morris

Record label based in Boulder, Colorado.

Secret Formula Records, Inc.
Email: gary1@secretformularecords.com
Website: http://secretformularecords.com
Website: https://www.facebook.com/secretformularecords

Genres: Classical; Jazz; New Age; Acid Classic Commercial Contemporary Electronic Non-Commercial Post Classical Dance Fusion Funk Hip-Hop Instrumental Jazz Lounge New Age Rock Relaxation Rock and Roll Soundtracks Techno Trance Trip Hop

Contact: Gary Farr

A bi-coastal record label with the corporate office in the State of Florida and the recording studio in Los Angeles California.

Secretly Canadian
213 S. Rogers
Bloomington, IN 47404
Email: info@secretlycanadian.com
Website: https://secretlycanadian.com
Website: https://www.facebook.com/SecretlyCanadian

Genres: Country; Folk; Hardcore; Indie; Pop; Punk; Rock; Roots

Record label based in Bloomington, Indiana.

Segue Records
Email: wayne@peacefulwaters.com
Website: https://www.peacefulwaters.com/segue-records

US Record Labels

Genres: All types of music

Contact: Wayne Warnecke

An independent music company concentrating on quality new music releases of all genres.

Sequoia Records
Website: http://www.sequoiarecords.com

Genres: Electronic; Folk; New Age; World; Ambient; Trance; Dance; Chill; Lounge; Celtic

Dedicated to creating music to enlighten the mind, nourish the soul and celebrate life. For 26 years, Sequoia has consistently created groundbreaking recordings that have defined and transcended Ambient, Worldbeat, Native/Drumming , Trance/Dance, Chill-Out/Lounge, Celtic and Healing/Meditative music.

SGNB Records
9971 E Ida Pl
Englewood, CO 80111
Email: info@sgnbrecords.com
Email: tracey@tacmusicmanagement.com
Website: http://sgnbrecords.com/
Website: https://tacmusicmanagement.com/

Genres: Country; Blues; Guitar based; Metal; Rock; Rock and Roll; Rockabilly; Roots; Singer-Songwriter; Americana

Contact: Tracey Chirhart

Indie record label service based in Denver CO. Label releases singles only and focuses on southern rock, hard rock, country and blues rock and metal. The label's focus is "new" sound of southern rock. Parent company offers artist management, consulting, marketing, promo, branding and tour planning/booking. No long-term contracts, artist keeps rights to their music and services available on a monthly basis or as needed depending on artists needs and goals.

Shady Records
Website: https://www.shadyrecords.com
Website: https://www.facebook.com/ShadyRecords

Genres: Hip-Hop; Rap; Urban

Record label specializing in hip hop music.

Shanachie Entertainment
37 East Clinton Street
Newton, NJ 07860
Email: facebook@shanachie.com
Website: http://www.shanachie.com
Website: https://www.facebook.com/shanachie.entertainment

Genres: Blues; Country; Electronic; Folk; Gospel; Jazz; R&B; Reggae; Singer-Songwriter; World

Record label based in New Jersey.

Shangri-La Projects, Inc.
PO Box 40116
Memphis, Tennessee 38174
Email: sherman@shangrilaprojects.com
Website: http://www.shangrilaprojects.com

Genres: Alternative Rock

Record label based in Memphis, Tennessee, with publishing and music tour arms to the business.

Shrapnel Records
Navato, CA
Email: shrapnel1@aol.com
Website: https://www.shrapnelrecords.com
Website: https://twitter.com/shrapnelrecords

Genres: Heavy Metal; Hard Rock; Blues; Progressive Metal; Blues Rock; Country; Guitar based; Jazz

Record label based in Navato, California.

Side One Dummy Records
Email: info@sideonedummy.com
Website: https://sideonedummy.com
Website: https://www.facebook.com/SideOneDummy

Genres: Punk; Reggae; Hardcore; Ska; Alternative

Contact: Bill Armstrong; Joe Sib

Record label based in Los Angeles, California.

Signature Sound Recordings
32 Masonic Street
Northampton, MA 01060
Fax: +1 (509) 691-0457
Email: info@signaturesounds.com
Website: http://www.signaturesounds.com
Website: https://www.facebook.com/SignatureSoundsRecordings

Genres: Pop; Rock; Roots; Singer-Songwriter; Americana; Modern Folk; Indie

Record label based in Northampton, Massachusetts.

Silver Blue Productions / Joel Diamond Entertainment
3940 Laurel Canyon Boulevard, Suite 441
Studio City, CA 91604
Email: JDiamond20@aol.com
Website: https://www.joeldiamond.com

Genres: All types of music

Record label and publishing company based in Studio City, California. Handles a wide range of music, including classical.

Silver Wave Records
Boulder, CO
Email: jamesm@silverwave.com
Website: https://www.silverwave.com
Website: https://www.facebook.com/silverwaverecords/

Genres: Contemporary; World; Regional; New Age

Independent music label, specialising in World, New Age, and contemporary North American Indian music.

Six Degrees Records
PO Box 411347
San Francisco, CA 94141
Email: info@sixdegreesrecords.com
Website: http://sixdegreesrecords.com
Website: https://www.facebook.com/sixdegreesrecords

Genres: Electronic; Latin; Pop; Rock; World; Ambient; Folk; Contemporary; Classical; Dance

Record label based in San Francisco. Produces and markets accessible, genre-bending records that explore world music traditions, modern dance grooves, electronic music, and overlooked pop gems. Not generally accepting unsolicited demos, unless "you are determined", in which case send a private link to your music. No attachments.

Six Lowa Records
Email: info@sixlowarecords.com
Email: beats@sixlowarecords.com
Website: http://sixlowarecords.com
Website: https://www.facebook.com/SixLowaRecords/

Genres: R&B; Rap; Reggae; Hip-Hop

An independent record label based in Lower Manhattan, New York that focuses heavy on the internet as a way to market, promote, and distribute digital music.

Skaggs Family Records
PO Box 2478
Hendersonville, TN 37077
Fax: +1 (615) 264-8899
Email: info@skaggsfamilyrecords.com
Website: https://skaggsfamilyrecords.com
Website: https://www.facebook.com/rickyskaggsofficial

Genres: Blues; Country; Roots; Christian

Record label based in Hendersonville, Tennessee.

Slip-N-Slide Records
Email: demos@slipnsliderecords.net
Email: ryan@slipnsliderecords.net
Website: https://www.slipnsliderecords.com
Website: https://soundcloud.com/officialslipnsliderecords

Genres: Hip-Hop; Pop; Rap; Reggae; Urban; R&B

Record label hailing from South Florida. Responsible for selling over 30 million records. Send demos by email.

Slumberland Records
PO Box 19029
Oakland CA, 94619
Email: demos@slumberlandrecords.com
Email: slr@slumberlandrecords.com
Website: http://www.slumberlandrecords.com
Website: https://www.facebook.com/SlumberlandRecords

Genres: Post Punk; Indie; Pop; Punk; Lo-fi; Shoegaze

Record label based in Oakland, California. Send query by email with links to music online. No MP3 attachments.

Slush Fund Recordings
Email: david@slushfund.co
Website: https://www.slushfund.co

Genres: Rock

Rock record label established in 2007.

Smog Veil Records
1521 Alton Rd #625
Miami Beach, FL 33139
Fax: +1 (904) 212-0401
Email: franklisa@aol.com
Website: https://www.smogveil.com
Website: https://www.facebook.com/Smog-Veil-Records-66696836527/

Genres: Underground Rock and Roll

Handles bombastic underground rock n' roll.

Sonic Safari Music
Jonkey Enterprises
663 West California Avenue
Glendale, CA 91203-1505
Email: chuck@sonicsafarimusic.com
Website: http://www.sonicsafarimusic.com
Website: https://www.facebook.com/SonicSafariMusic/

Genres: Ethnic; World; Traditional

Contact: Chuck Jonkey

Record label based in Glendale, California.

Sony Music Entertainment – Legacy Recordings
Website: https://www.legacyrecordings.com/
Website: https://www.facebook.com/LegacyRecordings/

Genres: Blues; Country; Folk; Jazz; Pop; R&B; Reggae; Rock; Hip-Hop; Gospel; Soundtracks; Ethnic; World

Re-releases and compilations / box-sets from the parent company's back catalogue. No submissions.

Sony Masterworks
Website: https://www.sonymusicmasterworks.com/

Genres: Classical; Jazz

Record label based in New York.

Sony Music Entertainment
25 Madison Avenue
New York, NY 10010
Website: https://www.sonymusic.com
Website: https://www.facebook.com/sonymusic/

Genres: All types of music

International music group with offices around the world. Only accepts demos submitted through an established music industry professional, such as a manager, lawyer, agent, producer, artist, programmer, or tastemaker.

Sony Music Latin
Website: https://www.sonymusiclatin.com
Website: https://www.facebook.com/sonymusiclatin

Genres: Latin

Latin music label.

Sony Music Nashville
Website: https://www.sonymusicnashville.com
Website: https://www.facebook.com/SonyMusicNashville/

Genres: Country

US Record Labels

Country label based in Nashville, Tennessee.

Sound Feelings
18375 Ventura Blvd. #8000
Tarzana, CA 91356
Email: information@soundfeelings.com
Website: http://www.soundfeelings.com
Website: https://www.facebook.com/soundfeelingspublishing

Genres: New Age; Pop; Relaxation

Contact: Howard Richman

Music therapy for transformation offers drug-free audio products for specific illnesses and conditions. Our recordings provide a music therapy alternative to traditional expressive arts therapy.

Southern Lord Recordings
Email: info@southernlord.com
Website: https://southernlord.com
Website: https://www.facebook.com/SLadmin

Genres: Metal; Hard Rock

Heavy metal label based in Los Angeles, California. Send demos as bandcamp stream or similar. No zip files, MP3, or WAV. Do not submit via social media.

Southland Records
PO Box 15086
Odessa, TX 79762
Email: realcountry@southlandrecords.com
Website: https://www.southlandrecords.com

Genres: Traditional Country; Swing; Gospel; Pop; Rock

Record label based in Odessa, Texas, specialising in Western Swing, traditional Country, gospel, pop, and rock.

Spinefarm Records
1755 Broadway
New York, NY 10019

UK OFFICE
Beaumont House,
Kensington Village,
Avonmore Rd.,

London W14 8TS

FINLAND OFFICE
Merimiehenkatu 36 D
00150 Helsinki
Finland
Email: info@spinefarmrecords.com
Email: contact@spinefarm.fi
Website: https://www.spinefarmrecords.com
Website: https://www.facebook.com/spinefarm

Genres: Hard Rock; Metal

Record label with offices in New York, London, and Helsinki.

Spiral Galaxy Entertainment
Los Angeles, CA 91343
Email: spiralgalaxyent@gmail.com
Website: https://spiralgalaxyent.com
Website: https://www.facebook.com/Spiral-Galaxy-Entertainment-237987439580429/

Genres: Dance; Jazz; Hip-Hop; Gospel; Pop; R&B

Contact: Reggie Calloway

Record label based in Los Angeles, California.

Spitslam
Website: https://slamjamz.com

Genres: Urban

Urban record label established in 1996.

Stackhouse & BluEsoterica
3516 Holmes Street
Kansas City, MO 64109
Email: jim@bluesoterica.com
Email: Stackhouse232@aol.com
Website: http://www.bluesoterica.com

Genres: Blues; World

Contact: Jim O'Neal

Record label based in Kansas City, Missouri.

Claim your free access to www.musicsocket.com: See p.211

Star Time Intl
Website: https://www.startimeintl.com
Website: https://www.facebook.com/StarTimeInternational

Genres: All types of music

Record label based in New York.

Stones Throw Records
2658 Griffith Park Boulevard #504
Los Angeles, CA 90039
Website: https://www.stonesthrow.com
Website: https://soundcloud.com/stonesthrow

Genres: All types of music

Record label based in Los Angeles, California.

Strange Music Inc.
Peppergreen Media
2248 Broadway #1127
New York, NY 10024
Website: http://www.strangemusic.com

Genres: Alternative

Record label based in New York.

Strictly Rhythm
New York
Email: demos@strictly.com
Website: http://strictly.com
Website: https://www.facebook.com/strictlyrhythm/

Genres: House

House record label. Send query by email.

Sub Pop Records
2013 Fourth Avenue, Third Floor
Seattle, WA 98121
Fax: +1 (206) 441-8245
Email: info@subpop.com
Website: https://www.subpop.com
Website: https://soundcloud.com/subpop/

Genres: Americana; Electronic; Folk; Indie; Metal; Pop; Rock; Punk; Singer-Songwriter

Record label based in Seattle, the original home of Nirvana, Soundgarden and Mudhoney. Send demos via Soundcloud. See Facebook page for details.

Subliminal Records
Email: tracks@subliminalrecords.com
Website: http://www.subliminalrecords.com
Website: https://www.facebook.com/subliminalrecords

Genres: Electronic; Dance; House; Techno

New York house and techno imprint. Send demos by email.

Suburban Noize Records
Burbank, CA
Website: https://suburbannoizerecords.com
Website: https://www.facebook.com/suburbannoizerecords

Genres: Hard Rock; Hip-Hop; Punk; Underground

Record label based in Burbank, California.

Sugar Hill Records
Website: https://www.sugarhillrecords.com
Website: https://www.facebook.com/sugarhillrecords

Genres: Blues; Roots; Americana

Label handling bluegrass, Americana and roots.

Sumerian Records
Email: info@sumerianrecords.com
Website: http://www.sumerianrecords.com
Website: https://www.facebook.com/SumerianRecords

Genres: All types of music

Record label based in Los Angeles, California.

Summit Records, Inc
PO Box 13692
Tempe, AZ 85284-3692
Email: sales@summitrecords.com
Website: https://www.summitrecords.com

Genres: Classical; Blues; Jazz

Record label founded in the late 1980s, based in Tempe, Arizona.

Sunnyside Records
Email: francois@sunnysiderecords.com
Website: http://www.sunnysiderecords.com
Website: https://www.facebook.com/SunnysideRecords

Genres: Jazz; Blues; World

Describes itself as a relaxed, independent label, with an acceptance of any jazz style.

Suretone Records
1411 5th Street, #200
Santa Monica, CA 91401
Website: http://www.suretone.com

Genres: Rock

Record label based in Santa Monica, California.

Surfview Records
Website: http://www.surfviewrecords.com

Genres: All types of music

Record label based in Phoenix, Arizona.

Swade Records
106 Virginia Road
Pittsburgh, PA 15237
Website: https://www.swaderecords.com

Genres: Alternative Modern Mainstream Americana Blues Garage Guitar based Rock Rock and Roll Ska

Contact: Tony Vinski

An independent record label founded in 2004 that is based in Pittsburgh, PA. We focus on, but are not limited to, rock & roll, alternative, indie, punk, and ska music. Most of our releases feature Pittsburgh musicians but our intention is not to be a Pittsburgh-only label by any means.

Symbiotic Records
Los Angeles, CA
Website: http://www.symbioticrecords.com
Website: https://www.facebook.com/symbioticrecords

Genres: All types of music

Contact: Eric Knight; Jerjan Alim

Full service record label based in Los Angeles, California. Send demo using form on website.

Team Love Records
New Paltz, NY
Email: info@team-love.com
Website: https://test.team-love.com
Website: https://twitter.com/teamloverecords

Genres: All types of music

Record label based in New Paltz, New York. Send submissions by email as Soundcloud or Bandcamp track / playlist. No Microsoft attachments or Google Drive links.

Tee Pee Records
Website: https://teepeerecords.com
Website: https://www.facebook.com/teepeerecords

Genres: Indie; Metal; Punk; Rock

New York-based label dealing in indie, metal, punk and rock.

Terminus Records
Atlanta, GA
Email: admin@terminusrecords.com
Website: https://terminusrecords.com
Website: https://www.facebook.com/TerminusRecords/

Genres: Rock; Modern Rock; Blues

Record label based in Atlanta, Georgia.

Thin Man Entertainment
Email: Submissions@ThinManEntertainment.com
Email: AR@ThinManEntertainment.com
Website: http://thinmanentertainment.com
Website: https://www.facebook.com/profile.php?id=100070572305110

US Record Labels

Genres: Alternative Rock; Gothic; Industrial; Jazz; Punk; Psychebilly; Underground

Record label focused on underground music of all genres. Send submissions by email.

Third Man Records
623 7th Avenue South
Nashville, TN 37203
Email: nashvillestore@thirdmanrecords.com
Website: https://thirdmanrecords.com
Website: https://www.facebook.com/ThirdManRecords/

Genres: All types of music

Record label based in Nashville, Tennessee. Considers itself "an innovator in the world of vinyl records and a boundary pusher in the world of recorded music".

Thrill Jockey Records
Email: orders@thrilljockey.com
Website: http://www.thrilljockey.com
Website: https://www.facebook.com/ThrillJockey

Genres: Electronic; Indie; Jazz; Pop; Rock

Record label with offices in the US and UK. Not currently accepting demos as at December 2020.

ThrillerTracks
Email: contact@thrillertracks.com
Website: https://www.thrillertracks.com

Genres: Electronic Ambient Instrumental Soundtracks

Contact: Shane Cormier

An indie music label, specializing in background production music for film and video. Our music has been featured in BMW and Lexus commercials in the Netherlands, Germany and Italy.

Thrive Records
Email: demos@thrivemusic.com
Email: info@thrivemusic.com
Website: https://www.thrivemusic.com

Genres: Alternative; Dance; Electronic; Indie; Rock

Send demo by email.

Throne of Blood Records
New York, NY
Email: james@throneofbloodmusic.com
Website: http://www.throneofbloodmusic.com
Website: https://www.facebook.com/tobrecnyc/

Genres: Electronic; Club; Disco; House

Record label based in New York, specialising in House, Electro, Disco, and Club music.

Thump Records
Email: customersupport@thumprecords.com
Website: https://thumprecords.com
Website: https://www.facebook.com/thumprecords

Genres: Dance; Electronic; Latin; Pop; R&B; Rap; Hip-Hop; Urban

Home of the World's Favorite Party Music! We specialize in music from the streets representing decades of great sounds.

Tommy Boy
Website: https://www.tommyboy.com
Website: https://twitter.com/TommyBoyRecords

Genres: Electronic; Hip-Hop; Latin Hip-Hop; Dance; Alternative; Pop

Hip Hop and Electronic label founded in New York City in 1981.

TommyBoy Entertainment LLC
New York, NY
Website: https://www.tommyboy.com
Website: https://twitter.com/TommyBoyRecords

Genres: Hip-Hop; Dance; Electronic; Alternative; Pop

Legendary Hip Hop and Electronic label founded in NYC in 1981.

Tooth & Nail Records
P.O. Box 12698
Seattle, WA 98111
Email: resume@toothandnail.com
Website: https://www.toothandnail.com
Website: https://www.facebook.com/toothandnail

Genres: Alternative; Rock

Record label based in Seattle, tracing its origins back to the early '90s punk and hardcore music scene. Send your best three tracks on CD by post.

Topshelf Records
540 NE Tillamook Street
Portland, OR 97212
Email: info@topshelfrecords.com
Website: https://www.topshelfrecords.com
Website: https://soundcloud.com/topshelfrecords

Genres: All types of music

Record label based in Portland, Oregon. Not accepting demos as at August 2022.

Toucan Cove Entertainment
800 Fifth Avenue #101-292
Seattle, WA 98104-3191
Website: https://toucancove.com
Website: https://twitter.com/toucancove

Genres: All types of music

Full service entertainment company.

Touch and Go Records
Po Box 25520
Chicago, IL 60625
Website: http://www.touchandgorecords.com

Genres: Alternative; Hardcore; Indie; Punk; Rock; Singer-Songwriter

Not currently accepting demos.

Triple Crown Records
PO Box 222132
Great Neck, NY 11022
Email: info@triplecrownrecords.com
Website: http://www.triplecrownrecords.com
Website: https://www.facebook.com/triplecrownrecords

Genres: Alternative; Rock

Record label based in Great Neck, New York.

Tuff City Music Group
Website: https://tuffcity.com
Website: https://www.facebook.com/TuffCityRecords/

Genres: Blues; R&B; Jazz; Funk; Soul; Hip-Hop

Originally rooted in hip-hop, has transitioned its focus toward rescuing thousands of blues, jazz, funk, soul and R&B treasures from obscurity.

Turkey Vulture Records
129 Phelps Avenue, Suite 240
Rockford, IL 61108
Email: info@turkeyvulturerecords.com
Website: http://www.turkeyvulturerecords.com
Website: https://www.facebook.com/turkeyvulturerecords

Genres: All types of music

A worldwide independent label specializing in rock, metal, hardcore, punk, emo, and alternative bands.

Ubiquity Recordings, Inc.
1010 West 17th Street
Costa Mesa, CA 92627
Email: michaelmcfadin@mc.com
Email: Enrique@ubiquityrecords.com
Website: http://www.ubiquityrecords.com
Website: https://www.facebook.com/ubiquityrecords

Genres: Electronic; Indie; Hip-Hop; Jazz; R&B; Rap; Latin Jazz; Funk

Contact: Michael McFadin / Enrique Estrella

Record label based in Costa Mesa, California.

US Record Labels

Ultra Music
Email: info@ultrarecords.com
Website: https://www.ultrarecords.com
Website: https://www.facebook.com/UltraRecordsOfficial/

Genres: Electronic; Pop; Rap; Hip-Hop; Reggae; World; Dance

Describes itself as "one step ahead in the world of dance music" and "the leading independent electronic label".

Undertow Records
Email: hello@undertowmusic.com
Website: http://undertowmusic.com
Website: http://facebook.com/undertowmusic

Genres: Blues; Indie; Rock; Roots

Contact: Bob Andrews; Jayne Ballantyne; Ward Gollings; Chris Grabau; Mark Ray

Unlikely to take on any new acts, so don't send CDs by post or MP3s by email. Send email query with links to your music online, but response not guaranteed.

Unfun Records
PO Box 40307
Berkeley, CA 94704
Email: johnny@unfunrecords.com
Email: unfunrecords@hotmail.com
Website: http://unfunrecords.com

Genres: All types of music

Record label based in California. Send demo on CD by post.

Union Entertainment Group (UEG), Inc.
Email: info@ueginc.com
Website: http://www.ueginc.com

Genres: All types of music

Record label based in the Los Angeles area since 1987, with offices in California, Texas, Florida, Washington, Canada, and Amsterdam.

United Riot Records
Email: UNITEDRIOT1@gmail.com
Email: unitedriotrec@aol.com
Website: https://unitedriotrecords.com
Website: https://www.facebook.com/unitedriotrecords
Website: https://myspace.com/unitedriotrecords

Genres: Hardcore; Punk; Rock and Roll; Ska; Metal

A label dedicated to the underground music scene. Mainly interested in Hardcore, Punk and Oi! but always interested in all types of music such as Rock n' Roll, Ska, Metal or just plain good music.

Universal Music Group Nashville
Website: https://www.umgnashville.com
Website: https://www.facebook.com/UMGNashville

Genres: Country; Rock; Americana

Record label based in Nashville, Tennessee.

Universal Music Group
2220 Colorado Avenue
Santa Monica, CA 90404
Email: communications@umusic.com
Website: https://www.universalmusic.com
Website: https://www.facebook.com/UniversalMusicGroup

Genres: All types of music

International music group. Accepts demos only through a manager, agent, producer, radio DJ or other industry professional.

Universal Music Latin Entertainment
Website: http://www.universalmusica.com
Website: https://www.facebook.com/universalmusica

Genres: Latin

A record company specialised in producing and distributing Latin Music in the US and Puerto Rico.

Access more listings online at *www.musicsocket.com*

US Record Labels 37

Vagrant Records
Website: https://vagrant.com
Website: https://www.facebook.com/vagrantrecords

Genres: All types of music

Record label based in California. Focuses on rock, but features artists in a variety of other genres including folk, soul, electronic, and pop.

Valley Entertainment
Email: jon@valley-entertainment.com
Email: erika@valley-entertainment.com
Website: https://www.valley-entertainment.com
Website: https://www.facebook.com/valleyent

Genres: Jazz; New Age; Rock; World; Blues; Country; Celtic; Instrumental

A privately owned record label that was founded in the mid-nineties. The label includes an eclectic repertoire from pop to alternative, with focus on singer-songwriters, modern Irish musicians and World music.

Van Richter
Email: manager@vanrichter.net
Email: vanrichterrec@gmail.com
Website: https://www.vanrichter.net
Website: https://www.facebook.com/vanrichter.net/

Genres: Industrial; Gothic; Ambient; Synthpop

Our Artists cover the entire spectrum of the Industrial sub genres including Aggro, Electro, Darkwave, Noise, and Ambient.

Varese Sarabande Records
Email: cary.mansfield@varesesarabande.com
Website: https://www.varesesarabande.com/

Genres: Soundtracks

Contact: Cary Mansfield

Record label of new and classic soundtracks.

Verve Label Group
Universal Music Group
2220 Colorado Ave
Santa Monica, CA 90404
Website: https://www.vervelabelgroup.com
Website: https://www.facebook.com/ververecords/

Genres: Jazz; Contemporary; Pop; R&B

Record label based in Santa Monica, California.

Victory Records
Fax: +1 (312) 666-8665
Email: info@victoryrecords.com
Website: https://victoryrecords.com
Website: https://www.facebook.com/VictoryRecords

Genres: Metal; Rock; Indie; Hardcore; Punk

Formed in 1989, it separated itself from the pack as the definitive independent label for punk, hardcore, emo, metal and alternative. Supplying 30 years of formative music to dichard audiences everywhere, the Chicago-bred and -based label cranked up the voices of three generations of iconoclasts and built a culture without compromise.

Vineyard Worship
Email: info@vineyardworship.com
Website: https://www.vineyardworship.com
Website: https://www.facebook.com/VineyardWorship

Genres: Christian

Record label releasing Christian music.

Viper Records
Website: https://www.viperrecords.com
Website: https://www.facebook.com/viperrecords/

Genres: Hip-Hop; Rap

A boutique indie label created to level an uneven playing field between artists and labels. Approach via online contact form. Tries to respond, but not always possible due to volume of submissions.

US Record Labels

Visionary Music Group
Website: http://www.teamvisionary.com
Website: https://www.facebook.com/VisionaryMusicGroup

Genres: Urban

Not accepting enquiries as at October 2022.

Warrior Records
7095 Hollywood Blvd., #826
Hollywood, CA 90028
Email: info@warriorrecords.com
Website: https://www.warriorrecords.com
Website: https://www.facebook.com/OfficialWarriorRecords/

Genres: All types of music

Contact: Jim Ervin

Accepts unsolicited submissions but does not review websites. Send three or four tracks and type all correspondence. Include SASE or email address for response, and picture/bio if available. Expect response to take at least 6-8 weeks.

Water Music Records
Los Angeles
Email: info@watermusicrecords.com
Website: http://watermusicrecords.com
Website: https://www.facebook.com/WaterMusicDance

Genres: Dance; Electronic; Pop; Rock

Record label based in Los Angeles, California.

West Clark Records
Email: westclarkrecords@gmail.com
Website: https://www.facebook.com/westclarkrecords
Website: https://westclarkrecords.bandcamp.com

Genres: Electronic Hard Heavy Non-Commercial Mainstream Underground Acoustic Alternative Club Dance Drum and Bass Dubstep Emo Garage Guitar based Hardcore Indie Lo-fi Metal Punk Remix Rock Rock and Roll Rockabilly Ska Surf Techno

A little label created in a basement in the suburbs of St. Louis with nothing more than a dream.

Yellow Dog Records
1910 Madison Avenue #671
Memphis, TN 38104
Website: http://yellowdogrecords.com
Website: http://facebook.com/ydrecords

Genres: Blues; Folk; Jazz; Roots; Soul; Americana

Record label based in Memphis, Tennessee.

*Access more listings online at **www.musicsocket.com***

UK Record Labels

For the most up-to-date listings of these and hundreds of other record labels, visit https://www.musicsocket.com/recordlabels

To claim your *free* access to the site, please see the back of this book.

2020 Vision Recordings Ltd
Website: https://www.2020recordings.com
Website: https://www.facebook.com/2020VisionRecordings/

Genres: Dance; Electronic

Send demos through online form on website.

3tone Records
Saint Nicholas Street
Bristol
BS1 1TG
Email: demo@3tonerecords.co.uk
Email: info@3tonerecords.co.uk
Website: http://www.3tonerecords.co.uk
Website: https://www.facebook.com/3toneRecords/

Genres: All types of music

Independent record label based in Bristol. Send demos by email.

Aardvark Records Ltd
75 Alderwood Parc
Penryn
Cornwall
TR10 8RL
Email: sophsweet@gmail.com
Email: mail@aardvarkrecords.co.uk
Website: http://www.aardvarkrecords.co.uk

Genres: Dance; Rock; Pop; Acoustic; Folk; New Age; World; Chill; Downtempo; Break Beat; Drum and Bass; Traditional Soul; Traditional R&B; Ambient Chill; Commercial Dance; House; Techno; Techno Trance; Alternative Rock; Progressive Rock; Blues; Celtic; Indie; Reggae; Soul

Contact: Andy Reeve; Sophie Sweatman

Record label based in Cornwall. Describes itself as a Fair Trade record label and music publisher; staunchly independent; and green. See website for demo submission guidelines.

Accidental Records Ltd
Email: info@accidentalrecords.com
Website: http://www.accidentalrecords.com
Website: https://www.facebook.com/accidentalrecords

Genres: All types of music

Send demos by email with the words "Demo submission" in the subject line and links to streaming music online. No audio files.

Acid Jazz Records
146 Bethnal Green Road
London
E2 6DG
Website: https://www.acidjazz.co.uk

Genres: All types of music, except: Black Metal; Metal; Rap

Record label based in London, founded in 1987 at the start of the "acieed" explosion.

Actual Size Music
Website: https://www.actualsizemusic.org.uk

Genres: Experimental

Artist run record label based in London, UK and releasing experimental material. Run as a means for the artists operating the label to release their own music, so does not sign other artists.

AD Music
5 Albion Road
Bungay
Suffolk
NR35 1LQ
Email: contact@admusicshop.com
Website: https://www.admusicshop.com
Website: https://www.facebook.com/ADmusiconline

Genres: Instrumental Electronic; Chill

Record label based in Bungay, Suffolk. Releases electronica, chill out and instrumental synth electronic music (not dance) only. No submissions.

Adapted Vinyl
Email: sb@adaptedvinyl.com
Website: http://www.adaptedvinyl.com

Genres: Electronic

Record label dedicated to releasing high quality electronic music.

Adasam Limited
Website: http://www.adasam.co.uk/

Genres: All types of music

Home to a number of independent record labels, covering a wide range of genres. See individual websites of labels for specific details.

Alcopop! Records
Email: jack@ilovealcopop.co.uk
Email: LukeAnR@hotmail.com
Website: https://ilovealcopop.co.uk
Website: https://www.facebook.com/ilovealcopop

Genres: Alternative; Indie

Record label founded in Oxford in 2006, home to independent music.

Alex Tronic Records
Email: info@alextronicrecords.co.uk
Website: http://www.alextronicrecords.co.uk
Website: https://www.facebook.com/Alex-Tronic-Records-Recording-Studios-281100465296557

Genres: Dance; Electronic; Downtempo; Ambient; House; Drum and Bass; Break Beat; Hip-Hop

Contact: Becki Bardot (A&R)

Record label based in Edinburgh, Scotland. Prefers to receive CDs in the post, but will accept links to music online by email. Will not download large files, however.

Almighty Records Limited
PO Box 414
Stroud
GL6 1HR
Email: info@almightyrecords.com
Website: https://www.almightyrecords.com
Website: https://www.facebook.com/AlmightyRecordLabel/

Genres: Dance; Pop

Record label based in Stroud, Gloucestershire.

Alter Ego Records
Email: home@alteregorecords.com
Website: http://www.alteregorecords.com
Website: http://www.label-worx.com/demo/alteregomusic

Genres: Trance; Progressive; House

Record label based in Cardiff. Send demos by uploading to DemoBox online only.

Amazon Records
Email: frank@amazonrecords.co.uk
Website: http://www.amazonrecords.co.uk
Website: https://www.facebook.com/amazonrecords/

Genres: Indie; Pop; Rock; Punk; Folk; Country

UK Record Labels

Once again taking up the challenge of signing new and interesting artists. Contact by email.

Amber Artists
Email: records@amberartists.com
Website: http://www.amberartists.com

Genres: Commercial; Contemporary; Pop

Independent artist management company and independent record company.

Ambiel
15 Hatch Lane
Chigford
London
E4 6LP
Email: pr@ambiel.co.uk
Website: https://ambielmusic.com
Website: https://www.facebook.com/ambielmusic

Genres: All types of music

Make contact through Facebook. Do not send submissions or artist/promo packs through contact form on website. Aims to listen to everything sent to them, but cannot respond to everyone.

The Animal Farm
4th Floor, Block A
Tower Bridge Business Complex
100 Clements Road
London
SE16 4DG
Email: info@theanimalfarm.co.uk
Website: http://www.theanimalfarm.co.uk
Website: https://www.facebook.com/theanimalfarmmusic

Genres: Indie; Pop; Rock; Acoustic; Alternative; Metal

An independently owned music company offering a wide range of creative and business services to artists and songwriters: produces and mixes records and writes songs in their two recording studios in London; manages artists and songwriters; run an independent record label and a publishing company and a booking agency. Send query with link to music online by email or via online contact form.

ARC Music Productions International
A & R Department
PO Box 111
East Grinstead
West Sussex
RH19 4FZ
Email: anr@arcmusic.co.uk
Email: info@arcmusic.co.uk
Website: https://www.arcmusic.co.uk
Website: https://www.facebook.com/arcmusicprod/

Genres: World; Folk; Celtic; Latin

Record label based in East Grinstead, West Sussex. Send demo as attachment by email (if less than 10MB), or by download site e.g. yousendit if larger. Alternatively send CD and info by post.

Ariwa Sounds Ltd
34 Whitehorse Lane
London
SE25 6RE
Email: info@ariwa.com
Email: ariwastudios@gmail.com
Website: https://www.ariwa.com
Website: https://www.facebook.com/Ariwasounds

Genres: Dub; Roots; Reggae; Electronic

Produces Dub, Lovers Rock, and Roots & Culture reggae music.

Armadillo Music Limited
PO Box 3055
Sturminster Newton
Dorset
DT10 2XA
Email: mail@bluearmadillo.com
Website: https://www.bluearmadillo.com
Website: https://www.facebook.com/Armadillo-Music-Ltd-538482406197055/

Genres: Americana; Blues; Rockabilly; Rock; Roots

Independent Roots & Blues Music Label based in Sturminster Newton, Dorset.

Claim your free access to www.musicsocket.com: See p.211

Armellodie
Glasgow
Scotland
Email: info@armellodie.com
Website: http://www.armellodie.com
Website: https://twitter.com/Armellotweet

Genres: Leftfield Rock; Indie; Avant-Garde

Record label based in Glasgow, Scotland, describing itself as "a tiny wee independent label, stable, collective, R.O.C.K consortium,".

Audiobulb Records
Sheffield
Email: contact@audiobulb.com
Website: https://www.audiobulb.com
Website: https://www.facebook.com/audiobulb/

Genres: Dance; Electronic Experimental Downtempo Avant-Garde Alternative Leftfield; Ambient

An exploratory music label designed to promote creativity in all its forms. Releases artist works on CD and download formats as well as multimedia works, VST, audio hardware and other creative tools. Works supported by this label often explore the interface between the electronic and natural world. We embrace the complexity of unique electronics, intricate acoustics and detailed microsounds.

Audiorec Limited
Lynton House
304 Bensham Lane
Thornton Heath
Surrey
CR7 7EQ
Email: info@audiorec.co.uk
Email: info@audiorec.co.in
Website: http://www.audiorec.co.uk

Genres: Regional

Record label handling Indian music, with offices in the UK and India.

b-unique
Website: https://www.b-uniquerecords.com/

Genres: Alternative; Indie; Rock

Small independent company formed in 2001. Has been involved in sales of over 100 million albums, 20 billion streams and countless number one singles across publishing and records.

Backwater Records
Website: https://backwaterrecords.com
Website: https://soundcloud.com/backwater-records

Genres: Alternative Country; Acid Folk; Psychedelic Pop Rock; Singer-Songwriter

Suffolk-based label releasing Suffolk-based bands/artists.

Bamboleo Records
London
Email: demos@bamboleorecords.com
Email: info@bamboleorecords.com
Website: http://www.bamboleorecords.com

Genres: House; Techno; Funk

Record label based in London. Send demos by email.

Banquet Records
52 Eden Street
Kingston
Surrey
KT1 1EE
Email: shop@banquetrecords.com
Website: https://www.banquetrecords.com/banquet-label
Website: https://www.facebook.com/banquetrecords/

Genres: Hardcore; Indie; Punk

Record shop in Kingston, Surrey, with its own record label.

Barely Breaking Even Records
Arch 376
10 Helmsley Place
London
E8 3SB
Email: staff@bbemusic.com
Website: https://www.bbemusic.com

Website: https://www.facebook.com/
bbcmusic/

Genres: Dance; Jazz; Funk; Techno; Garage; Hip-Hop; Disco

Record label based in London.

Basick Records
Email: info@basickrecords.com
Website: https://www.basickrecords.com
Website: https://soundcloud.com/basickrecords

Genres: Metal; Progressive

A fiercely heavy and progressive record label from London, UK.

Beggars Group
17-19 Alma Road
London
SW18 1AA
Email: banquet@beggars.com
Website: https://beggars.com

Genres: Indie

Record label with offices around the world.

Bella Union
120-124 Curtain Road
London
EC2A 3SQ
Email: simon@bellaunion.com
Email: mark@bellaunion.com
Website: https://bellaunion.com
Website: https://www.facebook.com/bellaunionrecs

Genres: All types of music

Contact: Simon

Not accepting unsolicited demos as at September 2020, due to overwhelming level of submissions.

Beta Recordings
Email: demos@john-b.com
Website: https://www.beta-recordings.com/
Website: https://www.facebook.com/betarecordings/

Genres: Dance; Drum and Bass; Techno; House; Atmospheric Drum and Bass; Melodic Drum and Bass; Electronic; Dance Rock

Contact: John B

Send soundcloud links by email.

Big Dada Recordings
PO Box 4296
London
SE11 4WW
Email: demos@ninjatune.net
Website: https://www.bigdada.com
Website: https://soundcloud.com/bigdadasound

Genres: Hip-Hop; Alternative Hip-Hop; Grime

Record label based in London. Started as an underground hip hop label, but now releases a full range of Black Music. Send query by email only with links to MP3 files, soundcloud, pages, or websites. No MP3 attachments. Response if interested. Do not chase for response.

Big Scary Monsters Recording Company
Email: connor@bsmrocks.com
Email: dave@bsmrocks.com
Website: https://bsmrocks.com/
Website: https://www.facebook.com/bigscarymonsters

Genres: Post Rock; Punk; Alternative; Hardcore; Acoustic

Record label based in Oxford. Send query by email describing your act and providing links to your music online.

Black Acre Records
Bristol
Email: hello@blackacrerecords.co.uk
Website: http://theblackacre.co.uk

Genres: Electronic

Electronic record label based in Bristol. Send query by email with links to music online.

Black Butter Records
London
Email: info@black-butter.co.uk
Email: demos@black-butter.co.uk
Website: https://www.black-butter.com
Website: https://soundcloud.com/black-butter-records

Genres: Dance; Hip-Hop; Urban

Record label based in London. Send query by email with "Demo" in the subject line, including Soundcloud links.

Black Tragick Records
Belfast
Email: blacktragickrecords@gmail.com
Website: https://www.facebook.com/blacktragickrecords
Website: https://twitter.com/blacktragician

Genres: Doom; Folk; Metal

Record label based in Belfast.

Blindsight Records
Email: info@blindsightrecords.co.uk
Website: http://www.blindsightrecords.co.uk
Website: https://soundcloud.com/blindsight-records

Genres: Rock; Electronic; Ambient; Post Rock; Hardcore; Metal

Record label based in the United Kingdom. For demo submissions make contact by email, or use Soundcloud.

Blue Shell Music
Derry
Email: jonny@blueshellmusic.com
Website: https://www.facebook.com/BlueShellMusicManagement

Genres: Pop

Record label and management based in Derry, Northern Ireland. Send query by email in first instance and submit demo upon request.

Blues Matters Records
PO Box 18
Bridgend
CF33 6YW
Email: alan@bluesmatters.com
Website: http://www.bluesmatters.com
Website: https://www.facebook.com/bluesmattersmagazine/

Genres: Blues; Rhythm and Blues

Contact: Alan Pearce

Describes itself as one of the most recognizable Blues magazines in the world.

Bohemian Jukebox
Email: recordings@bohemianjukebox.com
Website: https://www.bohemianjukebox.com
Website: https://soundcloud.com/bencalvert

Genres: Post Folk; Singer-Songwriter; Psychedelic; Alternative Acoustic; Leftfield Acoustic; Experimental

Contact: Ben Calvert

Record label with offices in Birmingham. Works with Post-Folk, Alternative and Psychedelic lyric-centric songwriters who have a way with poetics.

Bomber Music Ltd
125-135 Preston Road
London
BN1 6AF
Email: postbox@bombermusic.com
Website: https://www.bombermusic.com
Website: https://www.facebook.com/bombermusic

Genres: Punk; Rock and Roll; Rockabilly; Reggae; Ska; Underground;

Label set up in 2010 by an independent music company, describing itself as the UK's leading alternative music publisher.

Border Community
Website: http://www.bordercommunity.com
Website: https://soundcloud.com/border-community

Genres: Electronic

Record label based in London. Send streaming links via online contact form.

Boslevan Records
Email: boslevanrecords@gmail.com
Email: vinosangre@gmail.com
Website: https://boslevanrecords.co.uk
Website: https://www.facebook.com/BoslevanRecords

Genres: Hardcore; Indie; Punk; Punk Rock

DIY record label based in Cornwall.

Botchit & Scarper Records
Website: https://www.botchitandscarper.com
Website: https://www.facebook.com/botchit

Genres: Break Beat

Record label founded in 1995. Describes itself as unique in present times, in that it concentrates on artist development; and "has reinvented the way breakbeats impact the dance world".

Brain Bomb Productions (BBP)
Website: https://www.brainbomb.com/
Website: https://soundcloud.com/brainbomb

Genres: Ambient; Chill; Downtempo; Break Beat; House; Techno; Tribal; Trance; Drum and Bass

Contact: Luke Harrison

Small indie label that has grown organically over many years into a high impact producer of music audio and video productions.

BS1 Records
Email: info@bs1records.com
Website: https://bs1records.com
Website: https://soundcloud.com/bs1records

Genres: Drum and Bass

Drum & Bass label. Send email with links to music online for consideration.

Bucks Music Group
Roundhouse
212 Regents Park Road Entrance
London
NW1 8AW
Fax: +44 (0) 20 7229 6893
Email: recordings@bucksmusicgroup.co.uk
Email: info@bucksmusicgroup.co.uk
Website: http://www.bucksmusicgroup.com
Website: https://www.facebook.com/bucksmusicgroup/

Genres: All types of music

Independent music publisher based in London, operating a number of labels.

Burning Shed Limited
Unit B, Yarefield Park
Old Hall Road
Norwich
NR4 6FF
Email: support@burningshed.com
Website: https://burningshed.com

Genres: Ambient; Electronic; Singer-Songwriter; Progressive; Rock

Contact: Tim Bowness; Peter Chilvers; Pete Morgan

Online label and record store. Send demos by post or as emails with download links. No attachments. Response not guaranteed unless interested.

Bush Bash Recordings
London
Email: recordings@bushbash.biz
Website: https://www.bushbashrecordings.com
Website: https://facebook.com/BushBashrecs

Genres: Garage; Grime; Hip-Hop; House; R&B; Rap; Urban

Record label based in London.

BUT! Records
Email: jamesie@butgroup.com
Email: Nick.lyp@gmail.com
Website: http://www.butgroup.com
Website: https://www.youtube.com/user/TheBUTmusicGroup

Genres: Commercial Acoustic Alternative Mainstream Guitar based Pop Rock Singer-Songwriter

Contact: Allan James; Nick Robinson

UK Record Labels

Successful UK based Independant Record label with USA partner. International distribution. Roster available on website and YouTube Channel.

Button Up Records
51 King Street
Coatbridge
ML5 1JF
Email: buttonupinfo@hotmail.com
Website: https://www.buttonuprecords.co.uk/
Website: https://www.facebook.com/buttonuprecords

Genres: All types of music

Contact: Garry John Kane

Record label based in Coatbridge. Send query by email with links to music online or MP3s. We are very open minded.

Buzz Records
Email: studio@thebuzzgroup.co.uk
Website: https://thebuzzgroup.co.uk
Website: https://www.facebook.com/buzzpublicity

Genres: Alternative Roots; Blues; Country; Folk; Alternative Blues

A small independent alternative bluses label focusing on "music that has an insurgent twist and an original angle, dragging old-time sounds kicking and screaming into the 21st century." Focussing now on a single artist, so not taking on any new acts.

Buzzin' Fly Records
Website: http://www.buzzinfly.com
Website: https://www.facebook.com/buzzinflyrecords/

Genres: Electronic; House; Techno

Contact: Ben Watt

Record label based in London. On hiatus since 2013.

Candid Productions Ltd
16 Castelnau
Barnes
London
SW13 9RU
Email: enquiries@candidrecords.com
Website: http://www.candidrecords.com
Website: https://www.facebook.com/CandidRec/

Genres: Blues; Jazz; Mainstream Jazz; Modern Jazz; Swing; World Jazz

Send demo on CD by post, marked for the attention of the A&R Department. Receives a large volume of material so cannot respond personally to everything. Response if interested. Do not use the online contact form to send emails about submissions etc. as they will not reach the A&R Department.

Candlelight Records
Beaumont House
Kensington Village
Avonmore Rd
London
W14 8TS
Email: info@spinefarmrecords.com
Website: https://www.candlelightrecords.co.uk
Website: https://www.facebook.com/candlelightrecords/

Genres: Metal

Metal record label based in London, with offices in New York and Helsinki.

Caritas Records
Achmore
Moss Road
Ullapool
Ross-shire
IV26 2TF
Email: caritas-records@caritas-music.co.uk
Email: info@caritas-music.co.uk
Website: https://www.caritas-music.co.uk

Genres: Classical

Contact: Katharine Douglas

Record label handling Classical and Choral music.

Catskills Records
3 Brooker Street
Hove
BN3 3YX

Access more listings online at www.musicsocket.com

Email: info@catskillsrecords.com
Website: https://www.catskillsmusic.com
Website: https://www.facebook.com/catskillsrecords

Genres: All types of music

Record label based in London and Brighton.

Champion Records
181 High Street
Harlesden
London
NW10 4TE
Email: rob@championrecords.co.uk
Email: raj@championrecords.co.uk
Website: https://www.championrecords.co.uk
Website: https://www.facebook.com/championrecords/

Genres: Garage; House; Singer-Songwriter

Record label based in Harlesden, London.

Chandos Records Ltd
Chandos House
1 Commerce Park
Commerce Way
Colchester
Essex
CO2 8HX
Fax: +44 (0) 1206 225201
Website: https://www.chandos.net

Genres: Classical

Classical record label, based in Colchester, Essex.

Chemikal Underground Records
Glasgow
Email: info@chemikal.co.uk
Website: https://chemikal.co.uk
Website: https://soundcloud.com/chemikal-underground

Genres: Alternative

Record label based in Glasgow, Scotland.

Cherry Red Records
Power Road Studios
114 Power Road
London
W4 5PY
Fax: +44 (0) 20 8747 4030
Email: infonet@cherryred.co.uk
Email: ideas@cherryred.co.uk
Website: https://www.cherryred.co.uk
Website: https://www.facebook.com/CherryRedRecords

Genres: All types of music

A proudly independent record label making noise in West London for more than 40 years.

Chocolate Fireguard Music Ltd
PO Box 461
Huddersfield
West Yorkshire
HD5 8WL
Email: info@chocolatefireguard.co.uk
Website: http://www.chocolatefireguard.co.uk
Website: https://www.facebook.com/ChocolateFireguardMusic
Website: http://www.myspace.com/chocolatefireguardmusic

Genres: Dance; Electronic; Hip-Hop; Rock

Record label based in Huddersfield, West Yorkshire. Always looking for new music, so submit your tracks if you think they are right for this label after consulting the website.

Circuit Records
c/o Higher Rhythm Ltd
53-57 Nether Hall Road
Doncaster
South Yorkshire
DN1 2PG
Email: mail@circuitrecords.co.uk
Website: https://www.circuitrecords.co.uk
Website: https://www.facebook.com/circuitrecordsuk

Genres: All types of music

Record label from a Yorkshire based music and media company, also running a radio station, a recording studio, artist development programmes, live events, and lots of other things. Accepts approaches from artists from Yorkshire.

Circus Records

17 Chocolate Studios
7 Shepherdess Place
Shoreditch
London
N1 7LJ
Email: info@circus-records.co.uk
Website: https://circus-records.co.uk
Website: https://soundcloud.com/circusrecords

Genres: Electronic

Electronic record label based in Shoreditch, London. Send query by email with soundcloud links for up to two tracks.

Cityscape Records

Website: https://cityscaperecords.bandcamp.com

Genres: Electronic; Indie; Pop

A long established kitchen table label which has been championing DIY pop from a Bolton terrace since '96. Recording in glamorous locations such as the 'back room'.

Clue Records

Leeds
Email: info@cluerecords.com
Website: https://cluerecords.bandcamp.com
Website: https://www.facebook.com/ClueRecords

Genres: Alternative; Indie; Rock

An independent record label based in Leeds, UK. "We work with artists we adore and release music we love."

Commercially Inviable Records

41 Gristhorpe Road
Birmingham
B29
Email: info@cominrecords.com
Website: http://www.cominrecords.com
Website: https://www.facebook.com/cominrecords

Genres: Acoustic; Country; Folk

Record label based in Brimingham. No A&R policy as such, but anyone having some music they think might be suitable may get in touch using the contact form on the website.

Concrete Recordings

Website: http://www.concreterecordings.co.uk

Genres: Acoustic; Guitar based; Indie; Post Punk

Record label based in Manchester.

Confidential Records (UK) Ltd

Cadman Lane
SNAITH
EAST YORKSHIRE
DN14 9JR
Website: https://www.confidentialrecords.co.uk
Website: https://www.facebook.com/confidentialrecordsuk

Genres: All types of music

Record label based in Snaith, East Yorkshire. Maximum roster of 40. Check website to see if they currently have scope for taking on a new act.

Cooking Vinyl

12 & 13 Swainson Road
London
W3 7XB
Email: info@cookingvinyl.com
Website: https://www.cookingvinyl.com
Website: https://www.facebook.com/cookingvinylrecords/

Genres: All types of music

Record label based in London. Home to an eclectic mix of acclaimed artists.

Cr2 Records

Email: demos@cr2records.com
Email: info@cr2records.co.uk

Website: http://www.cr2records.co.uk
Website: https://soundcloud.com/cr2records

Genres: Dance; House; Techno; Electronic

Contact: Mark Brown

Send demos by email as private Soundcloud links, or via online submission system. No MP3 email attachments.

CRD Records Limited
TRURO
TR2 5YJ
Email: info@crdrecords.com
Website: https://www.crdrecords.com
Website: https://www.facebook.com/CRDrecords

Genres: Classical

Classical record label based in Truro, Cornwall.

Criminal Records
Email: pr@criminalrecords.cc
Website: http://www.criminalrecords.cc
Website: https://soundcloud.com/criminal-records

Genres: Indie; Rock; Electronic

Always on the lookout for good bands. Send email with links to your music online.

Critical Music
Email: badger@criticalmusic.com
Website: https://criticalmusic.com
Website: https://www.facebook.com/criticalmusicdnb

Genres: Drum and Bass; Electronic; Dance

Electronic dance music label committed to shining a light on the new generation of Drum & Bass artists. Submit demos via online form on website.

Crucial Records
Email: crlabelinfo@crucial-records.com
Website: http://www.crucial-records.com

Genres: All types of music

Mainly interested in rock, metal etc. music with social or political ideas being a big part of the song.

Cruise International Records
Alerton Grange Vale
Leeds
LS17 6LS
Email: info@cruisedigital.co.uk
Website: https://www.cruisedigital.co.uk
Website: https://www.facebook.com/cruisedigitalmusic/

Genres: All types of music

Record label based in Leeds, West Yorkshire. Send query through form on website.

D.O.R.
Website: https://dor.co.uk/contact/
Website: https://www.facebook.com/DORlabel/

Genres: Experimental

Experimental music for the future.

Dancing Turtle Records
London
Website: https://www.dancingturtle.com
Website: https://www.soundcloud.com/dancingturtle

Genres: Electronic; Experimental; Folk; Indie; World

Company based in London, incorporating a record label, film production company, creative agency and global news hub.

Dead by Mono Records
Email: info@deadbymono.com
Website: https://www.deadbymono.com
Website: https://www.facebook.com/DeadbyMonoRecords

Genres: Garage Rock Rhythm and Blues Rock and Roll Surf Rockabilly Psychebilly Punk Instrumental Blues Horror Alternative New Wave Psychedelic

UK Record Labels

Independent record label and mail order based in the UK. Dedicated to garage rock, surf music and rock 'n' roll since 2005.

Dead Happy Records
3B Castledown Avenue
Hastings
East Sussex
TN34 3RJ
Email: dave@deadhappyrecords.co.uk
Website: http://www.deadhappyrecords.co.uk

Genres: Dance; Indie; Trance

Label based in Hastings, East Sussex.

Defected
Email: demos@defected.com
Website: https://defected.com
Website: https://www.facebook.com/DefectedRecords

Genres: Dance; House

Record label based in London. Dedicated to the finest in house, from its label and numerous associated imprints, to its events and festivals.

Delphian Records
34 Wallace Avenue
The Meadows
Wallyford
East Lothian
EH21 8BZ
Email: info@delphianrecords.co.uk
Website: https://www.delphianrecords.com
Website: https://www.facebook.com/delphianrecords/

Genres: Classical

Contact: Paul Baxter

Describes itself as one of the UK's foremost independent classical record labels.

Deltasonic Records
Email: annheston@live.com
Website: http://deltasonicrecords.co.uk
Website: https://www.facebook.com/deltasonicrecords/

Genres: All types of music

Record label based in Liverpool, founded by a former Polygram music scout. Send Soundcloud link via contact form on website.

Denizen Recordings
Nottingham
Email: denizendemos@denizen.uk.com
Email: kristi@denizen.uk.com
Website: http://denizenrecordings.uk.com
Website: https://soundcloud.com/denizenrecordings

Genres: All types of music

Contact: Kristi Genovese

Send demos by email as MP3 attachments up to 10MB maximum, or upload to the dropbox.

Detour Records
PO Box 18
Midhurst
West Sussex
GU29 9YU
Fax: +44 (0) 1730 815422
Email: Detour@btinternet.com
Website: http://www.detour-records.co.uk
Website: https://www.facebook.com/pages/Detour-Records-Official/672613086164448

Genres: Punk

Label dealing in Mod and Punk. Send demo by post.

Dirtee Stank
14 Havelock Walk
London
SE23 3HG
Website: https://soundcloud.com/dirteestankrecordingsltd
Website: https://find-and-update.company-information.service.gov.uk/company/05579928

Genres: Hip-Hop; Garage; Rap; Grime; Urban

Record label based in London, intended to bridge the gap between indies, majors and the street.

Access more listings online at www.musicsocket.com

Dirty Hit
Email: info@dirtyhit.co.uk
Website: https://dirtyhit.co.uk
Website: https://www.facebook.com/DirtyHit/

Genres: Alternative

Independent record label formed in 2009, with a desire to develop and nurture homegrown artists. Frustration with outdated record company models means a commitment to long-term career building principals. Send query by email with links to music online.

Dirty Water Records
47 Moresby Road
Flat 2, top floor
London
E5 9LE
Email: label@dirtywaterclub.com
Website: https://www.dirtywaterrecords.co.uk
Website: https://www.facebook.com/dirtywaterrecords

Genres: Garage; Power Pop; Punk Rock; Rock and Roll; Rhythm and Blues

Record label based in London. Send query by email with links to music online. Also recommends sending a CD-R by post.

Dissention Records
Website: https://www.dissentionrecords.com
Website: https://twitter.com/dissentionmgmt

Genres: Punk; Alternative

Independent record label started in Boston but now based in the UK. Heavily influenced by punk rock music, specifically the DC hardcore scene.

Distinctive Records
Website: http://www.distinctiverecords.com
Website: https://www.facebook.com/distinctiverecs

Genres: Acid; Dance; House; Break Beat

proud upholder of Acid house and rave, and likes submissions form this genre.

Divine Art Record Company
176-178 Pontefract Road
Cudworth
Barnsley
S72 8BE
Email: info@divineartrecords.com
Website: https://divineartrecords.com

Genres: Classical

Classical music label with offices in the UK and US. See website for brochure on recording with the label, and the new project proposal form. No forms of current popular music. Offers both recording service arrangement and traditional royalty arrangement, covering up-front costs. See website for full details.

Dog Knights Productions
Email: info@dogknightsproductions.com
Email: dogknightsproductions@hotmail.co.uk
Website: https://dogknightsproductions.com/
Website: https://www.facebook.com/dogknights

Genres: Hardcore; Punk

UK-based independent record label.

Dome Records Ltd
Email: info@domerecords.co.uk
Website: http://www.domerecords.co.uk
Website: https://www.facebook.com/domerecords/

Genres: R&B; Soul

Describes itself as the UK home of Soul and R&B.

Domino Recording Company
Website: https://www.dominomusic.com
Website: https://soundcloud.com/dominorecordco

Genres: Alternative

Founded in Putney, South West London, in 1993. Send demos via Soundcloud.

Dorado Music
19A Douglas Street, Unit B
London
SW1P 4PA

US OFFICE:
4770 Biscayne Blvd. Suite 900
Miami, FL 33137
United States
Email: contact@dorado.net
Email: ollie@dorado.net
Website: https://dorado.net
Website: https://www.facebook.com/doradorecords/

Genres: Acid Jazz; Drum and Bass; Jazz; Electronic; Hip-Hop; Soul

Record label with offices in London and Florida.

Dr Johns Surgery Records
Email: drjohnssurgeryrecords@gmail.com
Website: https://www.facebook.com/drjohnssurgery1
Website: https://www.facebook.com/drjohnssurgery1

Genres: All types of music

Independent record label run for the artists, not personal gain. Submit demos via form on website.

Dramatico Entertainment Ltd
Box 214
Farnham
Surrey
GU10 5XZ
Email: mail@dramatico.com
Website: http://www.dramatico.com
Website: http://www.facebook.com/Dramatico

Genres: Alternative; Pop

Record label based in London. Unusual among record labels, it controls marketing and sales throughout much of the world by means of direct control from London, rather than licensing to other labels in other territories.

Drum With Our Hands
Email: info@drumwithourhands.com
Email: steve@drumwithourhands.com
Website: http://www.drumwithourhands.com
Website: https://www.facebook.com/DWOHrecords

Genres: Electronic; Alternative Folk; Classic Pop; Ambient

Contact: Andy; Steve

Indie/DIY record label from North Wales.

Earache London
Email: tim@earache.com
Email: dan.hardingham@earache.com
Website: https://www.earache.com

Genres: Metal

Send submissions via Artist Submission Form on website.

East Central One
Creeting House
All Saints Road
Creeting St Mary
Suffolk
IP6 8PR
Fax: +44 (0) 1449 726067
Email: enquiries@eastcentralone.com
Website: https://www.eastcentralone.com

Genres: All types of music, except: Dance

Contact: Steve Fernie; Helen Milner

Record label based in Ipswich, founded in 1998 by a former employee of EMI and BMG.

Eastzone Records
53 Corbet Avenue
Sprowston
Norwich
NR7 8HS
Website: http://www.eastzonerecords.co.uk

Genres: All types of music

Contact: Kingsley Harris

Record label based in Norwich.

End Of The Trail Records
Hastings
Email: kelly@endofthetrailcreative.co.uk
Website: https://www.endofthetrailcreative.co.uk
Website: https://www.facebook.com/endofthetrailcreative

Genres: All types of music

Management company and record label based in Hastings. Send demos by email.

Engineer Records
Email: label@engineerrecords.com
Email: info@engineerrecords.com
Website: https://www.engineerrecords.com
Website: https://www.facebook.com/engineerrecords

Genres: Hardcore Punk; Emo; Alternative; Indie

Independent, alternative record label from England since 1999 sending over 300 releases out to the world. Send query by email with bio, band pic, and any record artwork, with mp3s or links to music online. No large files.

Enhanced Music
20-24 Old Street
London
EC1V 9AB
Email: info@enhancedmusic.com
Email: shop@enhancedmusic.com
Website: https://www.enhancedmusic.com
Website: https://www.labelradar.com/labels/enhancedmusic/portal

Genres: Ambient; Chill; Electronic; Trance

Record label based in London. Send demos via online upload system. See website for link.

Escape Music Ltd
4 Cavendish Court
Dean Bank
Ferry Hill
Co. Durham
DL17 8PY
Email: contact@escape-music.com
Website: http://www.escape-music.com

Genres: Melodic Rock; Metal

Contact: Khalil Turk; Barrie Kirtly

Founded in 1994 as a partnership before becoming a limited company in 1996, the two founders first found common ground in the early eighties through a love of melodic rock.

Esoteric Recordings
Email: esotericrecordings@aol.com
Website: http://www.esotericrecordings.com
Website: https://www.facebook.com/EsotericRecordings/

Genres: Progressive Rock; Psychedelic Rock; Classic Rock; Electronic; Alternative Pop

Contact: Vicky Powell

The home of quality reissues in the Progressive, Classic Rock and Psychedelic genres.

Evil Twin Records
Email: info@eviltwinrecords.com
Website: http://www.eviltwinrecords.com
Website: https://eviltwinrecords.bandcamp.com

Genres: Electronic; Hip-Hop; Reggae; Soul

Record label concentrating mainly on hip-hop.

Expansion Records
London
Email: ralph@passionmusic.co.uk
Website: https://expansionrecords.com
Website: https://facebook.com/expansionrecs

Genres: Modern Soul; Classic Soul; Jazz; Funk

Contact: Ralph Tee

Record label describing itself as the UK's number one label for modern soul, classic soul, and smooth jazz.

F&G Dj Trade
Email: gavino@fgmusica.com
Website: http://www.fgmusica.com

Website: https://www.facebook.com/fgdjtrade

Genres: House; Electronic

Contact: Francesca Nesi; Gavino Prunas

Record label based in London.

Fabyl
London
Email: info@fabyl.co.uk
Website: https://www.facebook.com/FabylRecordings
Website: https://soundcloud.com/fabyl-1

Genres: Dance; Hip-Hop; Grime; Indie; Pop; Rock; Singer-Songwriter; Soul; Urban

Record label based in London, describing itself as a "bastard child of Rock and Hip Hop". Send query by email with links to music online.

Fantastic Plastic
Unit 6 Trident House
London
SE1 8QW
Email: info@fpmusic.org
Website: https://www.fpmusic.org
Website: https://www.facebook.com/fpmusicco

Genres: Alternative Guitar based

Independent record label also offering artist management and music publishing.

Far Out Recordings
Email: info@faroutrecordings.com
Website: https://www.faroutrecordings.com
Website: https://soundcloud.com/faroutrecs

Genres: Regional; Electronic

London-based record label dealing in Brazilian and electronic music.

Farmyard Records
Nottingham
Email: info@farmyardrecords.com
Website: http://www.farmyardrecords.com
Website: https://www.facebook.com/farmyardrecords

Genres: Indie; Pop; Soul; Alternative

Label, management, and promoters based in Nottingham.

Fast Static
Website: https://faststatic.co.uk
Website: https://www.facebook.com/FastStatic

Genres: Alternative

Independent record label and events collective.

Fat Hippy Records
c/o Captain Tom Music
11 – 15 Ann Street
Aberdeen
AB25 3LH
Email: info@fathippyrecords.co.uk
Website: http://www.fathippyrecords.co.uk
Website: https://www.facebook.com/fathippyrecords

Genres: All types of music

Independent record label based in Aberdeen, Scotland. Founded in 2002 to help raise the profile of the burgeoning North East Scotland music scene, and with the hope of overthrowing the "evil tyranny of the $ driven corporate music industry" and replacing it with their own "slightly nicer one".

FatCat Records UK
PO Box 3400
Brighton
BN1 4WG
Email: info@fat-cat.co.uk
Website: https://www.fat-cat.co.uk
Website: https://soundcloud.com/fatcatrecords

Genres: All types of music

Record label based in Brighton. Send demos by email as links to music online, or by post.

FatCat Records UK
PO Box 3400
Brighton
BN1 4WG

Email: info@fat-cat.co.uk
Website: http://www.fat-cat.co.uk
Website: https://soundcloud.com/fatcatrecords

Genres: All types of music

Record label with offices in the US and UK. Send email with links to music online. Also accepts physical demos by post.

FatCat Records
PO Box 3400
Brighton
BN1 4WG
Email: info@fat-cat.co.uk
Website: https://www.fat-cat.co.uk
Website: https://soundcloud.com/fatcatrecords

Genres: All types of music

Send submissions by email with brief description and private listening link, or by post.

Fellside Recordings
Website: https://www.fellside.com
Website: https://www.facebook.com/fellsiderecordings

Genres: Folk; Traditional; Roots

Record label specialising in Folk, Traditional and Roots music. A wide range of styles and presentation and an equally wide range of artists, from those well-established to those making their debut albums.

Fence Records
Website: http://www.fencerecords.com

Genres: Acoustic; Singer-Songwriter

Record label based in Anstruther, Fife.

Fiction Records
Website: https://fictionrecords.co.uk
Website: https://soundcloud.com/fictionrecords

Genres: All types of music

London-based record label originally founded in 1978 and then, after a period of inactivity, re-started in 2004.

Fierce Panda Records
Email: simon@fiercepanda.co.uk
Email: chris@fiercepanda.co.uk
Website: http://www.fiercepanda.co.uk
Website: https://www.facebook.com/fiercepanda

Genres: Indie; Rock

Indie rock label based in London. Approach by email with links to music on Soundcloud or Bandcamp or Facebook.

Fika Recordings
Email: demos@fikarecordings.com
Email: info@fikarecordings.com
Website: http://fikarecordings.com
Website: https://www.facebook.com/fikarecordings

Genres: Folk; Guitar based; Indie

Send query by email with bio, details of artists you like, bands you've played shows with, links to press or radio coverage, and links to streaming music online (e.g. Soundcloud or Bandcamp). Discriminates against artists based on their political beliefs.

Filter Records
19A Douglas Street, Unit B
London
SW1P 4PA
Email: contact@dorado.net
Website: http://www.dorado.net
Website: https://www.facebook.com/doradorecords/

Genres: Electronic

Concentrates on DJs and electronic music.

Fine Chooned
Email: info@finechooned.com
Website: http://www.finechooned.com
Website: http://soundcloud.com/fine-chooned

Genres: Electronic; Funky; Progressive; Tribal; Soulful; Urban; Club; House

UK Record Labels

Fresh progressive and funky tech house label from the UK. Featuring new but experienced house music producers.

Finger Lickin' Records
6 Windmill Street
London
W1T 2JB
Email: info@fingerlickin.co.uk
Website: http://www.fingerlickin.co.uk
Website: https://soundcloud.com/fingerlickinmanagement

Genres: Break Beat; Dance; Hip-Hop; Electronic

Record label based in London.

Fired Up Records
Lincoln
Email: sarahc@fireduprecords.com
Website: https://fireduprecords.com
Website: https://soundcloud.com/fireduprecords

Genres: Hard Dance

Contact: Sarah Curtis

Record label based in Lincoln, UK. Specialises in hard dance. Submit demo via online submission form.

First Night Records
Website: http://first-night-records.co.uk

Genres: Soundtracks

Contact: John Craig OBE

Mainly deals in theatre, film and TV soundtracks.

First Word Records
Email: info@firstwordrecords.com
Email: aly@firstwordrecords.com
Website: http://www.firstwordrecords.com
Website: https://www.facebook.com/firstwordrecords

Genres: Hip-Hop; Funk; Jazz; Soul; Reggae; Break Beat

Send demos on CD with bio by post, including SAE if return of CD required.

Flair Records
1st Floor
25 Commercial Street
Brighouse
HD6 1AF
Email: info@now-music.com
Website: https://www.now-music.com
Website: https://www.facebook.com/Now-Music-388961064509727/

Genres: Pop

Record label based in West Yorkshire, dealing with pop artists.

Flair Records
25 Commercial Street
Brighouse
HD6 1AF
Email: info@now-music.com
Website: http://www.now-music.com
Website: https://www.facebook.com/Now-Music-388961064509727/

Genres: Mainstream Pop; Acoustic

Contact: John Wagstaff

Pop label based in Brighouse, West Yorkshire.

Folkroom Records
Email: stephen@folkroom.co.uk
Email: ben@folkroom.co.uk
Website: http://folkroom.co.uk
Website: https://www.facebook.com/Folkroom

Genres: Folk

Folk label based in London. Acts are generally discovered by playing at the fortnightly live gigs. Best method of approach is therefore to apply to play at one of the gigs.

4AD
Email: demos@4ad.com
Email: 4ad@4ad.com
Website: https://www.4ad.com
Website: https://www.facebook.com/fourad

Genres: Alternative

Send demos by email.

Access more listings online at **www.musicsocket.com**

UK Record Labels 57

From Concentrate
Email: hello@fromconc.com
Website: https://www.facebook.com/fromconcentratemusic
Website: https://soundcloud.com/fromconcentrate

Genres: Garage; Pop; Soul

Record label and events collective.

Fury Records
PO Box 7187
Ringstead
Kettering
NN16 6DJ
Email: furyrecords@btconnect.com
Website: http://www.fury-records.com

Genres: Rockabilly; Rock and Roll

Record label based in Kettering, Northamptonshire. Specialises in all styles related to Rockabilly and Rock'n'Roll music.

Fuzzkill Records
Email: fuzzkillrecords@gmail.com
Website: https://www.facebook.com/FUZZKILLrecords
Website: https://twitter.com/FUZZKILLRECORDS

Genres: Garage; Lo-fi; Psychedelic Rock; Rock and Roll

Scottish record label and party planner.

Gerry Loves Records
Website: http://gerrylovesrecords.com
Website: https://twitter.com/gerryloves

Genres: All types of music

Describes itself as a "tiny DIY label producing quality musical artifacts". Send query using form on website, including links to streaming tracks. Listens to all demos, but cannot guarantee a response.

Gizeh Records
Manchester
Email: contact@gizehrecords.com
Website: https://gizehrecords.com

Website: https://www.facebook.com/gizehrecords

Genres: All types of music

An independent label based in Manchester.

Glasstone Records
Bath
Email: submit@glasstonerecords.com
Email: info@glasstonerecords.com
Website: https://glasstonerecords.com

Genres: Indie; Rock; Metal; Electronic; Punk; Electronic Punk; Alternative

Contact: Greg Brooker

Independent label based in Bath. Send music, plus EPK if you have one, in an email via dropbox (preferred), soundcloud, or youtube. Listens to everything but cannot guarantee response.

Gotham Records
Email: barry@barrytomes.com
Website: http://www.gotham-records.com
Website: https://www.facebook.com/barry.tomes

Genres: Pop; Rock; Dance; Reggae

Contact: Barry Tomes

Record label based in Birmingham.

Gravy
Email: info@gravyhq.com
Website: https://www.gravyhq.com
Website: https://www.facebook.com/GravyNorwich

Genres: Dance; Punk

A musical collective born in Norwich, UK.

Green Pepper Junction
Website: https://greenpepperjunction.com

Genres: All types of music

Contact: Asher Halle

Originally founded in the early seventies as a production company, now a record label based in Glasgow.

Claim your free access to ***www.musicsocket.com****: See p.211*

Greentrax Recordings
Cockenzie Business Hub
Edinburgh Road
Cockenzie
East Lothian
EH32 0XL
Email: info@greentrax.com
Website: https://www.greentrax.com
Website: https://www.facebook.com/greentrax/

Genres: Regional; Traditional; Celtic

Contact: Ian Green

Record label dealing in traditional Scottish, Celtic, and Gaelic music.

Groovin' Records
Email: groovin.records@phonecoop.coop
Website: http://www.groovinrecords.co.uk

Genres: Blues; Rhythm and Blues; Acoustic; Soul

Contact: AL Willard Peterson

Record label based in Merseyside, focusing on rhythm and blues.

Gruuv
Email: demos@gruuv.net
Email: label@gruuv.net
Website: https://soundcloud.com/gruuv
Website: https://www.facebook.com/gruuv

Genres: House; Techno

Send query by email with links to streaming or download links online.

Hand in Hive
Email: contact@handinhive.com
Website: http://www.handinhive.com
Website: https://www.facebook.com/handinhive

Genres: Indie; Pop

An independent music company, formed in 2014 by two friends with a shared love of music, specialising in records, management, publishing and sync.

Handsome Dad Records
Email: handsomedadrecords@gmail.com
Website: http://www.handsomedadrecords.com
Website: https://www.facebook.com/handsomedadrecords

Genres: All types of music

Record label releasing CDs and vinyl.

Harmor Records
London
Email: contact@harmorrecords.com
Website: https://harmorrecords.com

Genres: Alternative; Dance; Electronic; House; IDM

Submit demos through form on website.

Hassle Records
Email: mease@fulltimehobby.co.uk
Email: tom@fulltimehobby.co.uk
Website: http://www.hasslerecords.com
Website: https://www.facebook.com/HassleRecords/

Genres: Alternative; Emo; Hardcore; Indie Rock; Punk; Metal; Pop Punk

A fully independent record label based in London, UK. Releases heavy guitar music.

Headcount Records
Email: info@headcountrecords.co.uk
Website: https://www.headcountrecords.co.uk
Website: https://soundcloud.com/headcount-records

Genres: Funk; Hip-Hop; Rap; Soul

An independent record label dedicated to supporting and championing talent across a wide array of genres and releasing limited edition vinyl along with digital content. Send demos by email.

Heavenly Recordings
Email: daisy@heavenlyrecordings.com
Website: https://heavenlyrecordings.com
Website: https://www.facebook.com/HeavenlyRecordings

Genres: Indie; Alternative; Rhythm and Blues; Underground; Country Pop

Send submissions by email.

Helium Records
Bath
Website: https://www.heliumrecords.co.uk
Website: https://soundcloud.com/helium-records

Genres: Jazz; Pop

Independant record label set up by a producer and artist. Seeks to pursue invention and experimentation in writing, performing and recording.

Hit And Run Records
Email: Joe@hitandrunrecords.com
Website: https://www.facebook.com/hitandrunrecords

Genres: Pop Punk; Rock; Alternative

Independent record label from Birmingham, UK, specialising in Pop Punk, Rock and alternative music.

Holier Than Thou Records
Website: http://holierthanthou.co.uk
Website: https://twitter.com/HTTrecords

Genres: Rock; Indie; Alternative; Metal; Lo-fi; Punk; Hard Rock; Heavy Rock; Alternative Rock; Electronic Rock; Garage Lo-fi Rock; Progressive Rock; Glam; Melodic Metal; Progressive Metal; Power Metal; Gothic Metal; Melodic Thrash

Contact: David Begg, Label Manager

Established in June 1995, an independent record label. We focus on providing music promotion, PR and digital distribution for our clients. Working within a very strong and competitive market we arrange promotion campaigns for single, album releases and quality demos (downloads or CD) Our promotion and management activities generate, radio airplay , interviews, music review, live sessions, gigs and music sales.

Hope Recordings
Unit 4.16 The Paintworks
Bath Road
Bristol
BS4 3EH
Email: la@hoperecordings.com
Website: https://www.hoperecordings.com
Website: https://www.facebook.com/HopeRecordings/

Genres: Dance

Record label based in Bristol. Send demos as WeTransfer or Soundcloud links through online submission form.

Hospital Records
Unit 4 Bessemer Park
250 Milkwood Road
London
SE24 0HG
Fax: +44 (0) 20 8613 0401
Email: Chris@HospitalRecords.com
Email: Dan@HospitalRecords.com
Website: https://www.hospitalrecords.com
Website: https://www.facebook.com/hospitalrecords

Genres: Drum and Bass

Contact: Chris Goss

Record label based in London. Send demos via demo submission page on website. No demos by email.

Houndstooth
Email: houndstooth@fabriclondon.com
Website: https://www.houndstoothlabel.com
Website: https://soundcloud.com/HoundstoothLBL

Genres: Electronic

Artist-led electronic label based at a London nightclub.

House of Mythology
34 Trinity Crescent
London
SW17 7AE
Email: info@houseofmythology.com
Website: https://www.houseofmythology.com/

UK Record Labels

Website: https://www.facebook.com/HOMlabel/

Genres: Electronic; Rock; Avant-Garde; Experimental

Independent record label specialising in qualitative boundary-bursting electronic, rock, avant-garde and experimental music.

I Ka Ching Records
Email: ikaching@hotmail.co.uk
Website: https://ikaching.cymru
Website: https://www.facebook.com/Ikaching

Genres: All types of music

Independent record label based in Wales.

I'm Not From London
The Old Bus Depot
Upstairs 1st Floor
1 Fisher Gate Point
Lower Parliament Street
Nottingham
NG1 1GD
Email: info@imnotfromlondon.com
Website: https://www.imnotfromlondon.com
Website: https://soundcloud.com/imnotfromlondonrecords

Genres: Guitar based

A group of Nottingham based DIY promoters, regularly putting on gigs in Nottingham and sometimes in Leeds, Sheffield and Blackpool. Launched label in 2010 and released first record in 2011.

Iffy Folk Records
Glasgow
Email: iffyfolkrecords@gmail.com
Website: http://www.iffyfolkrecords.com
Website: https://www.facebook.com/iffyfolkrecords

Genres: Country; Folk; Indie; Psychebilly; Rock; Rockabilly

Record label based in Glasgow.

Ignition Records
London
Fax: +44 (0) 20 7258 0962
Website: https://ignitionrecords.co.uk
Website: https://twitter.com/IgnitionMusicUK

Genres: Alternative; Rock

Independent record label with offices in London and LA. Send query via online contact form, including links to as many of your social media accounts as possible.

IKonic Image
45 Staple Lodge Road
Email: shawndavis22@hotmail.com
Website: https://milwaukie2003.wixsite.com/ikonicimage
Website: https://twitter.com/VinylLike

Genres: Ambient; Electronic; Modern Glitch; Techno

Experimental music label specialising in deep ambient and hypnotic electronica, which goes into the realms of Modern glitch and intelligent techno.

In At The Eye Records
Email: info@iaterecords.com
Email: a&r@iaterecords.com
Website: http://www.iaterecords.com
Website: https://www.facebook.com/InAtTheEyeRecords

Genres: Alternative; Dance; Electronic; Indie; Pop; Rock; Shoegaze; Acoustic Alternative; Synthpop; Singer-Songwriter; Acoustic; Experimental; New Wave; Mainstream; Leftfield

Contact: Jase Burns

Send submissions by email with info and links. No attachments.

In the Nursery (ITN) Corporation
PO Box 1795
Sheffield
S3 7FF
Email: itn@inthenursery.com
Website: https://www.inthenursery.com

Access more listings online at www.musicsocket.com

UK Record Labels   61

Website: https://www.facebook.com/
INTHENURSERY

Genres: Soundtracks

Handles soundtracks and theme music for TV and film.

Infidelity Records
Email: demos@infidelityrecords.co.uk
Website: http://infidelityrecords.co.uk
Website: https://www.facebook.com/
Infidelityrecords

Genres: Drum and Bass

Record label specialising in D&B. Vocalists and producers can approach through through email.

Infinite Hive
Website: https://infinitehive.com
Website: https://www.facebook.com/
infinitehive

Genres: Indie; Metal; Punk; Rock

Contact: Mr John

Edinburgh-based Independent Record Label.

Innerground Records
Website: https://www.innergroundmusic.com
Website: https://soundcloud.com/
innergroundmusic

Genres: Dance; Drum and Bass

Record label based in London. Send demo via submission system on website.

Innersense Music
Website: http://www.innersenseworld.com

Genres: All types of music

Releases albums of relaxation and meditation.

Intuitive Productions
37 Cochrane Park Avenue
Newcastle upon Tyne
NE7 7JU
Email: kev@intuitive.productions
Website: http://intuitive.productions

Website: https://www.facebook.com/
IntuitiveProductions/

Genres: All types of music

Contact: Kevin Daley

Sound Production, Video Production, TV Production, Record Label, and Music Publisher.

Invisible Hands Music
40 Mortimer Street
London
W1W 7EQ
Email: sales@invisiblehands.co.uk
Website: http://www.invisiblehands.co.uk

Genres: All types of music

An independent record label based in the heart of Soho, London, England.

Invisiblegirl Records
Manchester
Email: julia@invisiblegirl.co.uk
Website: http://www.invisiblegirl.co.uk
Website: http://www.facebook.com/pages/
Invisiblegirl-Records/281793848983

Genres: All types of music

Independent record label, based in Manchester, and founded in 2006. Send demos by email as MP3 attachments.

Iron Man Records
Website: https://ironmanrecords.net
Website: https://twitter.com/IronManRecords

Genres: Alternative; Metal; Rock; Punk

Independent record label working out of Birmingham, Cardiff and London. The label also provides Tour Management Services to Musicians, Theatre groups and Film production companies.

ISHQ Records
Email: viveck@dnhartists.com
Website: http://www.ishqrecords.com
Website: https://www.facebook.com/
ballysagoomusic

Genres: Regional

Claim your free access to www.musicsocket.com: See p.211

Interested in Indian music with a Western crossover. S

Island Records
4 Pancras Square
Kings Cross
London
N1C 4AG
Website: https://www.islandrecords.co.uk

Genres: All types of music

Record label based in London.

istartedthefire records
Website: http://www.istartedthefire.co.uk
Website: https://www.facebook.com/istartedthefire

Genres: Acoustic; Alternative Country; Folk

Record label based in Cheltenham, Gloucestershire.

Jazz re:freshed
Email: sam@jazzrefreshed.com
Website: https://www.jazzrefreshed.com
Website: https://twitter.com/jazzrefreshed

Genres: Jazz

Contact: Sam Campbell

Record label with the intention to "challenge the elitism and prejudice within the jazz community that has kept jazz on the sidelines far too long, whilst bringing the incredibly diverse, colourful, expressive and creative world that is jazz to the people – live, fun and affordable."

Jeepster Recordings Ltd
Email: info@jeepster.co.uk
Website: https://jeepster.co.uk
Website: https://www.facebook.com/jeepsterrecordings

Genres: All types of music

Send demo by email with info and links to your music online.

JohnJohn Records
61b Stepney Green
London
E1 3LE
Email: theboss@johnjohnrecords.com
Website: http://www.johnjohnrecords.com

Genres: Folk; Jazz; World

Contact: Benoit Viellefon

Record label based in London.

Joof Recordings
Email: daniel@joof.co.uk
Email: gary@joof.co.uk
Website: https://www.joof.co.uk
Website: https://www.facebook.com/JOOFRecordings

Genres: Trance

Record label handling Trance only. Send demos by email.

JSNTGM (Just Say No To Government Music)
Email: andy@jsntgm.com
Website: https://jsntgm.com
Website: https://www.facebook.com/pages/category/Musician-Band/Just-Say-No-To-Government-Music-175595205810038/

Genres: Punk; Punk Rock; Ska Punk; Pop Punk; Post Punk; Underground; Psychebilly

Contact: Andy

Small independent non-profit-making label based in Blackpool. Established in the early nineties as a reaction against the mainstream music served up by the music industry.

Jungle Records
Suite B2 Livingstone Court
55 Peel Road
Wealdstone
Harrow
HA3 7QT
Email: enquiries@jungle-records.com
Website: https://www.jungle-records.net
Website: https://www.facebook.com/JungleRecords

Genres: All types of music

UK Record Labels

Record label based in London. Rarely signs new acts, and the only usually ones with an established sales base. Send query by email with links to music online, or submit CD by post. No MP3s by email.

Just Music
Just House
9 Gladwyn Road
London
SW15 1JY
Email: justmusic@justmusic.co.uk
Website: https://www.justmusic.co.uk
Website: https://soundcloud.com/justmusiclabel

Genres: Electronic; Acoustic; Ambient; Downtempo; Chill

Contact: John Benedict; Serena

Record label founded out of a belief that all music of artistic merit should have the opportunity to "enrich our lives". Accepts demos by post or email, but cannot return material or reply to unsuccessful submissions.

JW Music Limited
Email: https://jwmusic.uk
Website: https://facebook.com/jwmusichq

Genres: Electronic; House; Pop; R&B; Urban

Record label based in Carlisle. Also offers artist management, hosts branded events, and operates YouTube channel and radio show / podcast. Send demo through demo submission form on website.

K Dragon Records
Email: submissions@kdragonrecords.com
Email: kdragonrecords@gmail.com
Website: https://www.kdragonrecords.com
Website: https://www.facebook.com/KDragonRecords/

Genres: All types of music

Send demo by email with completed submission questionnaire (available on website).

KFM Records
Edinburgh
Email: info@kfmrecords.com
Website: http://www.kfmrecords.com

Genres: Electronic; Experimental; IDM; Post Rock; Shoegaze; Hip-Hop; Avant-Garde Rock; Experimental Rock

An Edinburgh-based label whose output ranges from hip-hop to art rock.

Killing Moon Records
Email: info@killing-moon.com
Website: https://killing-moon.com
Website: https://www.facebook.com/killingmoonrecords

Genres: Indie; Pop; Rock; Hardcore; Post Hardcore

Record label based in London. Accepts demos electronically.

King Prawn Records
Email: Info@kingprawnrecords.co.uk
Email: demo@kingprawnrecords.co.uk
Website: http://www.kingprawnrecords.co.uk
Website: https://www.facebook.com/kingprawnrecords/

Genres: Alternative; Indie; Metal; Rock

Send demos as streaming links by email.

Koothoomi Records
Email: koothoomi@live.co.uk
Website: http://www.koothoomi-records.com
Website: https://twitter.com/koothoomirecord

Genres: All types of music

Online record store and record label.

Kscope
Snapper Music plc
1st Floor
52 Lisson Street
London
NW1 5DF
Website: https://kscopemusic.com

Website: https://soundcloud.com/kscopemusic

Genres: Rock; Post Progressive

Record label based in London. Due to the high level of submissions, cannot answer all demo enquiries.

Kudos Records Limited
77 Fortess Road
Kentish Town
London
NW5 1AG
Email: info@kudosrecords.co.uk
Website: https://kudosrecords.co.uk
Website: https://www.facebook.com/kudosrecords

Genres: House; Leftfield; Hip-Hop; Jazz; Techno

London distributor that will work with artists willing to act as their own label.

Kufe Records Ltd
Fax: +44 (0) 20 8898 8649
Email: info@kuferecords.com
Website: https://www.kuferecords.com

Genres: Reggae; Classic R&B; Country

Specialised in Sixties & Modern R & B, Reggae, Soca and Country Music.

Lab Records
Email: info@labrecs.com
Website: https://labrecs.com
Website: https://www.facebook.com/labrecords/

Genres: Pop Rock; Acoustic; Alternative; Folk; Hip-Hop; Reggae; World

Pop-rock label based in Manchester. Send demo by post.

The Lab
Website: https://www.thelab.cc
Website: http://twitter.com/thelabcc

Genres: Acoustic; Alternative; Indie; Folk; Pop; Rock

We create and work on things that we love. Whether it be print, design, music, creative projects or event collaborations.

Lake
Email: info@fellside.com
Website: https://www.fellside.com
Website: https://www.facebook.com/lakerecords

Genres: Jazz; Mainstream; Traditional;

Contact: Paul and Linda Adams

Label started in 1984 to release Jazz. Focuses mainly (but not exclusively) on British mainstream and traditional styles.

The Leaf Label Ltd
PO Box 272
Leeds
LS19 9BP
Email: contact@theleaflabel.com
Website: http://www.theleaflabel.com
Website: https://www.facebook.com/theleaflabel

Genres: Alternative; Experimental

Record label based in Leeds. Send demo on CD, vinyl, or cassette. No emails with attachments. See website for full details.

Let Me Understand Records
Email: infolmurec@gmail.com
Website: https://www.facebook.com/lmurecords
Website: https://soundcloud.com/lmurecords

Genres: Electronic; House; Techno

Record label founded in 2018 by music industry veteran with decades of experience.

Lewis Recordings
95A Hackney Road
London
E2 8ET
Email: info@LewisRecordings.com
Website: http://www.lewisrecordings.com
Website: https://www.facebook.com/LewisRecordingsLDN

UK Record Labels

Genres: Alternative Hip-Hop; Rap; Electronic; Dubstep

Record label founded in 2001.

Lojinx
BCM Box 2676
London
WC1N 3XX
Website: https://www.lojinx.com
Website: https://soundcloud.com/lojinx

Genres: Alternative; Indie; Punk; Rock

A small, independent label based in London. Releases only a limited number of carefully considered records. No demos by post or email. Submit as Soundcloud links only.

Lucky Number Music Limited
Suite 3 Second Floor
344 Kingsland Road
London
E8 4DA
Email: contact@luckynumbermusic.com
Website: https://www.luckynumbermusic.com
Website: https://soundcloud.com/luckynumbermusic

Genres: Dance; Electronic; Indie; Pop; Singer-Songwriter

Independent music company based in London.

M1 Music Limited
Email: info@m1music.com
Website: http://www.m1music.com
Website: https://www.facebook.com/M1Music2001/
Website: https://myspace.com/m1musicltd

Genres: Hip-Hop; R&B; Reggae; Funk; Rap; Soul

No cover bands, just original acts. Send demo and any relevant links by email.

MaggotHouse Music
Email: ben@maggothouse.co.uk
Website: http://www.maggothouse.co.uk

Genres: Techno; Remix; Electronic; Experimental

Contact: Ben Neal

A small record label promoting and distributing the work of its artists, based in Cradley Heath in the West Midlands. Particularly interested in experimental music.

Make-That-A-Take Records
Dundee
Email: info@makethatatakerecords.com
Website: http://makethatatakerecords.com
Website: https://www.facebook.com/makethatatakerecords

Genres: Punk

DIY punk rock record label/collective based on the east coast of Scotland. Puts on punk shows and releases music. Send query by email with links to music online.

Malicious Damage
Email: info@maliciousdamage.co.uk
Website: http://www.maliciousdamage.biz
Website: https://www.facebook.com/groups/123103610446/
Website: https://myspace.com/maliciousdamage79

Genres: All types of music

Contact: Mike Coles

A totally independent record label releasing new and original music, without the commercial pressures and deadlines associated with a lot of bigger labels.

Manhaton Records
9 School Road
Twyford
Hampshire
SO21 1QQ
Email: arm@manhatonrecords.com
Website: https://www.manhatonrecords.com
Website: https://www.facebook.com/manhatonrecords2/

Genres: Blues; Jazz; Singer-Songwriter

Describes itself as one of Britain's leading record labels for contemporary blues, rock and roots music.

Claim your free access to **www.musicsocket.com**: *See p.211*

Manic Records UK
Email: info@manic-records.co.uk
Website: https://www.manic-records.co.uk

Genres: All types of music

We are an independent label, driven to introduce new and challenging music.

Metalbox Recordings
Email: anna@metalboxrecordings.com
Email: larry@metalboxrecordings.com
Website: http://metalboxrecordings.com
Website: http://www.facebook.com/MetalboxRecordings

Genres: Metal; Rock

Contact: Anna Di Laurenzio; Lawrence Paterson

Independent UK label formed in July 2010.

Midge Bitten Records
Website: https://www.fellside.com

Genres: Indie; Rock

Operators are now in semi-retirement, but the company has not been closed or sold.

Midhir Records
Northern Ireland
Email: info@midhirrecords.com
Website: http://www.midhirrecords.com
Website: https://twitter.com/midhir

Genres: Black Metal; Metal; Folk; Ambient; Experimental; Avant-Garde

Contact: Jon Hope

Record label of dark music.

Mighty Atom
Email: label@mightyatom.co.uk
Website: http://www.mightyatom.co.uk
Website: https://www.facebook.com/Mighty-Atom-Records-158656654146720/

Genres: Metal; Rock

Independent Record label based in South Wales that was at forefront of the Emo/Hardcore music scene in early 2000s.

Monomyth Records
Leeds
Email: Bob@monomythrecords.info
Website: https://www.monomythrecords.com
Website: https://www.facebook.com/Monomythrecords

Genres: All types of music

Record label / artist collective based in Leeds. Send query by email with links to music online.

Moshi Moshi Records
Email: hello@moshimoshimusic.com
Website: https://moshimoshimusic.com/
Website: https://www.facebook.com/moshimoshimusic

Genres: Alternative

Record label founded in 1998 by three friends who had jobs working for major record labels, to enable them to work with bands they loved but which didn't fit with the agenda of the companies they worked for. Went full-time in 2004.

Multiverse Music
Email: info@multiverse-music.com
Website: http://www.multiverse-music.com
Website: https://soundcloud.com/multiverse

Genres: Experimental; Electronic; Modern Classical; Soundtracks

A boutique music publisher and label house with a focus on experimental, electronic and modern classical music, as well as scores for feature films and trailers.

Navigator Records
Website: http://www.navigatorrecords.co.uk
Website: https://www.facebook.com/navigatorrecords

Genres: Acoustic; Folk; Singer-Songwriter; Traditional

Releases albums by artists on the contemporary folk scene.

9 Volt Records
Email: ac@9voltrecords.com
Email: martin@9voltrecords.com
Website: http://www.9voltrecords.com

Genres: Electronic

Contact: Adrian Collier; Martin Craig; Shaun Herbert; Gina Cole

Electronic label willing to reach out and look beyond the horizons of the genre. Send query by email with links to music online. No MP3 attachments. Response only if interested.

Nu Electro
Email: demos@nu-electro.com
Email: nu@nu-electro.com
Website: http://www.nu-electro.com
Website: https://soundcloud.com/nu-electro

Genres: Drum and Bass; Electronic; Techno; New Wave; Synthpop; Punk

Record label based in Maidenhead. Send soundcloud links by email.

Nu:Generation Music
Email: nugenerationmusic83@gmail.com
Website: https://linktr.ee/nugenerationmusic
Website: https://www.facebook.com/nugenerationmusic

Genres: Hip-Hop; Soul; Urban

Send query by email with EPK and links to music online.

Of Paradise Records
London
Email: info@ofparadiserecords.com
Website: https://www.facebook.com/OfParadiseRecords/
Website: https://soundcloud.com/ofparadiserecords

Genres: Dance

Dance label based in London. Send demos by email.

Payne Records
Email: support@paynerecords.com
Website: https://www.facebook.com/PayneRecords/
Website: https://twitter.com/paynerecords

Genres: All types of music

Record label launched in 2017. Send query by email with links to music online.

Peaceville Records
Website: https://peaceville.com
Website: https://soundcloud.com/peaceville
Website: http://www.myspace.com/peacevillerecords

Genres: Metal; Rock

Rock and metal label. Send submissions as links to music online via contact form on website.

Phono Sounds UK
London
Email: phonosounds@gmail.com
Website: https://soundcloud.com/phonosounds
Website: https://www.facebook.com/phonosounds

Genres: Electronic; Hip-Hop; Pop; R&B

Independent minded recording label based in London. Send query by email with links to music online.

Planet Records
Pendle Hawk Music
11 New Market Street
Colne
Lancashire
BB8 9BJ
Email: info@pendlehawkmusic.co.uk
Website: http://www.pendlehawkmusic.co.uk/Planet_Records.htm

Genres: Blues; Folk; Roots

Record label based in Colne, Lancashire.

Pretty Neat Records
London / Brighton
Email: prettyneatrecordings@googlemail.com
Website: http://www.8hz.co.uk/prettyneat

Website: https://soundcloud.com/pretty-neat-records

Genres: Chill; Drum and Bass; Dubstep; Electronic; Techno

Contact: Samuel Batt (A&R)

Record label based in London / Brighton. All profits go to charity.

A Priscilla Thing
Email: info@apriscillathing.co.uk
Website: http://apriscillathing.co.uk
Website: https://twitter.com/apriscillathing

Genres: Urban; Garage; R&B; Hip-Hop; House; Soul; Jazz

Independent urban music record label based in London, United Kingdom. The label distributes and produces music across a range of genres including; garage, R&B, hip-hop, house, neo-soul and nu jazz.

Project Melody
Email: info@projectmelodymusic.com
Website: https://www.projectmelodymusic.com
Website: https://www.facebook.com/projectmelodypm/

Genres: All types of music

A creative hub that provides expertise, resource and global content management in order to produce dynamic multi genre music and immersive content.

Push & Run
Email: bub@pushandrun.co.uk
Website: https://www.pushandrun.co.uk
Website: https://soundcloud.com/pushandrun

Genres: All types of music

Record label based in London. Send submissions by email.

Quickfix Recordings
Oxford and Bath
Email: quickfixmanagement@hotmail.com
Website: http://www.quickfixrecordings.com
Website: https://www.facebook.com/quickfixrecordings/

Genres: Indie

Independent record label, radio promoter, management company and gig promoter based in Oxford and Bath, UK.

Recoverworld Label Group
Email: demos@recoverworld.com
Website: http://www.recoverworld.com
Website: https://www.facebook.com/Recoverworld

Genres: Dance; Pop

An established and continually expanding collection of record labels, a publishing company, online record store and recording studio/mastering suite.

Red Eye Music
Website: http://www.redeyemusic.co.uk

Genres: Alternative Country; Americana; Blues; Folk; Singer-Songwriter

An independent Record Label and Music Production Company.

The Red Flag Recording Co.
The Basement
1 Star Street
London
W2 1QD
Email: info@redflagrecords.com
Email: info@playwrite.uk.com
Website: http://www.redflagrecords.com

Genres: Pop; Rock

Incubation label for its sister company, with a deliberately small roster. Believe in cultivation, development, and the creation of an environment in which artists can produce their best work.

Rekids Ltd
Email: loverekids@gmail.com
Website: https://rekids.com
Website: http://soundcloud.com/rekids

Genres: Electronic; House; Techno

Record label based in UK and Berlin, supporting international artists. Send all demos by email.

Access more listings online at www.musicsocket.com

UK Record Labels

REL Records Ltd
86 Causewayside
Edinburgh
EH9 1PY
Fax: +44 (0) 1316 624463
Email: online@relrecords.co.uk
Website: http://www.relrecords.co.uk

Genres: Celtic; Regional

Record label based in Edinburgh, handling Scottish and Celtic music.

Remixdj
Email: remixdj01@gmail.com
Website: https://remixdj.co.uk

Genres: Acoustic Alternative Avant-Garde Classic Commercial Electronic Experimental Funky Leftfield Mainstream Modern Non-Commercial Post Psychedelic Progressive Soulful Traditional Twisted Urban Uptempo Underground Tribal Ambient Blues Chill Classical Club Dance Deep Funk Disco Dub Fusion Funk Garage Guitar based Hip-Hop IDM Indie Instrumental Jazz Latin Lounge Pop Nostalgia Remix Soul Swing Techno Trance

An indie publishing outfit specialising in delivering audio products into prime retail positions.

Rhythmic Records
Email: info@rhythmic-records.co.uk
Website: https://www.rhythmic-records.co.uk
Website: https://www.facebook.com/RhythmicRecordsUK

Genres: Dance; Hip-Hop; House; Soul; Urban

Submit demos via online form.

Ridge Records Limited
1 York Street
Aberdeen
AB11 5DL
Fax: +44 (0) 1224 572598
Email: office@ridge-records.com
Website: https://www.ridge-records.com

Genres: Celtic; Traditional

Independent record label based in Aberdeen, Scotland.

River Rat Records
The River Lea
London
E5 9HQ
Email: info@riverratrecords.com
Website: https://www.riverratrecords.com
Website: https://www.facebook.com/riverratrecords/

Genres: Alternative; Folk; Blues

Female purveyors of alternative folk and blues music, hosting international live acts and releasing original music.

Rocket Recordings
Website: https://rocketrecordings.blogspot.com
Website: https://www.facebook.com/rocket.recordings.uk

Genres: Psychedelic; Space Doom; Kraut Rock; Acid Rock

Independent, UK based record label.

ROKiT Records
ROKiT House
Kingswood Business Park
Holyhead Road
Albrighton
Wolverhampton
WV7 3AU
Fax: +44 (0) 1902 374603
Email: info@rokrecords.com
Website: https://rokitrecords.info

Genres: Hip-Hop; Indie; R&B; Rock

Record label based in Wolverhampton. Describes itself as an innovative music company that utilises its advanced technology to support the music industry.

Rooftop Records
Liverpool
Email: emily@parrstreetstudios.com
Website: http://www.rooftoprecs.com
Website: https://www.facebook.com/RooftopRecordsLimited

70   UK Record Labels

Genres: All types of music

Independent label based in Liverpool, set on developing emerging artists.

Run Tingz Recordings
Email: bookings@runtingzrecordings.co.uk
Website: https://www.facebook.com/runtingzrecordings
Website: https://soundcloud.com/runtingzrecordings

Genres: Drum and Bass; Jungle

Send query by email with MP3 attachments or links to music online.

Saint Productions
Sheffield
Email: mark@saintproductions.co.uk
Website: http://saintproductions.co.uk

Genres: Dance; Pop

Record label based in Sheffield, Yorkshire.

Scylla Records
Email: rich@scyllarecords.com
Website: https://www.scyllarecords.com
Website: https://www.facebook.com/scyllarecords

Genres: Ambient; Metal; Pop; Punk; Rock

An independent UK record label.

Secret Records Ltd
15 Watling St
Fenny Stratford
Bletchley
Milton Keynes
MK2 2BU
Email: mail@secretrecordslimited.com
Website: https://secretrecordslimited.com
Website: https://www.facebook.com/secretrecordsltd/

Genres: Blues; Reggae; Black Origin Blue Beat Blues Fusion Folk Garage Guitar based Indie Instrumental Jazz Punk Reggae Reggaeton Rock Rock and Roll Rhythm and Blues Soul Acoustic Alternative Classic Acid Contemporary Hard Psychedelic Space Thrash Underground

A British independent record label based in London. The label currently specialises in live releases and older releases ranging across a number of genres including blues, reggae, rock, rock 'n' roll, psychedelic, soul and punk.

Originally started as a punk label, created in 1980 with the first release which reached number 20 in the UK album charts. As the 1990s came around the catalogue became less rooted in punk and become broader in genre choice. After 2000 the label began concentrating more on music DVD releases as well as live CD releases and continues to do so to this day.

Seeca Music Ltd
Fax: +44 (0) 20 3475 3101
Email: info@seeca.co.uk
Website: http://www.seeca.co.uk

Genres: Alternative

Publisher, label and Film & TV placement company. Send demo as MP3 attachment (max 7MB) to email giving brief description of band/artist/composer. Response only if interested.

Shock Records
Email: shockrecords@gmail.com
Website: https://shockrecords.wixsite.com/shock

Genres: Commercial Dance; Funky House; House; Trance

Send demos by email.

Signum Records
Unit 14
21 Wadsworth Road
Perivale
Middlesex
UB6 7LQ
Email: info@signumrecords.com
Website: https://signumrecords.com
Website: https://www.facebook.com/signumrecords

Genres: Classical

Access more listings online at www.musicsocket.com

Independent classical record label based in Perivale, Middlesex.

Silverwood Music Group
Website: https://www.silverword.co.uk

Genres: All types of music

Independent record label based in Wales. Has over 15 record labels in its catalogue, covering most genres of music.

Skinny Dog Records
Website: http://www.skinnydogrecords.com
Website: https://www.facebook.com/Skinny-Dog-Records-490311811128177/

Genres: Alternative; Punk; Rock

An independent record label based in Manchester, England, set up in 1999.

Skint Entertainment
PO Box 174
Brighton
BN1 4BA
Email: skint.demos@bmg.com
Website: https://www.skintentertainment.com/
Website: https://www.facebook.com/skintrecords

Genres: Dance

Record label based in Brighton. Send demos by email.

Snatch! Records
7 Bourne Court
Southend Road
Woodford Green
London
IG8 8HD
Email: contact@snatchrecords.com
Website: http://www.snatchrecords.com
Website: https://soundcloud.com/snatchrecords

Genres: House

Record label dealing in House music, based in London. "Expect slamming fresh house cuts from some of the most exciting talent in the scene." Send query via form on website with links to music online (wetransfer, dropbox, or soundcloud with active download).

Solar Distance
Email: demos@solardistance.com
Email: michele@solardistance.com
Website: http://www.solardistance.com
Website: https://soundcloud.com/solardistance

Genres: Electronic; Techno

Submit demos by email.

Soma Recordings Ltd
Acre House
35 Whitefield Road
Glasgow
G51 2YB
Email: info@somarecords.com
Website: https://www.somarecords.com
Website: https://www.facebook.com/SomaRecords/

Genres: Dance

Record label based in Glasgow, Scotland. Send email with soundcloud link to your two best tracks. No download links or MP3 files or any other kind of attachment.

Some Bizzare Records
Email: info@somebizzare.com
Website: http://www.somebizarre.com
Website: https://www.facebook.com/Some-Bizzare-141551249228568/

Genres: Alternative

"Bold and adventurous label".

Soul Jazz Records Ltd
7 Broadwick Street
Soho
London
W1F 0DA
Email: info@soundsoftheuniverse.com
Website: https://soundsoftheuniverse.com/sjr/
Website: https://www.facebook.com/Soul-Jazz-Records-Official-Page-118045430258/

UK Record Labels

Genres: Reggae; Dubstep; Leftfield; House; Techno; Electronic; Classic Disco; Hip-Hop; Post Punk; Funk; Soul; Jazz; Latin; Roots

Record shop, independent record label, book publisher, and occasional film company based in Soho, London.

Sound-Hub Records
7 King Street
Belper
Derbyshire
DE56 1PS
Email: info@sound-hub.com
Website: http://www.sound-hub.com
Website: https://www.facebook.com/SoundHubStudio

Genres: All types of music

Describe themselves as the "UK's leading independent label". Send details with YouTube or Soundcloud link via online web form, available on website. Only accepts submissions from the UK and Europe.

Sounds Of Meow
Email: contact@soundsofmeow.com
Website: https://soundsofmeow.com

Genres: Electronic Dance; Electronic Club; Commercial Dance; Melodic Techno; Underground House Techno; Melodic House Techno; Trance; Progressive House; Mainstream Dance

Deep/Tech/Club House, Trance and Melodic Techno music Label.
Was Established in 2020 to bring more and more music to this world.

Southern Records
Website: http://www.southern.com
Website: https://soundcloud.com/southern

Genres: Acoustic; Alternative; Folk; Rock

Independent record label formed in London in 1990.

Space Age Recordings
Website: http://www.spaceagerecordings.com

Genres: Experimental; Electronic

Record label based in Corby, Northamptonshire.

Squirrel Records
Leeds
Email: info@squirrelrecords.co.uk
Website: http://www.squirrelrecords.co.uk
Website: https://www.facebook.com/squirrelrecords
Website: http://www.myspace.com/squirrelrecords

Genres: Pop Punk; Rock and Roll; Lo-fi Indie; Guitar based; Alternative; New Wave

Contact: Darren; Caroline; Dicky; Chris Shake

Independent record label based in Leeds, Yorkshire. Specialises in mainly female-fronted bands.

Stereokill Recordings
Email: info@stereokillrecordings.com
Website: http://stereokillrecordings.com

Genres: All types of music

Independent record label run by "long standing music fanatics rather than by sharks and accountants".

Struggletown Records
Glasgow
Email: struggletownrecords@gmail.com
Website: http://www.struggletown.co.uk
Website: https://www.facebook.com/struggletownrecords

Genres: Pop Punk; Hardcore; Emo; Punk Rock

Small record label from Glasgow in Scotland dealing with pop-punk, hardcore, emo and punk rock.

Stunted Records & Management
6 Cliff Gardens
Scunthorpe
North Lincolnshire
DN15 7PJ

Fax: +44 (0) 1724 358966
Email: john@stuntedrecords.co.uk
Email: jill@stuntedrecords.co.uk
Website: http://www.stuntedrecords.co.uk
Website: http://www.myspace.com/stuntedrecords

Genres: Rock; Metal

Contact: John Clay

Send demos by post. Demos will not be returned. Include web address, contact phone numbers, press / photos, and any gigs / tour dates. Will respond if interested.

Subdust Music
Office 459
275 Deansgate
Manchester
M3 4EL
Email: admin(at)subdust.com
Website: https://www.subdust.com

Genres: Alternative; Electronic; Experimental; Mainstream; Urban; Commercial

Contact: Jason Holmes

An evolution of the normal record label model with collaborative production and artist releases with artist services including distribution and consultation. Send streaming links only by email.

Sugar Shack Records Ltd
c/o Crystal WM
19 Portland Square
Bristol
BS2 8SJ
Email: info@sugarshackrecords.co.uk
Email: mike@sugarshackrecords.co.uk
Website: http://www.sugarshackrecords.co.uk

Genres: Rock

Contact: Mike Darby

Always looking for great music. Send demos by post or by email.

Survival Records
P.O. BOX 2502
DEVIZES
WILTS
SN10 3ZN
Fax: +44 (0) 1380 860596
Email: survivalrecords@globalnet.co.uk
Website: http://www.survivalrecords.co.uk

Genres: Celtic

Contact: Anne-Marie Heighway; David Rome

Record label based in Devizes, Wiltshire.

Tangent Recordings
Email: demos@tangent-recordings.com
Email: office@tangent-recordings.com
Website: http://www.tangent-recordings.com

Genres: Drum and Bass

Send Soundcloud links by email.

Tenor Vossa Records Ltd
PO BOX 34803
London
W8 7OZ
Email: tenor.vossa@gmail.com
Website: http://www.tenorvossa.co.uk

Genres: Post Rock; Space Rock; Alternative Country

Record label based in London. Contact by email with any queries about release dates, back catalogue etc.

33 Jazz Records Ltd
Email: info@33jazz.com
Website: http://www.33jazz.com

Genres: Jazz

Record label specialising in jazz.

This and That Lab
Email: info@thisandthatlab.com
Website: http://thisandthatlab.com/
Website: https://www.facebook.com/thisandthatlab

Genres: Electronic; House; Techno

Record label and think tank combining music, art, and culture.

3 Bar Fire
Arch 462, Kingsland Viaduct
83 Rivington Street
London
EC2A 3AY
Email: hi@outpostmedia.co.uk
Website: http://3barfire.com

Genres: All types of music

Record label based in London. Send query by email with links to music online.

3 Beat Records
Liverpool
Website: https://www.threebeatrecords.co.uk
Website: https://soundcloud.com/3beat

Genres: Progressive; Dance; Trance; House; Funky House; Techno; Hardcore

Record store founded in 1989 in Liverpool, now also running a label and providing artist management services.

Tip Top Recordings
London
Email: tiptoprecs@gmail.com
Email: ben@tiptoprecordings.com
Website: https://www.tiptoprecs.com/contact
Website: http://www.facebook.com/tiptoprecs

Genres: Alternative; Indie; Punk

Record label based in London, Chicago, and Cambridge. Send query by email with links to music online.

TNS (That's Not Skanking) Records
Manchester
Email: info@tnsrecords.co.uk
Email: bev@tnsrecords.co.uk
Website: https://www.tnsrecords.co.uk
Website: https://www.facebook.com/group.php?gid=5735058846
Website: https://www.myspace.com/tnsrecords_uk

Genres: Punk; Ska; Underground

Not-for-profit label based in Manchester. Send query by email in first instance.

Tongue Master Records
PO Box 76066
London
W6 6LL
Email: info@tonguemaster.co.uk
Website: http://www.tonguemaster.co.uk
Website: https://twitter.com/TongueMasterRec

Genres: Indie

Independent record label based in London.

Topic Records
Proper Music Group
1 – 5 Applegarth Drive
Questor
Dartford
Kent
DA1 1JD
Email: lorraine.jones@propermusicgroup.com
Website: https://www.topicrecords.co.uk
Website: https://www.facebook.com/TopicRecords/

Genres: Folk Ethnic

Contact: Lorraine Jones

Traditonal folk label with a series of world ethnic music.

Tough Love Records
London
Email: info@toughloverecords.com
Website: http://toughloverecords.com
Website: https://www.facebook.com/ToughLoveRecordings/

Genres: Indie

Record label based in London.

Try Harder Records
20 Rosemary Close
High Wycombe
Bucks
HP12 4AG
Email: info@tryharderrecords.com
Website: http://www.tryharderrecords.com
Website: http://www.myspace.com/tryharderrecords

Genres: Alternative

Record label based in High Wycombe, Bucks.

TV Records Ltd
PO Box 34803
London
W8 7OZ
Email: tv.recordsltd@gmail.com
Email: tenor.vossa@gmail.com
Website: http://www.tenorvossa.co.uk
Website: https://www.facebook.com/TenorVossaAndTVRecords

Genres: Alternative Country; Lo-fi; Post Rock; Space Rock

Record label based in London.

Unpopular Music
Email: info@unpopularmusic.co.uk
Email: submissions@unpopularmusic.co.uk
Website: http://www.unpopularmusic.co.uk

Genres: Pop; Commercial Dance; Leftfield Electronic Experimental Downtempo Underground Ambient Break Beat Chill Dub Guitar based IDM Indie Instrumental Jazz Lo-fi Pop Ska Synthpop

Independent record label based in the UK. Open to submissions by email.

Viking Promotions
Email: viking_promo_music.uk@aol.com
Website: https://www.facebook.com/vikingpromotions

Genres: Acoustic; Blues; Country; Americana; Folk

Independent record label, promoter, and booking agency. Send query by email with links to music online.

Violette Records
Liverpool / Manchester / Paris
Email: matt@violetterecords.com
Website: http://violetterecords.com/
Website: https://www.facebook.com/violetterecords

Genres: Acoustic; Country; Blues; Folk; Indie; Lo-fi; Psychedelic Folk

Record label with offices in Liverpool, Manchester, and Paris. Send query by email with links to music online.

The Viper Label
Liverpool
Email: info@the-viper-label.co.uk
Website: http://www.the-viper-label.co.uk
Website: https://www.facebook.com/The-Viper-Label-484536141609241/

Genres: Indie; Pop; Alternative; Guitar based

Independent record label established in 1999 in Liverpool.

Wasted State Records
Email: info@wastedstate.com
Website: http://www.wastedstate.com
Website: https://www.facebook.com/wastedstate/

Genres: Indie; Metal; Psychebilly; Punk; Rock; Rock and Roll; Ska

Not actively looking for new signings, but if you want to get in touch, first check out existing releases to make sure your music fits the bill.

What Came First
Email: demos@wcfrecordings.com
Website: https://www.egglondon.co.uk/label/what-came-first

Genres: Electronic

Record label of electronic music. Send query by email with demo tracks as downloadable stream / wetransfer.

Wienerworld Limited
Unit 7
Freetrade House
Lowther Road
Stanmore
HA7 1EP
Email: info@wienerworld.com
Website: https://www.wienerworld.com

Genres: All types of music

UK Record Labels

Specialises in releasing, marketing, and distributing niche music content on DVD, Blu-Ray, CD, vinyl and digital formats.

A World Artists Love (AWAL)
Website: https://www.awal.com
Website: https://www.facebook.com/AWAL

Genres: All types of music

An alternative to the traditional music label, offering artists and independent labels a range of services without having to give up ownership or control.

World Circuit Records
Website: https://worldcircuit.co.uk
Website: https://www.facebook.com/WorldCircuitRecords

Genres: World; Regional

Record label formed in the mid 1980s and based in London, producing world music albums, and specialising in music from Cuba and West Africa.

Wrath Records
The Cardigan Centre
145-149 Cardigan Road
Leeds
LS6 1LJ
Email: info@wrathrecords.co.uk
Website: http://www.wrathrecords.co.uk

Genres: Leftfield; Alternative; Pop

A Leeds-based label bent on purveying quality leftfield alternative popular music.

Xtra Mile Recordings
Y16 – Access House
207-211 The Vale
Acton
London
W3 7QS
Email: info@xtramilerecordings.com
Website: https://www.xtramilerecordings.com
Website: https://soundcloud.com/xtramilerecordings

Genres: All types of music

Record label based in Acton, London.

Yala! Records
London
Email: info@yalarecords.com
Website: http://www.yalarecords.com
Website: https://www.facebook.com/yalarecords

Genres: Alternative; Electronic; Indie; Pop; Punk; Punk Rock; Rock

London-based label/club night founded in 2016. Send queries by email with links to music online.

Young Turks
London
Email: demos@theyoungturks.co.uk
Email: info@theyoungturks.co.uk
Website: https://theyoungturks.co.uk/
Website: https://www.facebook.com/youngturksrec/
Website: http://www.myspace.com/turkishdelights

Genres: Funk; Jazz; Punk

Record label based in London. Send demos by email.

Zube Records
Email: info@zuberecords.com
Website: https://www.zuberecords.com
Website: https://www.facebook.com/ZubeRecords/
Website: https://myspace.com/zuberecords/

Genres: Alternative; Acoustic; Electronic; Indie; Rock; Experimental

Independent record company based in London. Shares costs and profits 50/50 with artists. Releases acts in Rock, Acoustic, Electronica and Experimental. No cover material, pop, dance, garage, R&B, hip hop, techno, urban, rap or metal.

ZYX Records Ltd
Britania Way
Hanama House
London
NW10 7PR
Email: info@zyx.de

Website: https://zyx.de
Website: https://www.facebook.com/ OFFICIALZYXMUSIC

Genres: Dance; Electronic; Drum and Bass; Disco; Jazz; Blues; Soul; Country Rock; Country; World; Classic; New Age; House; Techno; R&B

Label with offices across Europe, based in Germany.

Canadian Record Labels

For the most up-to-date listings of these and hundreds of other record labels, visit https://www.musicsocket.com/recordlabels

*To claim your **free** access to the site, please see the back of this book.*

Beggars Group Canada
333 King Street East
Toronto, Ontario
M5A 0E1
Email: canada@beggars.com
Website: https://www.beggarsgroup.ca
Website: https://twitter.com/BeggarsCanada

Genres: Alternative; Pop; Rock

Record label based in Toronto, Ontario.

Borealis Records
Email: info@linusent.ca
Website: https://borealisrecords.com
Website: https://www.facebook.com/BorealisRecords/

Genres: Americana; Blues; Folk; Roots; Singer-Songwriter; World

A small dedicated independent record company founded by musicians for musicians located in downtown Toronto.

Drip Out Music Records
Email: dripoutrecords@gmail.com
Website: https://dripoutmusicrecords.bandzoogle.com/

Genres: All types of music

An Online independant Record Label and Artist Management Agency, founded in 2019.

Justin Time Records Inc.
482 av. Lansdowne
Westmount, QC
H3Y 2V2
Email: info@justin-time.com
Website: https://justin-time.com

Genres: Alternative; Blues; Folk; Gospel; Jazz; Rock; World

Record label based in Westmount, Quebec.

Mughal Music Group
3300 Bloor Street West, Suite 3140
11th Floor
Toronto, Ontario, M8X 2X3
Website: http://www.mughalentertainment.com
Website: https://www.facebook.com/mughalmusicgroup

Genres: R&B; Rap; Hip-Hop; Reggae; Urban; Soundtracks

A global music production company focused on music for film, television, fashion film, games and musical artists.

Nettwerk Records
1675 West 2nd Ave, 2nd Floor
Vancouver, BC V6J 1H3
Email: info@nettwerk.com
Website: http://www.nettwerk.com
Website: https://www.facebook.com/nettwerkmusicgroup

Canadian Record Labels

Genres: Acoustic; Folk; Singer-Songwriter

Record label with head office in Vancouver and other offices in the United States (Los Angeles, New York, Nashville, Boston), and Europe (London and Hamburg).

NorthernBlues Music Inc.
39 Birch Ave.
Ottawa ON
K1K 3G5
Email: info@northernblues.com
Website: http://www.northernblues.com
Website: https://www.facebook.com/NorthernBlues-Music-209455625926/

Genres: Blues; World; Roots; Gospel

Record label based in Ottowa, Ontario. Aims to be a friendly home to Canadian blues artists.

Open Road Recordings
Toronto, ON
Email: info@openroadrecordings.com
Website: http://www.openroadrecordings.com
Website: https://www.facebook.com/openroadrecordings

Genres: Country

A full service record company based in Toronto, Ontario, dedicated to country music. Offers marketing, promotion, publicity, A&R and licensing services.

Outside Music
7 Labatt Ave, Suite 210
Toronto, ON, M6K 1L4
Email: lloyd@outside-music.com
Email: evan@outside-music.com
Website: https://www.outside-music.com
Website: https://www.facebook.com/OutsideMusic/

Genres: All types of music

Contact: Lloyd Nishimura; Evan Newman

Label and management company based in Toronto.

Paper Bag Records
955 Queen St. W. Suite 116
Toronto, ON M6J 3X5
Email: shop@paperbagrecords.com
Website: http://paperbagrecords.com
Website: https://www.facebook.com/PaperBagRecords/

Genres: Alternative Rock

Alt rock label based in Toronto, Canada.

Sphere Music
Website: http://www.spheremusique.com
Website: https://www.facebook.com/spheremusique

Genres: All types of music

Record label based in Quebec.

True North Records
23 Griffin Street, P.O. Box 170
Waterdown, Ontario
L0R 2H0
Email: geoff@truenorthrecords.com
Email: brooke@truenorthrecords.com
Website: https://truenorthrecords.com
Website: https://www.facebook.com/tnrecords/

Genres: Blues; Country; Folk; Indie; Jazz; Reggae; Rock; Roots

Describes itself as "Canada's oldest independent record label and one of its largest."

Record Labels Index

This section lists record labels by their genres, with directions to the section of the book where the full listing can be found.

You can create your own customised lists of record labels using different combinations of these subject areas, plus over a dozen other criteria, instantly online at https://www.musicsocket.com.

*To claim your **free** access to the site, please see the back of this book.*

All types of music
  3tone Records (*UK*)
  Accidental Records Ltd (*UK*)
  Acid Jazz Records (*UK*)
  Adasam Limited (*UK*)
  All Star Music Corporation (*US*)
  Ambiel (*UK*)
  Aspenbeat LLC (*US*)
  AvatarDigi (*US*)
  Bella Union (*UK*)
  Big3 Records, Inc. (*US*)
  Bucks Music Group (*UK*)
  Button Up Records (*UK*)
  Catskills Records (*UK*)
  Cherry Red Records (*UK*)
  Circuit Records (*UK*)
  Confidential Records (UK) Ltd (*UK*)
  Cooking Vinyl (*UK*)
  Crucial Records (*UK*)
  Cruise International Records (*UK*)
  Deltasonic Records (*UK*)
  Denizen Recordings (*UK*)
  Dr Johns Surgery Records (*UK*)
  Drip Out Music Records (*Can*)
  East Central One (*UK*)
  Eastzone Records (*UK*)
  End Of The Trail Records (*UK*)
  ESP-Disk' Ltd (*US*)
  Fantasy Records (*US*)
  Fat Hippy Records (*UK*)
  FatCat Records UK (*UK*)
  FatCat Records UK (*UK*)
  FatCat Records (*UK*)
  Fiction Records (*UK*)
  Gerry Loves Records (*UK*)
  Gizeh Records (*UK*)
  Green Pepper Junction (*UK*)
  Handsome Dad Records (*UK*)
  I Ka Ching Records (*UK*)
  Innersense Music (*UK*)
  Intuitive Productions (*UK*)
  Invisible Hands Music (*UK*)
  Invisiblegirl Records (*UK*)
  Island Records (*UK*)
  Jeepster Recordings Ltd (*UK*)
  Jungle Records (*UK*)
  K Dragon Records (*UK*)
  !K7 Records (*US*)
  Koothoomi Records (*UK*)
  Light In The Attic (*US*)
  Malicious Damage (*UK*)
  Manic Records UK (*UK*)
  Monomyth Records (*UK*)
  Mosley Music Group (*US*)
  MRG Recordings (*US*)
  New Heights Entertainment (*US*)
  No Quarter (*US*)
  Noisy Poet Records (*US*)
  Not Not Fun (*US*)
  Omnivore Recordings (*US*)

Claim your free access to www.musicsocket.com: See p.211

Record Labels Index

Outside Music (Can)
Paper Garden Records (US)
Partisan Records (US)
Payne Records (UK)
pehr (US)
Phase One Network (US)
Photo Finish Records (US)
Playing In Traffic Records (US)
+1 Records (US)
Project Melody (UK)
Pure Noise (US)
Push & Run (UK)
Ramp Records (US)
Rampage Records (US)
Razor Sharp Records South, Inc. (US)
Red Bull Records (US)
Renaissance Records (US)
Rescue Records (US)
Rhino (US)
Rooftop Records (UK)
Segue Records (US)
Silver Blue Productions / Joel Diamond Entertainment (US)
Silverwood Music Group (UK)
Sony Music Entertainment (US)
Sound-Hub Records (UK)
Sphere Music (Can)
Star Time Intl (US)
Stereokill Recordings (UK)
Stones Throw Records (US)
Sumerian Records (US)
Surfview Records (US)
Symbiotic Records (US)
Team Love Records (US)
Third Man Records (US)
3 Bar Fire (UK)
Topshelf Records (US)
Toucan Cove Entertainment (US)
Turkey Vulture Records (US)
Unfun Records (US)
Union Entertainment Group (UEG), Inc. (US)
Universal Music Group (US)
Vagrant Records (US)
Warrior Records (US)
Wienerworld Limited (UK)
A World Artists Love (AWAL) (UK)
Xtra Mile Recordings (UK)

Acid
Backwater Records (UK)
Distinctive Records (UK)
Dorado Music (US) (US)
Dorado Music (UK)
Rocket Recordings (UK)
Secret Formula Records, Inc. (US)
Secret Records Ltd (UK)

Acoustic
Aardvark Records Ltd (UK)
Abet Publishing (US)
The Animal Farm (UK)
Big Scary Monsters Recording Company (UK)
Bohemian Jukebox (UK)
Boosweet Records (US)
BUT! Records (UK)
Commercially Inviable Records (UK)
Concrete Recordings (UK)
Favored Nations Entertainment (US)
Fence Records (UK)
Flair Records (UK)
Groovin' Records (UK)
Heartland Recordings (US)
In At The Eye Records (UK)
istartedthefire records (UK)
Just Music (UK)
Lab Records (UK)
The Lab (UK)
Meloden Nashville (US)
Navigator Records (UK)
Nettwerk Records (Can)
Red House Records (US)
Red Parlor Records (US)
Remixdj (UK)
Secret Records Ltd (UK)
Southern Records (UK)
Viking Promotions (UK)
Violette Records (UK)
West Clark Records (US)
Zube Records (UK)

Alternative
Aardvark Records Ltd (UK)
Abet Publishing (US)
Alcopop! Records (UK)
The Animal Farm (UK)
Audiobulb Records (UK)
b-unique (UK)
Backwater Records (UK)
BackWords Recordings (US)
Beggars Group Canada (Can)
Better Looking Records (US)
Big Dada Recordings (UK)
Big Scary Monsters Recording Company (UK)
Bohemian Jukebox (UK)
Boosweet Records (US)
BUT! Records (UK)
Buzz Records (UK)
Chemikal Underground Records (UK)
Clue Records (UK)
Dead by Mono Records (UK)

Record Labels Index

Dirty Hit (*UK*)
Dissention Records (*UK*)
Domino Recording Company (*UK*)
Dramatico Entertainment Ltd (*UK*)
Drum With Our Hands (*UK*)
Eclipse Records, inc. (*US*)
Emperor Jones Records (*US*)
Engineer Records (*UK*)
Esoteric Recordings (*UK*)
Fantastic Plastic (*UK*)
Farmyard Records (*UK*)
Fast Static (*UK*)
Fat Wreck Chords (*US*)
4AD (*UK*)
Glasstone Records (*UK*)
Harmor Records (*UK*)
Hassle Records (*UK*)
Heavenly Recordings (*UK*)
Hit And Run Records (*UK*)
Holier Than Thou Records (*UK*)
Ignition Records (*UK*)
In At The Eye Records (*UK*)
Iron Man Records (*UK*)
istartedthefire records (*UK*)
Justin Time Records Inc. (*Can*)
King Prawn Records (*UK*)
La Corporación Muzic (*US*)
Lab Records (*UK*)
The Lab (*UK*)
The Leaf Label Ltd (*UK*)
Lewis Recordings (*UK*)
Lojinx (*UK*)
Manifesto Records, Inc. (*US*)
Meloden Nashville (*US*)
Moshi Moshi Records (*UK*)
Oglio Entertainment (*US*)
Paper Bag Records (*Can*)
Parasol (*US*)
Park the Van Records (*US*)
Pinch Hit Records (*US*)
Pop Cautious Records (*US*)
Pravda Records (*US*)
Razor & Tie (*US*)
Red Eye Music (*UK*)
Remixdj (*UK*)
Righteous Babe Records (*US*)
River Rat Records (*UK*)
Roadrunner Records, Inc. (*US*)
S-Curve Records (*US*)
Secret Records Ltd (*UK*)
Seeca Music Ltd (*UK*)
Shangri-La Projects, Inc. (*US*)
Side One Dummy Records (*US*)
Skinny Dog Records (*UK*)
Some Bizzare Records (*UK*)

Southern Records (*UK*)
Squirrel Records (*UK*)
Strange Music Inc. (*US*)
Subdust Music (*UK*)
Swade Records (*US*)
Tenor Vossa Records Ltd (*UK*)
Thin Man Entertainment (*US*)
Thrive Records (*US*)
Tip Top Recordings (*UK*)
Tommy Boy (*US*)
TommyBoy Entertainment LLC (*US*)
Tooth & Nail Records (*US*)
Touch and Go Records (*US*)
Triple Crown Records (*US*)
Try Harder Records (*UK*)
TV Records Ltd (*UK*)
The Viper Label (*UK*)
West Clark Records (*US*)
Wrath Records (*UK*)
Yala! Records (*UK*)
Zube Records (*UK*)

Ambient
Aardvark Records Ltd (*UK*)
Abet Publishing (*US*)
Alex Tronic Records (*UK*)
Audiobulb Records (*UK*)
Blindsight Records (*UK*)
Brain Bomb Productions (BBP) (*UK*)
Burning Shed Limited (*UK*)
Drum With Our Hands (*UK*)
Enhanced Music (*UK*)
IKonic Image (*UK*)
Just Music (*UK*)
Midhir Records (*UK*)
Remixdj (*UK*)
Rhombus Records (*US*)
Scylla Records (*UK*)
Sequoia Records (*US*)
Six Degrees Records (*US*)
ThrillerTracks (*US*)
Unpopular Music (*UK*)
Van Richter (*US*)

Americana
Armadillo Music Limited (*UK*)
Borealis Records (*Can*)
Heartland Recordings (*US*)
Meloden Nashville (*US*)
Memphis International Records (*US*)
New West Records LLC (*US*)
Palm Pictures (*US*)
PS Classics (*US*)
R.O.A.D. (Riding on a Dream) Records (*US*)
Rainman Records (*US*)
Red Eye Music (*UK*)

Claim your free access to www.musicsocket.com: See p.211

Red Parlor Records (US)
Rhombus Records (US)
Rounder Records (US)
S-Curve Records (US)
SGNB Records (US)
Signature Sound Recordings (US)
Sub Pop Records (US)
Sugar Hill Records (US)
Swade Records (US)
Universal Music Group Nashville (US)
Viking Promotions (UK)
Yellow Dog Records (US)

Atmospheric
Beta Recordings (UK)

Avant-Garde
Amulet Records, Inc. (US)
Armellodie (UK)
Audiobulb Records (UK)
BackWords Recordings (US)
House of Mythology (UK)
K2B2 Records (US)
KFM Records (UK)
Midhir Records (UK)
Remixdj (UK)
Rhombus Records (US)

Black Metal
Midhir Records (UK)
Roadrunner Records, Inc. (US)

Black Origin
Secret Records Ltd (UK)

Blue Beat
Secret Records Ltd (UK)

Blues
Aardvark Records Ltd (UK)
Armadillo Music Limited (UK)
Basin Street Records (US)
Blue Wave Records (US)
Blues Matters Records (UK)
Boosweet Records (US)
Borealis Records (Can)
Buzz Records (UK)
Candid Productions Ltd (UK)
Dead by Mono Records (UK)
East of Sideways Music (US)
Ecko Records (US)
Favored Nations Entertainment (US)
Fedora (US)
GNP Crescendo Records (US)
Groovin' Records (UK)
Harmonized Records (US)
Justin Time Records Inc. (Can)
K2B2 Records (US)
Knitting Factory Records (US)
Malaco Music Group (US)
Manhaton Records (UK)

Mega Truth Records (US)
Megawave Records (US)
Meloden Nashville (US)
Memphis International Records (US)
New West Records LLC (US)
NorthernBlues Music Inc. (Can)
Orange Recordings (US)
Parliament Record Group (US)
Planet Records (UK)
Putumayo World Music (US)
R.O.A.D. (Riding on a Dream) Records (US)
Rainman Records (US)
Red Eye Music (UK)
Red House Records (US)
Red Parlor Records (US)
Remixdj (UK)
Rhombus Records (US)
River Rat Records (UK)
Rounder Records (US)
SCI Fidelity Records (US)
Secret Records Ltd (UK)
SGNB Records (US)
Shanachie Entertainment (US)
Shrapnel Records (US)
Skaggs Family Records (US)
Sony Music Entertainment - Legacy Recordings (US)
Stackhouse & BluEsoterica (US)
Sugar Hill Records (US)
Summit Records, Inc (US)
Sunnyside Records (US)
Swade Records (US)
Terminus Records (US)
True North Records (Can)
Tuff City Music Group (US)
Undertow Records (US)
Valley Entertainment (US)
Viking Promotions (UK)
Violette Records (UK)
Yellow Dog Records (US)
ZYX Records Ltd (UK)

Break Beat
Aardvark Records Ltd (UK)
Alex Tronic Records (UK)
Botchit & Scarper Records (UK)
Brain Bomb Productions (BBP) (UK)
Distinctive Records (UK)
Finger Lickin' Records (UK)
First Word Records (UK)
Unpopular Music (UK)

Celtic
Aardvark Records Ltd (UK)
ARC Music Productions International (UK)

Greentrax Recordings (*UK*)
REL Records Ltd (*UK*)
Ridge Records Limited (*UK*)
Sequoia Records (*US*)
Survival Records (*UK*)
Valley Entertainment (*US*)
Chill
Aardvark Records Ltd (*UK*)
Abet Publishing (*US*)
AD Music (*UK*)
Brain Bomb Productions (BBP) (*UK*)
Enhanced Music (*UK*)
Just Music (*UK*)
New Earth Records (*US*)
NexGen Music Group, LLC (*US*)
Palm Pictures (*US*)
Pretty Neat Records (*UK*)
Quango Music Group (*US*)
Remixdj (*UK*)
Sequoia Records (*US*)
Unpopular Music (*UK*)
Christian
Heartland Recordings (*US*)
Heaven's Disciples, LLC (*US*)
Integrity Music (*US*)
Meloden Nashville (*US*)
Pendulum Records (*US*)
Primarily A Cappella (*US*)
Provident Label Group (*US*)
Reunion Records (*US*)
Rockzion Records (*US*)
Skaggs Family Records (*US*)
Vineyard Worship (*US*)
Classic
Drum With Our Hands (*UK*)
Esoteric Recordings (*UK*)
Expansion Records (*UK*)
Kufe Records Ltd (*UK*)
Rainman Records (*US*)
Remixdj (*UK*)
Secret Formula Records, Inc. (*US*)
Secret Records Ltd (*UK*)
Soul Jazz Records Ltd (*UK*)
ZYX Records Ltd (*UK*)
Classical
Abet Publishing (*US*)
American Gramaphone (*US*)
BackWords Recordings (*US*)
Boosweet Records (*US*)
Caritas Records (*UK*)
Chandos Records Ltd (*UK*)
CRD Records Limited (*UK*)
Delphian Records (*UK*)
Divine Art Record Company (*UK*)
Favored Nations Entertainment (*US*)

K2B2 Records (*US*)
Multiverse Music (*UK*)
Remixdj (*UK*)
Secret Formula Records, Inc. (*US*)
Signum Records (*UK*)
Six Degrees Records (*US*)
Sony Masterworks (*US*)
Summit Records, Inc (*US*)
Club
Fine Chooned (*UK*)
Phunk Junk Records Inc (*US*)
Remixdj (*UK*)
Sounds Of Meow (*UK*)
Throne of Blood Records (*US*)
West Clark Records (*US*)
Commercial
Aardvark Records Ltd (*UK*)
Amber Artists (*UK*)
BUT! Records (*UK*)
Meloden Nashville (*US*)
Remixdj (*UK*)
Secret Formula Records, Inc. (*US*)
Shock Records (*UK*)
Sounds Of Meow (*UK*)
Subdust Music (*UK*)
Unpopular Music (*UK*)
Contemporary
Amber Artists (*UK*)
Ecko Records (*US*)
Favored Nations Entertainment (*US*)
5 Points Records (*US*)
Heads Up International (*US*)
Island Records (US) (*US*)
Knitting Factory Records (*US*)
Meloden Nashville (*US*)
Mountain Apple Company (*US*)
Om Records (*US*)
Primarily A Cappella (*US*)
Pyramid Records (*US*)
Rhombus Records (*US*)
S-Curve Records (*US*)
Secret Formula Records, Inc. (*US*)
Secret Records Ltd (*UK*)
Silver Wave Records (*US*)
Six Degrees Records (*US*)
Verve Label Group (*US*)
Country
Amazon Records (*UK*)
Arista Nashville (*US*)
Atlan-Dec/Grooveline Records (*US*)
Backwater Records (*UK*)
Boosweet Records (*US*)
Broken Bow Records (*US*)
Buzz Records (*UK*)
Columbia Nashville (*US*)

Claim your free access to www.musicsocket.com: See p.211

Record Labels Index

Commercially Inviable Records (*UK*)
East of Sideways Music (*US*)
GNP Crescendo Records (*US*)
Heartland Recordings (*US*)
Heavenly Recordings (*UK*)
Iffy Folk Records (*UK*)
istartedthefire records (*UK*)
Knitting Factory Records (*US*)
Kufe Records Ltd (*UK*)
Mailboat Records (*US*)
Meloden Nashville (*US*)
Memphis International Records (*US*)
Mercury Nashville (*US*)
New Pants Publishing (*US*)
New West Records LLC (*US*)
Open Road Recordings (*Can*)
Pravda Records (*US*)
Pyramid Records (*US*)
Quarterback Records (*US*)
Rebel Records (*US*)
Red Eye Music (*UK*)
Robbins Entertainment (*US*)
Saddle Creek (*US*)
Secretly Canadian (*US*)
SGNB Records (*US*)
Shanachie Entertainment (*US*)
Shrapnel Records (*US*)
Skaggs Family Records (*US*)
Sony Music Entertainment - Legacy Recordings (*US*)
Sony Music Nashville (*US*)
Southland Records (*US*)
Tenor Vossa Records Ltd (*UK*)
True North Records (*Can*)
TV Records Ltd (*UK*)
Universal Music Group Nashville (*US*)
Valley Entertainment (*US*)
Viking Promotions (*UK*)
Violette Records (*UK*)
ZYX Records Ltd (*UK*)
Dance
2020 Vision Recordings Ltd (*UK*)
76Label Music (*US*)
Aardvark Records Ltd (*UK*)
Alex Tronic Records (*UK*)
Almighty Records Limited (*UK*)
Audiobulb Records (*UK*)
Barely Breaking Even Records (*UK*)
Berman Brothers (*US*)
Beta Recordings (*UK*)
Black Butter Records (*UK*)
Boosweet Records (*US*)
Casablanca Records (*US*)
Chocolate Fireguard Music Ltd (*UK*)
Cr2 Records (*UK*)

Craniality Sounds (*US*)
Critical Music (*UK*)
Dead Happy Records (*UK*)
Defected (*UK*)
Dim Mak Records (*US*)
Distinctive Records (*UK*)
eenie meenie records (*US*)
Fabyl (*UK*)
Finger Lickin' Records (*UK*)
Fired Up Records (*UK*)
5 Points Records (*US*)
GNP Crescendo Records (*US*)
Gotham Records (*UK*)
Gravy (*UK*)
Harmor Records (*UK*)
Hope Recordings (*UK*)
In At The Eye Records (*UK*)
Innerground Records (*UK*)
King Street Sounds (*US*)
Loveslap! Recordings (*US*)
Lucky Number Music Limited (*UK*)
NexGen Music Group, LLC (*US*)
Of Paradise Records (*UK*)
Om Records (*US*)
Palm Pictures (*US*)
Phunk Junk Records Inc (*US*)
Radikal Records (*US*)
Recoverworld Label Group (*UK*)
Remixdj (*UK*)
Rhythmic Records (*UK*)
Robbins Entertainment (*US*)
Saint Productions (*UK*)
Secret Formula Records, Inc. (*US*)
Sequoia Records (*US*)
Shock Records (*UK*)
Six Degrees Records (*US*)
Skint Entertainment (*UK*)
Soma Recordings Ltd (*UK*)
Sounds Of Meow (*UK*)
Spiral Galaxy Entertainment (*US*)
Subliminal Records (*US*)
3 Beat Records (*UK*)
Thrive Records (*US*)
Thump Records (*US*)
Tommy Boy (*US*)
TommyBoy Entertainment LLC (*US*)
Ultra Music (*US*)
Unpopular Music (*UK*)
Water Music Records (*US*)
West Clark Records (*US*)
ZYX Records Ltd (*UK*)
Dancehall
Deep Funk
Remixdj (*UK*)

Disco
 Barely Breaking Even Records (*UK*)
 Remixdj (*UK*)
 Soul Jazz Records Ltd (*UK*)
 Throne of Blood Records (*US*)
 ZYX Records Ltd (*UK*)
Doom
 Black Tragick Records (*UK*)
 Rocket Recordings (*UK*)
Downtempo
 Aardvark Records Ltd (*UK*)
 Alex Tronic Records (*UK*)
 Audiobulb Records (*UK*)
 Brain Bomb Productions (BBP) (*UK*)
 Just Music (*UK*)
 NexGen Music Group, LLC (*US*)
 Unpopular Music (*UK*)
Drum and Bass
 Aardvark Records Ltd (*UK*)
 Alex Tronic Records (*UK*)
 Beta Recordings (*UK*)
 Brain Bomb Productions (BBP) (*UK*)
 BS1 Records (*UK*)
 Critical Music (*UK*)
 Dorado Music (US) (*US*)
 Dorado Music (*UK*)
 Hospital Records (*UK*)
 Infidelity Records (*UK*)
 Innerground Records (*UK*)
 NexGen Music Group, LLC (*US*)
 Nu Electro (*UK*)
 Palm Pictures (*US*)
 Pretty Neat Records (*UK*)
 Run Tingz Recordings (*UK*)
 Tangent Recordings (*UK*)
 West Clark Records (*US*)
 ZYX Records Ltd (*UK*)
Dub
 Ariwa Sounds Ltd (*UK*)
 Remixdj (*UK*)
 Unpopular Music (*UK*)
Dubstep
 Lewis Recordings (*UK*)
 NexGen Music Group, LLC (*US*)
 Pretty Neat Records (*UK*)
 Soul Jazz Records Ltd (*UK*)
 West Clark Records (*US*)
Electronic
 2020 Vision Recordings Ltd (*UK*)
 76Label Music (*US*)
 Abet Publishing (*US*)
 AD Music (*UK*)
 Adapted Vinyl (*UK*)
 Alex Tronic Records (*UK*)
 Alpha Pup Records (*US*)

 Aphagia Recordings (*US*)
 Ariwa Sounds Ltd (*UK*)
 Audiobulb Records (*UK*)
 BackWords Recordings (*US*)
 Beta Recordings (*UK*)
 Bifocal Media (*US*)
 Black Acre Records (*UK*)
 Blindsight Records (*UK*)
 Blue Jackel Entertainment (*US*)
 Border Community (*UK*)
 Burning Shed Limited (*UK*)
 Buzzin' Fly Records (*UK*)
 Casablanca Records (*US*)
 Chocolate Fireguard Music Ltd (*UK*)
 Circus Records (*UK*)
 Cityscape Records (*UK*)
 Cr2 Records (*UK*)
 Criminal Records (*UK*)
 Critical Music (*UK*)
 Dancing Turtle Records (*UK*)
 Dim Mak Records (*US*)
 Dorado Music (*UK*)
 Drum With Our Hands (*UK*)
 East of Sideways Music (*US*)
 eenie meenie records (*US*)
 Enhanced Music (*UK*)
 Esoteric Recordings (*UK*)
 Evil Twin Records (*UK*)
 F&G Dj Trade (*UK*)
 Far Out Recordings (*UK*)
 Filter Records (*UK*)
 Fine Chooned (*UK*)
 Finger Lickin' Records (*UK*)
 5 Points Records (*US*)
 Glasstone Records (*UK*)
 GNP Crescendo Records (*US*)
 Harmonized Records (*US*)
 Harmor Records (*UK*)
 Holier Than Thou Records (*UK*)
 Houndstooth (*UK*)
 House of Mythology (*UK*)
 IKonic Image (*UK*)
 In At The Eye Records (*UK*)
 Just Music (*UK*)
 JW Music Limited (*UK*)
 KFM Records (*UK*)
 King Street Sounds (*US*)
 Knife Fight Media (*US*)
 Knitting Factory Records (*US*)
 La Corporación Muzic (*US*)
 Let Me Understand Records (*US*)
 Lewis Recordings (*UK*)
 Lucky Number Music Limited (*UK*)
 MaggotHouse Music (*UK*)
 Megawave Records (*US*)

88   Record Labels Index

Multiverse Music (*UK*)
New Earth Records (*US*)
NexGen Music Group, LLC (*US*)
9 Volt Records (*UK*)
Nu Electro (*UK*)
Oglio Entertainment (*US*)
Om Records (*US*)
One Little Independent Records US (*US*)
Palm Pictures (*US*)
Phono Sounds UK (*UK*)
Phunk Junk Records Inc (*US*)
Pi Recordings (*US*)
Plug Research (*US*)
Pretty Neat Records (*UK*)
Quango Music Group (*US*)
Quark Records (*US*)
Radikal Records (*US*)
raSa Music (*US*)
Rekids Ltd (*UK*)
Remixdj (*UK*)
Robbins Entertainment (*US*)
Ropeadope Records (*US*)
Saddle Creek (*US*)
SCI Fidelity Records (*US*)
Secret Formula Records, Inc. (*US*)
Sequoia Records (*US*)
Shanachie Entertainment (*US*)
Six Degrees Records (*US*)
Solar Distance (*UK*)
Soul Jazz Records Ltd (*UK*)
Sounds Of Meow (*UK*)
Space Age Recordings (*UK*)
Sub Pop Records (*US*)
Subdust Music (*UK*)
Subliminal Records (*US*)
This and That Lab (*UK*)
Thrill Jockey Records (*US*)
ThrillerTracks (*US*)
Thrive Records (*US*)
Throne of Blood Records (*US*)
Thump Records (*US*)
Tommy Boy (*US*)
TommyBoy Entertainment LLC (*US*)
Ubiquity Recordings, Inc. (*US*)
Ultra Music (*US*)
Unpopular Music (*UK*)
Water Music Records (*US*)
West Clark Records (*US*)
What Came First (*UK*)
Yala! Records (*UK*)
Zube Records (*UK*)
ZYX Records Ltd (*UK*)
Emo
Engineer Records (*UK*)
Hassle Records (*UK*)

Revelation Records (*US*)
Struggletown Records (*UK*)
West Clark Records (*US*)
Ethnic
Sonic Safari Music (*US*)
Sony Music Entertainment - Legacy Recordings (*US*)
Topic Records (*UK*)
Experimental
Actual Size Music (*UK*)
Amulet Records, Inc. (*US*)
Aphagia Recordings (*US*)
Audiobulb Records (*UK*)
Bohemian Jukebox (*UK*)
D.O.R. (*UK*)
Dancing Turtle Records (*UK*)
House of Mythology (*UK*)
Hydra Head Records (*US*)
In At The Eye Records (*UK*)
KFM Records (*UK*)
The Leaf Label Ltd (*UK*)
MaggotHouse Music (*UK*)
Midhir Records (*UK*)
Multiverse Music (*UK*)
NexGen Music Group, LLC (*US*)
No Sleep (*US*)
Remixdj (*UK*)
Space Age Recordings (*UK*)
Subdust Music (*UK*)
Unpopular Music (*UK*)
Zube Records (*UK*)
Extreme
Rotten Records (*US*)
Folk
Aardvark Records Ltd (*UK*)
Acony Records (*US*)
Amazon Records (*UK*)
ARC Music Productions International (*UK*)
Backwater Records (*UK*)
Black Tragick Records (*UK*)
Blue Jackel Entertainment (*US*)
Bohemian Jukebox (*UK*)
Boosweet Records (*US*)
Borealis Records (*Can*)
Buzz Records (*UK*)
Commercially Inviable Records (*UK*)
Dancing Turtle Records (*UK*)
Drum With Our Hands (*UK*)
Emperor Jones Records (*US*)
Fellside Recordings (*UK*)
Fika Recordings (*UK*)
Folkroom Records (*UK*)
GNP Crescendo Records (*US*)
Heartland Recordings (*US*)

Record Labels Index

Iffy Folk Records (*UK*)
istartedthefire records (*UK*)
JohnJohn Records (*UK*)
Justin Time Records Inc. (*Can*)
Knitting Factory Records (*US*)
Lab Records (*UK*)
The Lab (*UK*)
Mailboat Records (*US*)
Meloden Nashville (*US*)
Memphis International Records (*US*)
Midhir Records (*UK*)
Navigator Records (*UK*)
Nettwerk Records (*Can*)
New Pants Publishing (*US*)
New West Records LLC (*US*)
NYC Records (*US*)
Oh Boy Records (*US*)
One Little Independent Records US (*US*)
Orange Recordings (*US*)
Parasol (*US*)
Planet Records (*UK*)
Pop Cautious Records (*US*)
Putumayo World Music (*US*)
Razor & Tie (*US*)
Rebel Records (*US*)
Red Eye Music (*UK*)
Red House Records (*US*)
Rhombus Records (*US*)
Righteous Babe Records (*US*)
River Rat Records (*UK*)
Ropeadope Records (*US*)
Rounder Records (*US*)
Secret Records Ltd (*UK*)
Secretly Canadian (*US*)
Sequoia Records (*US*)
Shanachie Entertainment (*US*)
Signature Sound Recordings (*US*)
Six Degrees Records (*US*)
Sony Music Entertainment - Legacy Recordings (*US*)
Southern Records (*UK*)
Sub Pop Records (*US*)
Topic Records (*UK*)
True North Records (*Can*)
Viking Promotions (*UK*)
Violette Records (*UK*)
Yellow Dog Records (*US*)

Funk
Bamboleo Records (*UK*)
Barely Breaking Even Records (*UK*)
Expansion Records (*UK*)
First Word Records (*UK*)
Headcount Records (*UK*)
M1 Music Limited (*UK*)
NexGen Music Group, LLC (*US*)

Remixdj (*UK*)
Secret Formula Records, Inc. (*US*)
Soul Jazz Records Ltd (*UK*)
Tuff City Music Group (*US*)
Ubiquity Recordings, Inc. (*US*)
Young Turks (*UK*)

Funky
Craniality Sounds (*US*)
Fine Chooned (*UK*)
Meloden Nashville (*US*)
Remixdj (*UK*)
Rhombus Records (*US*)
Shock Records (*UK*)
3 Beat Records (*UK*)

Fusion
Remixdj (*UK*)
Rhombus Records (*US*)
Secret Formula Records, Inc. (*US*)
Secret Records Ltd (*UK*)

Garage
Barely Breaking Even Records (*UK*)
Bush Bash Recordings (*UK*)
Champion Records (*UK*)
Dead by Mono Records (*UK*)
Dirtee Stank (*UK*)
Dirty Water Records (*UK*)
From Concentrate (*UK*)
Fuzzkill Records (*UK*)
Holier Than Thou Records (*UK*)
NexGen Music Group, LLC (*US*)
A Priscilla Thing (*UK*)
Remixdj (*UK*)
Secret Records Ltd (*UK*)
Swade Records (*US*)
West Clark Records (*US*)

Glam
Holier Than Thou Records (*UK*)

Glitch
Aphagia Recordings (*US*)
IKonic Image (*UK*)

Gospel
Ecko Records (*US*)
Heartland Recordings (*US*)
Integrity Music (*US*)
Justin Time Records Inc. (*Can*)
Malaco Music Group (*US*)
Megawave Records (*US*)
Meloden Nashville (*US*)
NorthernBlues Music Inc. (*Can*)
Parliament Record Group (*US*)
Pendulum Records (*US*)
Polo Grounds Music (*US*)
Provident Label Group (*US*)
Pyramid Records (*US*)
Razor & Tie (*US*)

Claim your free access to www.musicsocket.com: See p.211

Record Labels Index

Shanachie Entertainment (*US*)
Sony Music Entertainment - Legacy Recordings (*US*)
Southland Records (*US*)
Spiral Galaxy Entertainment (*US*)

Gothic
Holier Than Thou Records (*UK*)
Invisible Records (*US*)
Thin Man Entertainment (*US*)
Van Richter (*US*)

Grime
Big Dada Recordings (*UK*)
Bush Bash Recordings (*UK*)
Dirtee Stank (*UK*)
Fabyl (*UK*)

Guitar based
BackWords Recordings (*US*)
BUT! Records (*UK*)
Concrete Recordings (*UK*)
Fantastic Plastic (*UK*)
Fika Recordings (*UK*)
I'm Not From London (*UK*)
Meloden Nashville (*US*)
Remixdj (*UK*)
Secret Records Ltd (*UK*)
SGNB Records (*US*)
Shrapnel Records (*US*)
Squirrel Records (*UK*)
Swade Records (*US*)
Unpopular Music (*UK*)
The Viper Label (*UK*)
West Clark Records (*US*)

Hard
Fired Up Records (*UK*)
Holier Than Thou Records (*UK*)
Hydra Head Records (*US*)
Prosthetic Records (*US*)
Secret Records Ltd (*UK*)
Shrapnel Records (*US*)
Southern Lord Recordings (*US*)
Spinefarm Records (*US*)
Suburban Noize Records (*US*)
West Clark Records (*US*)

Hardcore
Banquet Records (*UK*)
Bifocal Media (*US*)
Big Scary Monsters Recording Company (*UK*)
Blindsight Records (*UK*)
Boslevan Records (*UK*)
Dog Knights Productions (*UK*)
Engineer Records (*UK*)
Hassle Records (*UK*)
Hydra Head Records (*US*)
Jade Tree (*US*)

Killing Moon Records (*UK*)
Kung Fu Records (*US*)
No Sleep (*US*)
Psychopathic Records (*US*)
Revelation Records (*US*)
Rotten Records (*US*)
Secretly Canadian (*US*)
Side One Dummy Records (*US*)
Struggletown Records (*UK*)
3 Beat Records (*UK*)
Touch and Go Records (*US*)
United Riot Records (*US*)
Victory Records (*US*)
West Clark Records (*US*)

Heavy
Holier Than Thou Records (*UK*)
Pavement Music (*US*)
Prosthetic Records (*US*)
Shrapnel Records (*US*)
West Clark Records (*US*)

Hip-Hop
Alex Tronic Records (*UK*)
Alpha Pup Records (*US*)
Asylum Records (*US*)
Atlan-Dec/Grooveline Records (*US*)
Barely Breaking Even Records (*UK*)
Bifocal Media (*US*)
Big Dada Recordings (*UK*)
Black Butter Records (*UK*)
Boosweet Records (*US*)
Bush Bash Recordings (*UK*)
Chocolate Fireguard Music Ltd (*UK*)
Delicious Vinyl LLC (*US*)
Dim Mak Records (*US*)
Dirtee Stank (*UK*)
Dorado Music (*UK*)
East of Sideways Music (*US*)
Evil Twin Records (*UK*)
Fabyl (*UK*)
Finger Lickin' Records (*UK*)
First Word Records (*UK*)
Freddie Records (*US*)
Grim Reality Entertainment, LLC (*US*)
Headcount Records (*UK*)
iHipHop Distribution (*US*)
Island Records (US) (*US*)
KFM Records (*UK*)
Kudos Records Limited (*UK*)
Lab Records (*UK*)
Lewis Recordings (*UK*)
M1 Music Limited (*UK*)
Mughal Music Group (*Can*)
NexGen Music Group, LLC (*US*)
No Sleep (*US*)
Nu:Generation Music (*UK*)

Access more listings online at www.musicsocket.com

Oglio Entertainment (US)
Om Records (US)
One Little Independent Records US (US)
Palm Pictures (US)
Parliament Record Group (US)
Penalty Entertainment (US)
Pendulum Records (US)
Phono Sounds UK (UK)
Polo Grounds Music (US)
A Priscilla Thing (UK)
Psychopathic Records (US)
Pyramid Records (US)
Quality Control (US)
RCA Records (US)
Remixdj (UK)
Rhymesayers Entertainment (US)
Rhythmic Records (UK)
ROKiT Records (UK)
Secret Formula Records, Inc. (US)
Shady Records (US)
Six Lowa Records (US)
Slip-N-Slide Records (US)
Sony Music Entertainment - Legacy Recordings (US)
Soul Jazz Records Ltd (UK)
Spiral Galaxy Entertainment (US)
Suburban Noize Records (US)
Thump Records (US)
Tommy Boy (US)
TommyBoy Entertainment LLC (US)
Tuff City Music Group (US)
Ubiquity Recordings, Inc. (US)
Ultra Music (US)
Viper Records (US)

Horror
Dead by Mono Records (UK)

House
Aardvark Records Ltd (UK)
Alex Tronic Records (UK)
Alter Ego Records (UK)
Bamboleo Records (UK)
Beta Recordings (UK)
Brain Bomb Productions (BBP) (UK)
Bush Bash Recordings (UK)
Buzzin' Fly Records (UK)
Champion Records (UK)
Cr2 Records (UK)
Craniality Sounds (US)
Defected (UK)
Distinctive Records (UK)
F&G Dj Trade (UK)
Fine Chooned (UK)
Gruuv (UK)
Harmor Records (UK)
JW Music Limited (UK)

Kudos Records Limited (UK)
Let Me Understand Records (UK)
Loveslap! Recordings (US)
NexGen Music Group, LLC (US)
Phunk Junk Records Inc (US)
A Priscilla Thing (UK)
Rekids Ltd (UK)
Rhythmic Records (UK)
Shock Records (UK)
Snatch! Records (UK)
Soul Jazz Records Ltd (UK)
Sounds Of Meow (UK)
Strictly Rhythm (US)
Subliminal Records (US)
This and That Lab (UK)
3 Beat Records (UK)
Throne of Blood Records (US)
ZYX Records Ltd (UK)

House
Aardvark Records Ltd (UK)
Alex Tronic Records (UK)
Alter Ego Records (UK)
Bamboleo Records (UK)
Beta Recordings (UK)
Brain Bomb Productions (BBP) (UK)
Bush Bash Recordings (UK)
Buzzin' Fly Records (UK)
Champion Records (UK)
Cr2 Records (UK)
Craniality Sounds (US)
Defected (UK)
Distinctive Records (UK)
F&G Dj Trade (UK)
Fine Chooned (UK)
Gruuv (UK)
Harmor Records (UK)
JW Music Limited (UK)
Kudos Records Limited (UK)
Let Me Understand Records (UK)
Loveslap! Recordings (US)
NexGen Music Group, LLC (US)
Phunk Junk Records Inc (US)
A Priscilla Thing (UK)
Rekids Ltd (UK)
Rhythmic Records (UK)
Shock Records (UK)
Snatch! Records (UK)
Soul Jazz Records Ltd (UK)
Sounds Of Meow (UK)
Strictly Rhythm (US)
Subliminal Records (US)
This and That Lab (UK)
3 Beat Records (UK)
Throne of Blood Records (US)
ZYX Records Ltd (UK)

Claim your free access to www.musicsocket.com: See p.211

IDM
  Harmor Records (*UK*)
  KFM Records (*UK*)
  Phunk Junk Records Inc (*US*)
  Remixdj (*UK*)
  Unpopular Music (*UK*)
Indie
  Aardvark Records Ltd (*UK*)
  Alcopop! Records (*UK*)
  Alpha Pup Records (*US*)
  Amazon Records (*UK*)
  The Animal Farm (*UK*)
  Armellodie (*UK*)
  b-unique (*UK*)
  BackWords Recordings (*US*)
  Banquet Records (*UK*)
  Beggars Group (*UK*)
  Better Looking Records (*US*)
  Boslevan Records (*UK*)
  Cityscape Records (*UK*)
  Clue Records (*UK*)
  Concrete Recordings (*UK*)
  Criminal Records (*UK*)
  Dancing Turtle Records (*UK*)
  Dead Happy Records (*UK*)
  Dim Mak Records (*US*)
  Downtown Music (*US*)
  eenie meenie records (*US*)
  Emperor Jones Records (*US*)
  Engineer Records (*UK*)
  Fabyl (*UK*)
  Farmyard Records (*UK*)
  Fierce Panda Records (*UK*)
  Fika Recordings (*UK*)
  Glasstone Records (*UK*)
  Hand in Hive (*UK*)
  Hassle Records (*UK*)
  Heavenly Recordings (*UK*)
  Holier Than Thou Records (*UK*)
  Iffy Folk Records (*UK*)
  In At The Eye Records (*UK*)
  Infinite Hive (*UK*)
  Island Records (US) (*US*)
  Killing Moon Records (*UK*)
  King Prawn Records (*UK*)
  The Lab (*UK*)
  Lojinx (*UK*)
  Lovitt Records (*US*)
  Lucky Number Music Limited (*UK*)
  Manifesto Records, Inc. (*US*)
  Meloden Nashville (*US*)
  Midge Bitten Records (*UK*)
  New West Records LLC (*US*)
  Nine Mile Records (NMR) (*US*)
  No Sleep (*US*)
  One Little Independent Records US (*US*)
  Orange Recordings (*US*)
  Palm Pictures (*US*)
  Parasol (*US*)
  Pinch Hit Records (*US*)
  Plug Research (*US*)
  Polyvinyl Record Co. (*US*)
  Pop Cautious Records (*US*)
  Q Division Records (*US*)
  Quickfix Recordings (*UK*)
  Razor & Tie (*US*)
  Reach Out International Records (ROIR) (*US*)
  Relapse Records (*US*)
  Remixdj (*UK*)
  ROKiT Records (*UK*)
  Ropeadope Records (*US*)
  Rough Trade US (*US*)
  S-Curve Records (*US*)
  Saddle Creek (*US*)
  Secret Records Ltd (*UK*)
  Secretly Canadian (*US*)
  Signature Sound Recordings (*US*)
  Slumberland Records (*US*)
  Squirrel Records (*UK*)
  Sub Pop Records (*US*)
  Tee Pee Records (*US*)
  Thrill Jockey Records (*US*)
  Thrive Records (*US*)
  Tip Top Recordings (*UK*)
  Tongue Master Records (*UK*)
  Touch and Go Records (*US*)
  Tough Love Records (*UK*)
  True North Records (*Can*)
  Ubiquity Recordings, Inc. (*US*)
  Undertow Records (*US*)
  Unpopular Music (*UK*)
  Victory Records (*US*)
  Violette Records (*UK*)
  The Viper Label (*UK*)
  Wasted State Records (*UK*)
  West Clark Records (*US*)
  Yala! Records (*UK*)
  Zube Records (*UK*)
Industrial
  Aphagia Recordings (*US*)
  Thin Man Entertainment (*US*)
  Van Richter (*US*)
Instrumental
  AD Music (*UK*)
  Aphagia Recordings (*US*)
  BackWords Recordings (*US*)
  Dancing Cat Records (*US*)
  Dead by Mono Records (*UK*)
  Heads Up International (*US*)

Heaven's Disciples, LLC (*US*)
Red House Records (*US*)
Remixdj (*UK*)
Secret Formula Records, Inc. (*US*)
Secret Records Ltd (*UK*)
ThrillerTracks (*US*)
Unpopular Music (*UK*)
Valley Entertainment (*US*)
Jazz
Amherst Record Sales, Inc. (*US*)
Arkadia Entertainment Corp (*US*)
Atlan-Dec/Grooveline Records (*US*)
Barely Breaking Even Records (*UK*)
Basin Street Records (*US*)
Blue Jackel Entertainment (*US*)
Boosweet Records (*US*)
Candid Productions Ltd (*UK*)
Cexton Records (*US*)
Chiaroscuro Records (*US*)
Dorado Music (US) (*US*)
Dorado Music (*UK*)
East of Sideways Music (*US*)
Expansion Records (*UK*)
Favored Nations Entertainment (*US*)
First Word Records (*UK*)
GNP Crescendo Records (*US*)
Harmonized Records (*US*)
Heads Up International (*US*)
Helium Records (*UK*)
HighNote Records (*US*)
Jazz re:freshed (*UK*)
JohnJohn Records (*UK*)
Justin Time Records Inc. (*Can*)
K2B2 Records (*US*)
Knitting Factory Records (*US*)
Kudos Records Limited (*UK*)
Lake (*UK*)
Malaco Music Group (*US*)
Manhaton Records (*UK*)
Megawave Records (*US*)
Memphis International Records (*US*)
Newvelle Records (*US*)
NYC Records (*US*)
Palmetto Records (*US*)
Pi Recordings (*US*)
Posi-Tone (*US*)
PRA Records (*US*)
Primarily A Cappella (*US*)
A Priscilla Thing (*UK*)
Remixdj (*UK*)
Reservoir Music (*US*)
Rhombus Records (*US*)
Righteous Babe Records (*US*)
Ropeadope Records (*US*)
Rounder Records (*US*)

Secret Formula Records, Inc. (*US*)
Secret Records Ltd (*UK*)
Shanachie Entertainment (*US*)
Shrapnel Records (*US*)
Sony Music Entertainment - Legacy Recordings (*US*)
Sony Masterworks (*US*)
Soul Jazz Records Ltd (*UK*)
Spiral Galaxy Entertainment (*US*)
Summit Records, Inc (*US*)
Sunnyside Records (*US*)
Thin Man Entertainment (*US*)
33 Jazz Records Ltd (*UK*)
Thrill Jockey Records (*US*)
True North Records (*Can*)
Tuff City Music Group (*US*)
Ubiquity Recordings, Inc. (*US*)
Unpopular Music (*UK*)
Valley Entertainment (*US*)
Verve Label Group (*US*)
Yellow Dog Records (*US*)
Young Turks (*UK*)
ZYX Records Ltd (*UK*)
Jungle
Run Tingz Recordings (*UK*)
Kraut
Rocket Recordings (*UK*)
Latin
ARC Music Productions International (*UK*)
Basin Street Records (*US*)
Blue Jackel Entertainment (*US*)
Boosweet Records (*US*)
Capitol Latin (*US*)
East of Sideways Music (*US*)
Freddie Records (*US*)
GNP Crescendo Records (*US*)
Heads Up International (*US*)
La Corporación Muzic (*US*)
Nacional Records (*US*)
Palm Pictures (*US*)
Pendulum Records (*US*)
Putumayo World Music (*US*)
Remixdj (*UK*)
Rhombus Records (*US*)
Righteous Babe Records (*US*)
Six Degrees Records (*US*)
Sony Music Latin (*US*)
Soul Jazz Records Ltd (*UK*)
Thump Records (*US*)
Tommy Boy (*US*)
Ubiquity Recordings, Inc. (*US*)
Universal Music Latin Entertainment (*US*)
Leftfield
Armellodie (*UK*)

Record Labels Index

Audiobulb Records (*UK*)
Bohemian Jukebox (*UK*)
In At The Eye Records (*UK*)
Kudos Records Limited (*UK*)
Remixdj (*UK*)
Soul Jazz Records Ltd (*UK*)
Unpopular Music (*UK*)
Wrath Records (*UK*)

Lo-fi
Fuzzkill Records (*UK*)
Holier Than Thou Records (*UK*)
Slumberland Records (*US*)
Squirrel Records (*UK*)
TV Records Ltd (*UK*)
Unpopular Music (*UK*)
Violette Records (*UK*)
West Clark Records (*US*)

Lounge
Remixdj (*UK*)
Secret Formula Records, Inc. (*US*)
Sequoia Records (*US*)

Mainstream
BUT! Records (*UK*)
Candid Productions Ltd (*UK*)
Decca Records US (*US*)
Flair Records (*UK*)
In At The Eye Records (*UK*)
Lake (*UK*)
Meloden Nashville (*US*)
Remixdj (*UK*)
Sounds Of Meow (*UK*)
Subdust Music (*UK*)
Swade Records (*US*)
West Clark Records (*US*)

Melodic
BackWords Recordings (*US*)
Beta Recordings (*UK*)
Escape Music Ltd (*UK*)
Gearhead Records (*US*)
Holier Than Thou Records (*UK*)
Meloden Nashville (*US*)
Sounds Of Meow (*UK*)

Metal
The Animal Farm (*UK*)
Basick Records (*UK*)
Black Tragick Records (*UK*)
Blindsight Records (*UK*)
Boosweet Records (*US*)
Candlelight Records (*UK*)
Earache London (*UK*)
Escape Music Ltd (*UK*)
Favored Nations Entertainment (*US*)
Glasstone Records (*UK*)
Hassle Records (*UK*)
Holier Than Thou Records (*UK*)

Hydra Head Records (*US*)
Infinite Hive (*UK*)
Invisible Records (*US*)
Iron Man Records (*UK*)
Island Records (US) (*US*)
King Prawn Records (*UK*)
Knife Fight Media (*US*)
Knitting Factory Records (*US*)
Metalbox Recordings (*UK*)
Midhir Records (*UK*)
Mighty Atom (*UK*)
Nuclear Blast America (*US*)
Pavement Music (*US*)
Peaceville Records (*UK*)
Prosthetic Records (*US*)
Rainman Records (*US*)
Razor & Tie (*US*)
Relapse Records (*US*)
Roadrunner Records, Inc. (*US*)
Rotten Records (*US*)
Scylla Records (*UK*)
SGNB Records (*US*)
Shrapnel Records (*US*)
Southern Lord Recordings (*US*)
Spinefarm Records (*UK*)
Stunted Records & Management (*UK*)
Sub Pop Records (*US*)
Tee Pee Records (*US*)
United Riot Records (*US*)
Victory Records (*US*)
Wasted State Records (*UK*)
West Clark Records (*US*)

Modern
Better Looking Records (*US*)
Candid Productions Ltd (*UK*)
Expansion Records (*UK*)
IKonic Image (*UK*)
Meloden Nashville (*US*)
Multiverse Music (*UK*)
Remixdj (*UK*)
Signature Sound Recordings (*US*)
Swade Records (*US*)
Terminus Records (*US*)

MOR
Meloden Nashville (*US*)

Mystical
BackWords Recordings (*US*)

New Age
Aardvark Records Ltd (*UK*)
Favored Nations Entertainment (*US*)
New Earth Records (*US*)
raSa Music (*US*)
Rhombus Records (*US*)
Secret Formula Records, Inc. (*US*)
Sequoia Records (*US*)

Access more listings online at **www.musicsocket.com**

Record Labels Index

Silver Wave Records (*US*)
Sound Feelings (*US*)
Valley Entertainment (*US*)
ZYX Records Ltd (*UK*)
New Wave
   Dead by Mono Records (*UK*)
   Gearhead Records (*US*)
   In At The Eye Records (*UK*)
   Meloden Nashville (*US*)
   Nu Electro (*UK*)
   Squirrel Records (*UK*)
Non-Commercial
   Blue Wave Records (*US*)
   Remixdj (*UK*)
   Secret Formula Records, Inc. (*US*)
   West Clark Records (*US*)
Nostalgia
   Remixdj (*UK*)
Pop
   76Label Music (*US*)
   Aardvark Records Ltd (*UK*)
   Abet Publishing (*US*)
   ABKCO Music & Records Inc. (*US*)
   Aeronaut Records (*US*)
   Almighty Records Limited (*UK*)
   Alpha Pup Records (*US*)
   Amazon Records (*UK*)
   Amber Artists (*UK*)
   Amherst Record Sales, Inc. (*US*)
   The Animal Farm (*UK*)
   Atlan-Dec/Grooveline Records (*US*)
   Backwater Records (*UK*)
   Basin Street Records (*US*)
   Beggars Group Canada (*Can*)
   Berman Brothers (*US*)
   Blue Shell Music (*UK*)
   Boosweet Records (*US*)
   BUT! Records (*UK*)
   Cityscape Records (*UK*)
   Delicious Vinyl LLC (*US*)
   Dim Mak Records (*US*)
   Dirty Water Records (*UK*)
   Downtown Music (*US*)
   Dramatico Entertainment Ltd (*UK*)
   Drum With Our Hands (*UK*)
   East of Sideways Music (*US*)
   eenie meenie records (*US*)
   Esoteric Recordings (*UK*)
   Fabyl (*UK*)
   Farmyard Records (*UK*)
   5 Points Records (*US*)
   Flair Records (*UK*)
   Flair Records (*UK*)
   From Concentrate (*UK*)
   Gearhead Records (*US*)

   GNP Crescendo Records (*US*)
   Gotham Records (*UK*)
   Hand in Hive (*UK*)
   Hassle Records (*UK*)
   Heavenly Recordings (*UK*)
   Helium Records (*UK*)
   Hit And Run Records (*UK*)
   In At The Eye Records (*UK*)
   Island Records (US) (*US*)
   Jade Tree (*US*)
   JSNTGM (Just Say No To Government Music) (*UK*)
   JW Music Limited (*UK*)
   Killing Moon Records (*UK*)
   Kung Fu Records (*US*)
   La Corporación Muzic (*US*)
   Lab Records (*UK*)
   The Lab (*UK*)
   Lucky Number Music Limited (*UK*)
   Mailboat Records (*US*)
   Manifesto Records, Inc. (*US*)
   Meloden Nashville (*US*)
   New Pants Publishing (*US*)
   NexGen Music Group, LLC (*US*)
   Nine Mile Records (NMR) (*US*)
   One Little Independent Records US (*US*)
   Palm Pictures (*US*)
   Parasol (*US*)
   Park the Van Records (*US*)
   Peek-A-Boo Records (*US*)
   Pendulum Records (*US*)
   Phono Sounds UK (*UK*)
   Pinch Hit Records (*US*)
   Polo Grounds Music (*US*)
   Poptown Records (*US*)
   Pravda Records (*US*)
   PS Classics (*US*)
   Q Division Records (*US*)
   Radikal Records (*US*)
   Rainman Records (*US*)
   Razor & Tie (*US*)
   RCA Records (*US*)
   Recoverworld Label Group (*UK*)
   The Red Flag Recording Co. (*UK*)
   Remixdj (*UK*)
   Reunion Records (*US*)
   Rhombus Records (*US*)
   Robbins Entertainment (*US*)
   S-Curve Records (*US*)
   Saint Productions (*UK*)
   Schoolboy Records (*US*)
   Scylla Records (*UK*)
   Secretly Canadian (*US*)
   Signature Sound Recordings (*US*)
   Six Degrees Records (*US*)

Claim your free access to www.musicsocket.com: See p.211

Slip-N-Slide Records (US)
Slumberland Records (US)
Sony Music Entertainment - Legacy Recordings (US)
Sound Feelings (US)
Southland Records (US)
Spiral Galaxy Entertainment (US)
Squirrel Records (UK)
Struggletown Records (UK)
Sub Pop Records (US)
Thrill Jockey Records (US)
Thump Records (US)
Tommy Boy (US)
TommyBoy Entertainment LLC (US)
Ultra Music (US)
Unpopular Music (UK)
Verve Label Group (US)
The Viper Label (UK)
Water Music Records (US)
Wrath Records (UK)
Yala! Records (UK)

Post
Big Scary Monsters Recording Company (UK)
Blindsight Records (UK)
Bohemian Jukebox (UK)
Concrete Recordings (UK)
JSNTGM (Just Say No To Government Music) (UK)
KFM Records (UK)
Killing Moon Records (UK)
Kscope (UK)
Remixdj (UK)
Secret Formula Records, Inc. (US)
Slumberland Records (US)
Soul Jazz Records Ltd (UK)
Tenor Vossa Records Ltd (UK)
TV Records Ltd (UK)

Power
Dirty Water Records (UK)
Gearhead Records (US)
Holier Than Thou Records (UK)

Progressive
Aardvark Records Ltd (UK)
Alter Ego Records (UK)
Aphagia Recordings (US)
Basick Records (UK)
Burning Shed Limited (UK)
Esoteric Recordings (UK)
Fine Chooned (UK)
Holier Than Thou Records (UK)
Kscope (UK)
Remixdj (UK)
Rhombus Records (US)
Shrapnel Records (US)

Sounds Of Meow (UK)
3 Beat Records (UK)

Psychebilly
Dead by Mono Records (UK)
Iffy Folk Records (UK)
JSNTGM (Just Say No To Government Music) (UK)
Thin Man Entertainment (US)
Wasted State Records (UK)

Psychedelic
Backwater Records (UK)
BackWords Recordings (US)
Bohemian Jukebox (UK)
Dead by Mono Records (UK)
Esoteric Recordings (UK)
Fuzzkill Records (UK)
Remixdj (UK)
Rocket Recordings (UK)
Secret Records Ltd (UK)
Violette Records (UK)

Punk
Amazon Records (UK)
Banquet Records (UK)
Bifocal Media (US)
Big Scary Monsters Recording Company (UK)
Bomber Music Ltd (UK)
Boslevan Records (UK)
Concrete Recordings (UK)
Crosscheck Records (US)
Dead by Mono Records (UK)
Detour Records (UK)
Dim Mak Records (US)
Dirty Water Records (UK)
Dischord Records (US)
Dissention Records (UK)
Dog Knights Productions (UK)
Engineer Records (UK)
Fat Wreck Chords (US)
Gearhead Records (US)
Glasstone Records (UK)
Gravy (UK)
Hassle Records (UK)
Hit And Run Records (UK)
Holier Than Thou Records (UK)
Infinite Hive (UK)
Iron Man Records (UK)
Island Records (US) (US)
Jade Tree (US)
JSNTGM (Just Say No To Government Music) (UK)
Knife Fight Media (US)
Knitting Factory Records (US)
Kung Fu Records (US)
Lojinx (UK)

Access more listings online at www.musicsocket.com

Record Labels Index   97

Lookout! Records (US)
Lovitt Records (US)
Make-That-A-Take Records (UK)
Manifesto Records, Inc. (US)
Nitro Records (US)
Nu Electro (UK)
One Little Independent Records US (US)
Orange Recordings (US)
Radical Records (US)
Reach Out International Records (ROIR) (US)
Revelation Records (US)
Righteous Babe Records (US)
Rotten Records (US)
Scylla Records (UK)
Secret Records Ltd (UK)
Secretly Canadian (US)
Side One Dummy Records (US)
Skinny Dog Records (UK)
Slumberland Records (US)
Soul Jazz Records Ltd (UK)
Squirrel Records (UK)
Struggletown Records (UK)
Sub Pop Records (US)
Suburban Noize Records (US)
Tee Pee Records (US)
Thin Man Entertainment (US)
Tip Top Recordings (UK)
TNS (That's Not Skanking) Records (UK)
Touch and Go Records (US)
United Riot Records (US)
Victory Records (US)
Wasted State Records (UK)
West Clark Records (US)
Yala! Records (UK)
Young Turks (UK)

RampB
Aardvark Records Ltd (UK)
ABKCO Music & Records Inc. (US)
Amherst Record Sales, Inc. (US)
Atlan-Dec/Grooveline Records (US)
Basin Street Records (US)
Berman Brothers (US)
Boosweet Records (US)
Brunswick Record Corporation (US)
Bush Bash Recordings (UK)
Dome Records Ltd (UK)
Ecko Records (US)
Heaven's Disciples, LLC (US)
Island Records (US) (US)
JW Music Limited (UK)
Kufe Records Ltd (UK)
M1 Music Limited (UK)
Malaco Music Group (US)
Memphis International Records (US)

Mughal Music Group (Can)
New Pants Publishing (US)
Parliament Record Group (US)
Pendulum Records (US)
Phono Sounds UK (UK)
Polo Grounds Music (US)
Pravda Records (US)
A Priscilla Thing (UK)
Pyramid Records (US)
RCA Records (US)
ROKiT Records (UK)
S-Curve Records (US)
Shanachie Entertainment (US)
Six Lowa Records (US)
Slip-N-Slide Records (US)
Sony Music Entertainment - Legacy Recordings (US)
Spiral Galaxy Entertainment (US)
Thump Records (US)
Tuff City Music Group (US)
Ubiquity Recordings, Inc. (US)
Verve Label Group (US)
ZYX Records Ltd (UK)

Rap
Asylum Records (US)
Atlan-Dec/Grooveline Records (US)
Bifocal Media (US)
Boosweet Records (US)
Bush Bash Recordings (UK)
Crosscheck Records (US)
Delicious Vinyl LLC (US)
Dim Mak Records (US)
Dirtee Stank (UK)
East of Sideways Music (US)
Freddie Records (US)
Grim Reality Entertainment, LLC (US)
Headcount Records (UK)
Heaven's Disciples, LLC (US)
Island Records (US) (US)
La Corporación Muzic (US)
Lewis Recordings (UK)
M1 Music Limited (UK)
Mughal Music Group (Can)
New Pants Publishing (US)
Oglio Entertainment (US)
Om Records (US)
One Little Independent Records US (US)
Pendulum Records (US)
Polo Grounds Music (US)
Psychopathic Records (US)
Pyramid Records (US)
Shady Records (US)
Six Lowa Records (US)
Slip-N-Slide Records (US)
Thump Records (US)

Claim your free access to www.musicsocket.com: See p.211

98 Record Labels Index

Ubiquity Recordings, Inc. (US)
Ultra Music (US)
Viper Records (US)
Reggae
Aardvark Records Ltd (UK)
Ariwa Sounds Ltd (UK)
Bomber Music Ltd (UK)
Delicious Vinyl LLC (US)
Easy Star Records (US)
Evil Twin Records (UK)
First Word Records (UK)
Gotham Records (UK)
Heaven's Disciples, LLC (US)
Kufe Records Ltd (UK)
La Corporación Muzic (US)
Lab Records (UK)
M1 Music Limited (UK)
Megawave Records (US)
Mughal Music Group (Can)
Palm Pictures (US)
Polo Grounds Music (US)
Pyramid Records (US)
raSa Music (US)
Reach Out International Records (ROIR) (US)
Rhombus Records (US)
Secret Records Ltd (UK)
Shanachie Entertainment (US)
Side One Dummy Records (US)
Six Lowa Records (US)
Slip-N-Slide Records (US)
Sony Music Entertainment - Legacy Recordings (US)
Soul Jazz Records Ltd (UK)
True North Records (Can)
Ultra Music (US)
Reggaeton
Heaven's Disciples, LLC (US)
Polo Grounds Music (US)
Secret Records Ltd (UK)
Regional
Audiorec Limited (UK)
Far Out Recordings (UK)
Greentrax Recordings (UK)
ISHQ Records (UK)
Mountain Apple Company (US)
NorthSide (US)
REL Records Ltd (UK)
Silver Wave Records (US)
World Circuit Records (UK)
Relaxation
Secret Formula Records, Inc. (US)
Sound Feelings (US)
Remix
MaggotHouse Music (UK)
Remixdj (UK)
West Clark Records (US)
Rhythm and Blues
Atlan-Dec/Grooveline Records (US)
Blues Matters Records (UK)
Dead by Mono Records (UK)
Dirty Water Records (UK)
Groovin' Records (UK)
Heaven's Disciples, LLC (US)
Heavenly Recordings (UK)
Secret Records Ltd (UK)
Rock and Roll
Bomber Music Ltd (UK)
Dead by Mono Records (UK)
Dirty Water Records (UK)
Fury Records (UK)
Fuzzkill Records (UK)
Gearhead Records (US)
Meloden Nashville (US)
Rainman Records (US)
Secret Formula Records, Inc. (US)
Secret Records Ltd (UK)
SGNB Records (US)
Smog Veil Records (US)
Squirrel Records (UK)
Swade Records (US)
United Riot Records (US)
Wasted State Records (UK)
West Clark Records (US)
Rock
Aardvark Records Ltd (UK)
Abet Publishing (US)
ABKCO Music & Records Inc. (US)
Aeronaut Records (US)
Amazon Records (UK)
Amherst Record Sales, Inc. (US)
The Animal Farm (UK)
Aphagia Recordings (US)
Armadillo Music Limited (UK)
Armellodie (UK)
Atlan-Dec/Grooveline Records (US)
b-unique (UK)
Backwater Records (UK)
BackWords Recordings (US)
Basin Street Records (US)
Beggars Group Canada (Can)
Beta Recordings (UK)
Better Looking Records (US)
Better Looking Records (US)
Big Scary Monsters Recording Company (UK)
Blindsight Records (UK)
Boosweet Records (US)
Boslevan Records (UK)
Broken Arrow Records (US)

Access more listings online at www.musicsocket.com

Record Labels Index

Burning Shed Limited (*UK*)
BUT! Records (*UK*)
Chocolate Fireguard Music Ltd (*UK*)
Clue Records (*UK*)
Criminal Records (*UK*)
Dead by Mono Records (*UK*)
Delicious Vinyl LLC (*US*)
Dim Mak Records (*US*)
Dirty Water Records (*UK*)
Dischord Records (*US*)
Downtown Music (*US*)
East of Sideways Music (*US*)
Eclipse Records, inc. (*US*)
eenie meenie records (*US*)
Escape Music Ltd (*UK*)
Esoteric Recordings (*UK*)
Fabyl (*UK*)
Fat Wreck Chords (*US*)
Favored Nations Entertainment (*US*)
Fierce Panda Records (*UK*)
Fuzzkill Records (*UK*)
Gearhead Records (*US*)
Glasstone Records (*UK*)
GNP Crescendo Records (*US*)
Gotham Records (*UK*)
Harmonized Records (*US*)
Hassle Records (*UK*)
Hit And Run Records (*UK*)
Holier Than Thou Records (*UK*)
House of Mythology (*UK*)
Hydra Head Records (*US*)
Iffy Folk Records (*UK*)
Ignition Records (*UK*)
In At The Eye Records (*UK*)
Infinite Hive (*UK*)
Invisible Records (*US*)
Iron Man Records (*UK*)
Island Records (US) (*US*)
Jade Tree (*US*)
JSNTGM (Just Say No To Government Music) (*UK*)
Justin Time Records Inc. (*Can*)
KFM Records (*UK*)
Killing Moon Records (*UK*)
King Prawn Records (*UK*)
Knife Fight Media (*US*)
Knitting Factory Records (*US*)
Kscope (*UK*)
Kung Fu Records (*US*)
La Corporación Muzic (*US*)
Lab Records (*UK*)
The Lab (*UK*)
Lojinx (*UK*)
Lookout! Records (*US*)
Mailboat Records (*US*)

Manifesto Records, Inc. (*US*)
Mega Truth Records (*US*)
Megawave Records (*US*)
Meloden Nashville (*US*)
Metalbox Recordings (*UK*)
Midge Bitten Records (*UK*)
Mighty Atom (*UK*)
New Pants Publishing (*US*)
New West Records LLC (*US*)
Nine Mile Records (NMR) (*US*)
Nitro Records (*US*)
Nuclear Blast America (*US*)
Oglio Entertainment (*US*)
Om Records (*US*)
Omnium Records (*US*)
One Little Independent Records US (*US*)
Orange Recordings (*US*)
Palm Pictures (*US*)
Paper Bag Records (*Can*)
Parasol (*US*)
Park the Van Records (*US*)
Pavement Music (*US*)
Peaceville Records (*UK*)
Peek-A-Boo Records (*US*)
Plug Research (*US*)
Polyvinyl Record Co. (*US*)
Pop Cautious Records (*US*)
Poptown Records (*US*)
Pravda Records (*US*)
Prosthetic Records (*US*)
Pyramid Records (*US*)
Q Division Records (*US*)
Radical Records (*US*)
Rainman Records (*US*)
Razor & Tie (*US*)
RCA Records (*US*)
Reach Out International Records (ROIR) (*US*)
The Red Flag Recording Co. (*UK*)
Red Parlor Records (*US*)
Relapse Records (*US*)
Reunion Records (*US*)
Revelation Records (*US*)
Rhombus Records (*US*)
Righteous Babe Records (*US*)
Roadrunner Records, Inc. (*US*)
Rocket Recordings (*UK*)
Rockzion Records (*US*)
ROKiT Records (*UK*)
Ropeadope Records (*US*)
Rough Trade US (*US*)
Rounder Records (*US*)
S-Curve Records (*US*)
Saddle Creek (*US*)
SCI Fidelity Records (*US*)

Claim your free access to www.musicsocket.com: See p.211

Scylla Records (*UK*)
Secret Formula Records, Inc. (*US*)
Secret Records Ltd (*UK*)
Secretly Canadian (*US*)
SGNB Records (*US*)
Shangri-La Projects, Inc. (*US*)
Shrapnel Records (*US*)
Signature Sound Recordings (*US*)
Six Degrees Records (*US*)
Skinny Dog Records (*UK*)
Slush Fund Recordings (*US*)
Sony Music Entertainment - Legacy Recordings (*US*)
Southern Lord Recordings (*US*)
Southern Records (*UK*)
Southland Records (*US*)
Spinefarm Records (*US*)
Struggletown Records (*UK*)
Stunted Records & Management (*UK*)
Sub Pop Records (*US*)
Suburban Noize Records (*US*)
Sugar Shack Records Ltd (*UK*)
Suretone Records (*US*)
Swade Records (*US*)
Tee Pee Records (*US*)
Tenor Vossa Records Ltd (*UK*)
Terminus Records (*US*)
Thin Man Entertainment (*US*)
Thrill Jockey Records (*US*)
Thrive Records (*US*)
Tooth & Nail Records (*US*)
Touch and Go Records (*US*)
Triple Crown Records (*US*)
True North Records (*Can*)
TV Records Ltd (*UK*)
Undertow Records (*US*)
Universal Music Group Nashville (*US*)
Valley Entertainment (*US*)
Victory Records (*US*)
Wasted State Records (*UK*)
Water Music Records (*US*)
West Clark Records (*US*)
Yala! Records (*UK*)
Zube Records (*UK*)
ZYX Records Ltd (*UK*)

Rockabilly
Armadillo Music Limited (*UK*)
Bomber Music Ltd (*UK*)
Dead by Mono Records (*UK*)
Fury Records (*UK*)
Iffy Folk Records (*UK*)
Meloden Nashville (*US*)
Memphis International Records (*US*)
Pravda Records (*US*)
Rainman Records (*US*)

SGNB Records (*US*)
West Clark Records (*US*)

Roots
Acony Records (*US*)
Ariwa Sounds Ltd (*UK*)
Armadillo Music Limited (*UK*)
Blue Jackel Entertainment (*US*)
Borealis Records (*Can*)
Buzz Records (*UK*)
Fellside Recordings (*UK*)
Heartland Recordings (*US*)
Memphis International Records (*US*)
New West Records LLC (*US*)
NorthernBlues Music Inc. (*Can*)
NorthSide (*US*)
Oh Boy Records (*US*)
Parasol (*US*)
Planet Records (*UK*)
R.O.A.D. (Riding on a Dream) Records (*US*)
RCA Records (*US*)
Rebel Records (*US*)
Red House Records (*US*)
Rounder Records (*US*)
Secretly Canadian (*US*)
SGNB Records (*US*)
Signature Sound Recordings (*US*)
Skaggs Family Records (*US*)
Soul Jazz Records Ltd (*UK*)
Sugar Hill Records (*US*)
True North Records (*Can*)
Undertow Records (*US*)
Yellow Dog Records (*US*)

Shoegaze
In At The Eye Records (*UK*)
KFM Records (*UK*)
Slumberland Records (*US*)

Singer-Songwriter
Backwater Records (*UK*)
BackWords Recordings (*US*)
Bohemian Jukebox (*UK*)
Borealis Records (*Can*)
Broken Arrow Records (*US*)
Burning Shed Limited (*UK*)
BUT! Records (*UK*)
Champion Records (*UK*)
Downtown Music (*US*)
eenie meenie records (*US*)
Fabyl (*UK*)
Fence Records (*UK*)
Heartland Recordings (*US*)
In At The Eye Records (*UK*)
Lucky Number Music Limited (*UK*)
Manhaton Records (*UK*)
Meloden Nashville (*US*)

Navigator Records (*UK*)
Nettwerk Records (*Can*)
Om Records (*US*)
One Little Independent Records US (*US*)
Parasol (*US*)
Razor & Tie (*US*)
Red Eye Music (*UK*)
Red House Records (*US*)
Red Parlor Records (*US*)
Ropeadope Records (*US*)
S-Curve Records (*US*)
SCI Fidelity Records (*US*)
SGNB Records (*US*)
Shanachie Entertainment (*US*)
Signature Sound Recordings (*US*)
Sub Pop Records (*US*)
Touch and Go Records (*US*)

Ska
Bomber Music Ltd (*UK*)
JSNTGM (Just Say No To Government Music) (*UK*)
Side One Dummy Records (*US*)
Swade Records (*US*)
TNS (That's Not Skanking) Records (*UK*)
United Riot Records (*US*)
Unpopular Music (*UK*)
Wasted State Records (*UK*)
West Clark Records (*US*)

Soul
Aardvark Records Ltd (*UK*)
Dome Records Ltd (*UK*)
Dorado Music (*UK*)
Ecko Records (*US*)
Evil Twin Records (*UK*)
Expansion Records (*UK*)
Fabyl (*UK*)
Farmyard Records (*UK*)
First Word Records (*UK*)
From Concentrate (*UK*)
Groovin' Records (*UK*)
Headcount Records (*UK*)
M1 Music Limited (*UK*)
Malaco Music Group (*US*)
NexGen Music Group, LLC (*US*)
Nu:Generation Music (*UK*)
Parliament Record Group (*US*)
Pravda Records (*US*)
A Priscilla Thing (*UK*)
R.O.A.D. (Riding on a Dream) Records (*US*)
Remixdj (*UK*)
Rhythmic Records (*UK*)
Secret Records Ltd (*UK*)
Soul Jazz Records Ltd (*UK*)
Tuff City Music Group (*US*)

Yellow Dog Records (*US*)
ZYX Records Ltd (*UK*)

Soulful
Fine Chooned (*UK*)
Red Parlor Records (*US*)
Remixdj (*UK*)

Soundtracks
Aphagia Recordings (*US*)
Artists' Addiction Records (*US*)
First Night Records (*UK*)
GNP Crescendo Records (*US*)
In the Nursery (ITN) Corporation (*UK*)
Mughal Music Group (*Can*)
Multiverse Music (*UK*)
Palm Pictures (*US*)
PS Classics (*US*)
Secret Formula Records, Inc. (*US*)
Sony Music Entertainment - Legacy Recordings (*US*)
ThrillerTracks (*US*)
Varese Sarabande Records (*US*)

Space
Rocket Recordings (*UK*)
Secret Records Ltd (*UK*)
Tenor Vossa Records Ltd (*UK*)
TV Records Ltd (*UK*)

Spoken Word
BackWords Recordings (*US*)

Surf
Dead by Mono Records (*UK*)
West Clark Records (*US*)

Swing
Candid Productions Ltd (*UK*)
Cexton Records (*US*)
Memphis International Records (*US*)
Remixdj (*UK*)
Southland Records (*US*)

Synthpop
In At The Eye Records (*UK*)
Nu Electro (*UK*)
Unpopular Music (*UK*)
Van Richter (*US*)

Techno
Aardvark Records Ltd (*UK*)
Bamboleo Records (*UK*)
Barely Breaking Even Records (*UK*)
Beta Recordings (*UK*)
Brain Bomb Productions (BBP) (*UK*)
Buzzin' Fly Records (*UK*)
Cr2 Records (*UK*)
Gruuv (*UK*)
IKonic Image (*UK*)
Kudos Records Limited (*UK*)
Let Me Understand Records (*UK*)
MaggotHouse Music (*UK*)

Nu Electro (UK)
Pretty Neat Records (UK)
Rekids Ltd (UK)
Remixdj (UK)
Secret Formula Records, Inc. (US)
Solar Distance (UK)
Soul Jazz Records Ltd (UK)
Sounds Of Meow (UK)
Subliminal Records (US)
This and That Lab (UK)
3 Beat Records (UK)
West Clark Records (US)
ZYX Records Ltd (UK)

Thrash
Holier Than Thou Records (UK)
Roadrunner Records, Inc. (US)
Secret Records Ltd (UK)

Traditional
Aardvark Records Ltd (UK)
BackWords Recordings (US)
Fellside Recordings (UK)
Greentrax Recordings (UK)
Heads Up International (US)
Lake (UK)
Mountain Apple Company (US)
Navigator Records (UK)
Red House Records (US)
Remixdj (UK)
Rhombus Records (US)
Ridge Records Limited (UK)
Sonic Safari Music (US)
Southland Records (US)

Trance
Aardvark Records Ltd (UK)
Alter Ego Records (UK)
Brain Bomb Productions (BBP) (UK)
Dead Happy Records (UK)
Enhanced Music (UK)
Joof Recordings (UK)
New Earth Records (US)
Phunk Junk Records Inc (US)
Remixdj (UK)
Secret Formula Records, Inc. (US)
Sequoia Records (US)
Shock Records (UK)
Sounds Of Meow (UK)
3 Beat Records (UK)

Tribal
Brain Bomb Productions (BBP) (UK)
Fine Chooned (UK)
Remixdj (UK)

Trip Hop
Secret Formula Records, Inc. (US)

Twisted
Remixdj (UK)

Underground
Bomber Music Ltd (UK)
Craniality Sounds (US)
Grim Reality Entertainment, LLC (US)
Heavenly Recordings (UK)
JSNTGM (Just Say No To Government Music) (UK)
NexGen Music Group, LLC (US)
Pavement Music (US)
Remixdj (UK)
Secret Records Ltd (UK)
Smog Veil Records (US)
Sounds Of Meow (UK)
Suburban Noize Records (US)
Thin Man Entertainment (US)
TNS (That's Not Skanking) Records (UK)
Unpopular Music (UK)
West Clark Records (US)

Uptempo
Remixdj (UK)

Urban
Atlan-Dec/Grooveline Records (US)
Black Butter Records (UK)
Bush Bash Recordings (UK)
Dirtee Stank (UK)
Downtown Music (US)
East of Sideways Music (US)
Fabyl (UK)
Fine Chooned (UK)
Freddie Records (US)
Island Records (US) (US)
JW Music Limited (UK)
La Corporación Muzic (US)
Mughal Music Group (Can)
Nu:Generation Music (UK)
Om Records (US)
Penalty Entertainment (US)
Pendulum Records (US)
Polo Grounds Music (US)
A Priscilla Thing (UK)
Pyramid Records (US)
Quality Control (US)
Razor & Tie (US)
RCA Records (US)
Remixdj (UK)
Rhythmic Records (UK)
Shady Records (US)
Slip-N-Slide Records (US)
Spitslam (US)
Subdust Music (UK)
Thump Records (US)
Visionary Music Group (US)

World
Aardvark Records Ltd (UK)
Abet Publishing (US)

Access more listings online at www.musicsocket.com

Record Labels Index

ARC Music Productions International (*UK*)
Arkadia Entertainment Corp (*US*)
Blue Jackel Entertainment (*US*)
Borealis Records (*Can*)
Candid Productions Ltd (*UK*)
Dancing Cat Records (*US*)
Dancing Turtle Records (*UK*)
GNP Crescendo Records (*US*)
Heads Up International (*US*)
JohnJohn Records (*UK*)
Justin Time Records Inc. (*Can*)
Knitting Factory Records (*US*)
Lab Records (*UK*)
Luaka Bop (*US*)
Megawave Records (*US*)
New Earth Records (*US*)
NorthernBlues Music Inc. (*Can*)
Omnium Records (*US*)
One Little Independent Records US (*US*)
Palm Pictures (*US*)
Primarily A Cappella (*US*)
Putumayo World Music (*US*)
raSa Music (*US*)
Razor & Tie (*US*)
Rhombus Records (*US*)
Ropeadope Records (*US*)
Sequoia Records (*US*)
Shanachie Entertainment (*US*)
Silver Wave Records (*US*)
Six Degrees Records (*US*)
Sonic Safari Music (*US*)
Sony Music Entertainment - Legacy Recordings (*US*)
Stackhouse & BluEsoterica (*US*)
Sunnyside Records (*US*)
Ultra Music (*US*)
Valley Entertainment (*US*)
World Circuit Records (*UK*)
ZYX Records Ltd (*UK*)

Claim your free access to www.musicsocket.com: See p.211

US Managers

For the most up-to-date listings of these and hundreds of other managers, visit https://www.musicsocket.com/managers

*To claim your **free** access to the site, please see the back of this book.*

21st Century Artists, Inc.
853 Broadway, Suite 1607
New York, NY 10003
Email: info@21stca.com
Website: http://21stca.com

Represents: Artists/Bands

Genres: Folk; Rock; Roots

New York based management company representing artists dealing in folk music, rock, and roots.

25 Artist Agency
25 Music Square West
Nashville, TN 37203
Fax: +1 (615) 687-6699
Email: david@25ent.com
Email: dara@25ent.com
Website: https://www.25ccm.com/
Website: https://www.instagram.com/25artistagency/

Represents: Artists/Bands

Genres: Christian

Contact: David Breen; Dara Easterday; Todd Thomas

Christian record label, based in Nashville, Tennessee.

ACA Music & Entertainment
705 Larry Court
Waukesha, WI 53186
Fax: +1 (262) 790-9149
Email: info@acaentertainment.com
Website: http://acaentertainment.com
Website: https://www.facebook.com/AcaMusicEntertainment/

Represents: Artists/Bands; DJs; Tribute Acts

Genres: All types of music

Describes itself as the oldest and largest provider of live entertainment in the Midwest.

Act 1 Entertainment
28 Price Street
Patchogue, NY 11772
Email: info@act1entertainment.net
Email: karl@act1entertainment.net
Website: http://act1entertainment.net
Website: https://www.facebook.com/Act1Inc/

Represents: Artists/Bands; Comedians; DJs; Tribute Acts

Genres: Jazz; R&B; Soul; Blues; Swing; Roots; Rockabilly; Country; Reggae; Classic Rock

Contact: Karl BD Reamer

Management company based in Patchogue, New York.

Advanced Alternative Media (AAM)
New York / Los Angeles
Email: info@aaminc.com
Website: http://www.aaminc.com
Website: https://www.facebook.com/AdvancedAlternativeMedia

Represents: Artists/Bands; Producers; Songwriters; Sound Engineers

Genres: Alternative; Pop; Rock; Indie

Management company with offices in New York, London, and Los Angeles.

Aesthetic V
Website: https://www.vickyhamilton.com

Represents: Artists/Bands

Genres: All types of music

Contact: Vicky Hamilton

Management by long time Grammy Award-Winning music industry executive and personal manager, responsible for developing or managing such acts as Guns 'N' Roses, Mötley Crüe, Poison, Faster Pussycat and many others. Also offers consultancy service.

Allure Media Entertainment Group
34 East Germantown Pike, Suite 112
Norristown, PA 19401
Website: http://indiemusicpublicity.com
Website: https://www.facebook.com/alluremediaent

Represents: Artists/Bands

Genres: Hip-Hop; Pop; Rock; R&B; Alternative Rock

Provides publicity and marketing solutions for indie artists and labels.

American Artists Entertainment Group
29 Royal Palm Pointe Suite 5
Vero Beach, Florida 32960
Email: online@aaeg.com
Website: https://aaeg.com

Website: https://www.facebook.com/aaegcom/
Website: https://myspace.com/aaeg

Represents: Artists/Bands

Genres: Country; Pop; R&B; Rock

Management company with offices in Vero Beach, Florida, New York, and Hollywood. Has a 45-year history in the performing arts, and today serves over 16 countries and over 100 cities worldwide.

American International Artists, Inc.
356 Pine Valley Road
Hoosick Falls, NY 12090
Fax: +1 (518) 686-1960
Email: cynthia@aiartists.com
Website: https://aiartists.com
Website: https://www.instagram.com/aiartists/

Represents: Artists/Bands; Film / TV Composers

Genres: Classical; Jazz

Contact: Cynthia Herbst

Management company based in Hoosick Falls, NY. Devoted to the building and development of international careers of its world-class composers and jazz and classical performers, and to the development and co-ordination of special projects.

AMW Group Inc.
Website: https://www.amworldgroup.com
Website: https://facebook.com/amwgrp

Represents: Artists/Bands

Genres: All types of music

We have worked with promoting music for over 24 years. We work with different clients including major and independent labels, artists and producers. If you're looking for modern and effective ways to promote your music you have come to the right place.

APA (Agency for the Performing Arts)
10585 Santa Monica Blvd.
Los Angeles, CA 90025
Website: https://www.apa-agency.com

Represents: Artists/Bands

Genres: All types of music

Management company with offices in Los Angeles, Nashville, New York, Atlanta, Toronto, and London.

Apex Talent Group
8383 Wilshire Blvd., Suite 800
Beverly Hills, CA 90211

Email: music@apextalentgroup.com
Email: info@apextalentgroup.com
Website: https://apextalentgroup.com

Represents: Artists/Bands; DJs; Songwriters

Genres: Alternative; Dance; Indie; Pop; Rock; Singer-Songwriter; Electronic

Contact: Richard Makarewicz

Offers full-service artist development. Connections with major record labels, A&Rs, music publishing, playlist curators, and promoters help our clients achieve success in the music business.

Arslanian & Associates, Inc.
6671 Sunset Boulevard, Suite 1502
Hollywood, CA 90028
Email: oscar@discoverhollywood.com
Website: http://www.arslanianassociates.com

Represents: Artists/Bands

Genres: Classic Rock

Contact: Oscar Arslanian; Nyla Arslanian

Management company based in Hollywood, California.

Artist Representation and Management (ARM) Entertainment
Email: info@armentertainment.com
Website: https://armentertainment.com

Represents: Artists/Bands

Genres: Blues; Country; Classic Rock; Metal

Entertainment business with a focus on 70s, 80s, and 90s rock.

Backer Entertainment
Email: info@backerentertainment.com
Website: https://backerentertainment.com

Represents: Artists/Bands; Tribute Acts

Genres: All types of music

Manages mainly tribute acts for events.

Backstage Entertainment
Email: staff@backstageentertainment.net
Website: https://backstageentertainment.net
Website: https://www.facebook.com/BackstageEntertainment

Represents: Artists/Bands

Genres: All types of music

Contact: Paul Loggins

Artist management/marketing firm which specialises in working with independent artists, and aims to bridge the gap between radio, print and social media.

BBA Management & Booking
Email: info@bbabooking.com
Website: https://www.bbabooking.com
Website: https://www.facebook.com/bbabooking

Represents: Artists/Bands

Genres: Jazz; Classical; Rock; Latin

Contact: Michael Mordecai; Laura Mordecai

Management and booking for jazz, classical, and versatile party bands in Central Texas.

Big Beat Productions, Inc.
1515 University Drive, Suite 106
Coral Springs, FL 33071
Fax: +1 (954) 755-8733
Email: talent@bigbeatproductions.com
Website: http://www.bigbeatproductions.com

US Managers

Website: https://www.facebook.com/bigbeatproductions/

Represents: Artists/Bands; Comedians; DJs

Genres: Contemporary; Classic Rock; R&B; Disco; Regional; Jazz; Country

Contact: Richard Lloyd; Gary Ladka; Elissa Solomon

Management company based in Coral Springs, Florida.

Big Hassle Management
New York and Los Angeles
Email: weinstein@bighassle.com
Email: jim@bighassle.com
Website: https://www.bighassle.com

Represents: Artists/Bands

Genres: Indie; Pop; Rock; Alternative

Contact: Ken Weinstein

Management company with offices in New York and Los Angeles.

Big Noise
11 South Angell Street, Suite 336
Providence, RI 02906
Email: algomes@bignoisenow.com
Email: al@bignoisenow.com
Website: http://www.bignoisenow.com

Represents: Artists/Bands

Genres: All types of music

Contact: Al Gomes; A. Michelle

Award-winning Music Firm specialising in artist development, project management, career strategies, and promotion and publicity. Based in Providence, Rhode Island. Looking for artists who are unique, talented, professional, and ready to launch. Considers all genres. Query by phone or email in first instance. Must be at least 18.

Bill Silva Management
Website: https://www.billsilvaentertainment.com

Represents: Artists/Bands; Songwriters

Genres: All types of music

Contact: Bill Silva

Management company based in West Hollywood, California.

Bitchin' Entertainment
1750 Collard Valley Road
Cedartown, GA 30125
Email: Ty@BitchinEntertainment.com
Email: Rodney@BitchinEntertainment.com
Website: http://www.bitchinentertainment.com

Represents: Artists/Bands; Tribute Acts

Genres: Rock; Pop; R&B; Funk; Urban; Hip-Hop; Rap; Instrumental; Jazz; Classical; Ambient; World; Experimental; House; Trance; Electronic; Techno; Alternative; Metal; Punk; Gothic; Country; Americana; Blues; Folk; Singer-Songwriter; Spoken Word

Management company based in Cedartown, Georgia. Send query by email with link to your music online. See website for full submission guidelines, and details of who to approach regarding specific genres. For unsolicited demos, a submission code must be obtained before submitting.

Black Dot Management
Fax: +1 (323) 777-8169
Email: info@blkdot.com
Website: http://www.blkdot.com

Represents: Artists/Bands; Producers; Songwriters; Sound Engineers; Studio Musicians; Studio Technicians

Genres: Jazz; R&B; Urban; Contemporary

Contact: Raymond A. Shields II; Patricia Shields

Management company handling jazz, R&B, and urban.

Blind Ambition Management, Ltd
894 Barton Woods Rd
Atlanta, GA 30307
Email: info@blindambitionmgt.com

Website: http://www.blindambitionmgt.com
Website: https://www.facebook.com/
BlindAmbitionManagement

Represents: Artists/Bands; Film / TV Composers; Songwriters

Genres: Blues; Gospel; Roots; Folk; Singer-Songwriter

Management company based in Atlanta, Georgia, providing career management, business management, creative guidance, publicity, legal, and marketing services for recording artists and music-related businesses.

Booking Entertainment
Two Park Avenue 20th Floor
New York, NY 10016
Email: agents@bookingentertainment.com
Website: https://www.bookingentertainment.com
Website: https://www.facebook.com/profile.php?id=100057634982148

Represents: Artists/Bands

Genres: Pop; Rock; Jazz; R&B; Contemporary

Books big name entertainment for private parties, public concerts, corporate events, and fundraisers.

Brick Wall Management
39 West 32nd Street, Suite 1403
New York, NY 10001
Fax: +1 (212) 202-4582
Website: https://www.brickwallmgmt.com

Represents: Artists/Bands; Producers

Genres: Country; Pop; Rock; Singer-Songwriter

Contact: Michael Solomon; Rishon Blumberg

Management company based in New York.

Brilliant Corners Artist Management
2069 Mission Street, Suite A
San Francisco, CA 94110

SEATTLE OFFICE:
1434-C Elliott Ave W
Seattle, WA 98119
Email: info@brilliantcorners.com
Website: https://brilliantcorners.com
Website: https://www.facebook.com/brilliantcornersmgmt

Represents: Artists/Bands

Genres: Indie; Rock; Singer-Songwriter

Management company with offices in San Francisco and Seattle.

Brilliant Productions
Email: nancy@brilliant-productions.com
Website: https://brilliant-productions.com
Website: https://www.youtube.com/user/itsbrilliant

Represents: Artists/Bands

Genres: Blues; Regional; Roots; Americana

Contact: Nancy Lewis-Pegel

Music booking and management for roots / blues / Southern / jam / Americana music.

The Brokaw Company
4135 Bakman Avevenue
North Hollywood, CA 91602
Email: jobrok@aol.com
Email: db@brokawco.com
Website: http://brokawcompany.com

Represents: Artists/Bands

Genres: Country; Hip-Hop; Pop; Christian; Rock

Contact: Joel Brokaw; David Brokaw; Sanford Brokaw

Management company based in North Hollywood, California. As well as handling music artists, has also handled publicity for hit shows such as The Cosby Show and Roseanne.

Bsquared MGMT
Email: bsquaredmgmt@gmail.com
Website: https://www.bsquaredmgmt.com
Website: http://facebook.com/bsquaredmgmt1

Represents: Artists/Bands

Genres: All types of music

Artist Branding, Artist Development, Booking, Playlisting, Social Media MGMT and More...

Bulletproof Artist Management
241 Main Street
Easthampton, MA 01027
Email: patty@bulletproofartists.com
Website: https://bulletproofartists.com
Website: https://twitter.com/bproofmgmt

Represents: Artists/Bands; Producers

Genres: Country; Pop; Rock; Folk

Contact: Patty Romanoff

Management company based in Easthampton, Massachusetts.

Burgess World Co.
PO Box 646
Mayo, MD 21106-0646
Email: info@burgessworldco.com
Website: http://www.burgessworldco.com

Represents: Artists/Bands; Producers; Sound Engineers

Genres: Alternative; Blues; Jazz; Rock; Singer-Songwriter

Management company based in Mayo, Maryland. Originally founded to manage producers and engineers, but in the nineties expanded into artist management.

C Management
Email: info@studioexpresso.com
Website: http://www.studioexpresso.com/CHome.htm

Represents: Artists/Bands; Film / TV Composers; Producers; Songwriters; Sound Engineers; Studio Technicians; Supervisors

Genres: All types of music

Management company representing producers, mixers, engineers, songwriters, arrangers, magicians, and musicians.

Cantaloupe Music Productions, Inc.
157 West 79 Street
New York, NY 10024-6415
Email: ellenazorin@gmail.com
Website: https://www.cantaloupeproductions.com
Website: https://www.facebook.com/CantaloupeMusicProductions

Represents: Artists/Bands

Genres: Regional; Latin; World; Jazz; Blues; Swing

Contact: Ellen Azorin, President

Handles Brazilian music, Argentine tango, and other Latin-American music.

Career Artist Management (CAM)
Los Angeles, CA
Fax: +1 (424) 230-7839
Website: http://www.camanagement.com

Represents: Artists/Bands

Genres: Pop; Rock

Management company based in Los Angeles, California.

Case Entertainment Group Inc.
119 N. Wahsatch Ave
Colorado Springs, CO 80903
Fax: +1 (719) 634-2274
Email: rac@crlr.net
Website: https://newpants.com
Website: http://www.oldpants.com

Represents: Artists/Bands

Genres: Rock; Pop; Country; Folk; R&B; Rap

Contact: Robert Case

Management company based in Colorado Springs, Colorado.

CEC Management
15 Driftwood Drive
Port Washington, NY 11050

Represents: Artists/Bands; Producers

Genres: Rock; Indie; Pop; Alternative; Americana; Blues; Electronic; Jazz

Management company with offices in New York and London.

Celebrity Enterprises (CE) Inc.
137 Saddle Spur Trail,
Tijeras, NM 87059
Email: info@worldstageevents.com
Website: https://www.ent123.com

Represents: Artists/Bands

Genres: All types of music

Provides acts for corporate events and fundraisers, performing arts centres and casinos, and other special events.

Celebrity Talent Agency Inc.
111 East 14th Street Suite 249
New York, NY 10003
Fax: +1 (201) 837-9011
Email: markg@celebritytalentagency.com
Email: alinak@celebritytalentagency.com
Website: https://www.celebritytalentagency.com
Website: https://www.facebook.com/CelebrityTalentAgency/

Represents: Artists/Bands; Comedians; DJs

Genres: Dance; Hip-Hop; R&B; Latin; Reggae; Jazz; Gospel

Contact: Mark Green; Alina Kim

Talent agency with offices in New York and London.

Century Artists Management Agency, LLC
711 West End Avenue, Suite 3CS
New York, New York 10025
Email: phorton@centuryarts.com
Website: https://www.camatalent.com
Website: https://twitter.com/centuryartists

Represents: Artists/Bands; Producers; Songwriters

Genres: All types of music

Contact: Paul E. Horton, President

Offers strategic brand management for artists in music, television, film, and the performing arts. Seeking established and new talent.

Chaney Gig Affairs (CGA)
California
Email: ChaneyGigAffairs@gmail.com
Website: https://www.chaneygigaffairs.com
Website: https://www.facebook.com/ChaneyGigAffairs/

Represents: Artists/Bands

Genres: Jazz; R&B; Soul

Provides Music and Artist Management Services; Web Design, EPKs and Video/Media Content Creation; and Event Management.

Chapman & Co. Management
Fax: +1 (818) 788-9525
Email: info@chapmanmanagement.com
Email: steve@chapmanmanagement.com
Website: https://www.chapmanmanagement.com

Represents: Artists/Bands

Genres: Contemporary Jazz

Contact: Steve Chapman

Management company concentrating on smooth, contemporary jazz.

Ciulla Management, Inc.
Website: https://ciullamgmt.com

Represents: Artists/Bands

Genres: Rock; Metal

Contact: Tony Ciulla

Management company handling rock/metal artists.

Collin Artists
1099 N. Mar Vista Ave
Pasadena, CA 91104
Email: collinartists@gmail.com
Website: http://www.collinartists.com

112   US Managers

Represents: Artists/Bands

Genres: Instrumental Jazz; Latin; World; Blues; R&B; Swing; Contemporary Jazz

Contact: Barbara Collin

Management company based in Pasadena, California.

Concerted Efforts
PO Box 440326
Somerville MA, 02144
Fax: +1 (617) 209-1300
Email: concerted@concertedefforts.com
Website: https://concertedefforts.com

Represents: Artists/Bands

Genres: Blues; Folk; Jazz; Gospel; Soul; Singer-Songwriter; Rock; World

Music booking agency based in Somerville, Massachusetts.

Creative Artists Agency (CAA)
2000 Avenue of the Stars
Los Angeles, CA 90067
Fax: +1 (424) 288-2900
Website: https://www.caa.com
Website: https://www.instagram.com/creativeartistsagency/

Represents: Artists/Bands

Genres: All types of music

Talent agency with offices across the US, as well as in the UK, China, and Europe.

Crush Music Media Management
Email: info@crushmusic.com
Website: https://www.crushmusic.com

Represents: Artists/Bands; Producers; Songwriters

Genres: All types of music

Full service music company based in New York and Los Angeles

Culler Talent Management
48 Kelley Ave
Battle Creek, MI 49017

Email: chandlerculler@gmail.com
Website: https://www.linkedin.com/in/chandler-culler-913972a8

Represents: Variety Artists

Genres: All types of music

Contact: Chandler Culler

Provides talent management and event booking for all types of entertainers from all over.

Cumberland Music Collective
Nashville, TN
Email: lee@cmcartists.com
Email: andrew@cmcartists.com
Website: https://www.kcaartists.com
Website: https://www.facebook.com/KeithCaseAndAssociates

Represents: Artists/Bands

Genres: All types of music

Contact: Lee Olsen; Andrew Bestick; Chase Decraene

A new kind of music agency: one that puts the artists, agents and clients first – with the understanding that good business relies on good partnerships founded on mutual respect and integrity, designed for the success of all. To that end, it is a big tent with a boutique approach to artist representation, welcoming all genres of music.

D. Bailey Management, Inc.
17815 Gunn Hwy Suite 5
Odessa, FL 33556
Fax: +1 (813) 960-4662
Email: dennis@dbaileymanagement.com
Website: https://www.dbaileymanagement.com
Website: https://www.facebook.com/dbaileymanagement

Represents: Artists/Bands

Genres: Pop; R&B; Rock

Contact: Dennis Bailey

Live entertainment, event management, and artist management, based in Odessa, Florida.

Access more listings online at www.musicsocket.com

US Managers 113

DAS Communications Ltd
83 Riverside Drive
New York, NY 10024
Website: https://www.bloomberg.com/
profile/company/0835448D:US

Represents: Artists/Bands; Producers;
Songwriters

Genres: Hip-Hop; Pop; Rock

Management company based in New York.

Dave Kaplan Management
1126 South Coast Highway 101
Encinitas, CA 92024
Fax: +1 (760) 944-7808
Email: demo@surfdog.com
Website: https://surfdog.com
Website: https://www.facebook.com/
surfdogrecords/

Represents: Artists/Bands

Genres: Rock

Contact: Dave Kaplan; Scott Seine

Management company based in Encinitas, California. Also runs associated record label. Accepts submissions by post marked for the attention of A&R, but prefers links by email (no MP3 attachments).

David Belenzon Management, Inc.
PO Box 5000 PMB 67,
Rancho Santa Fe, CA 92067

Fax: +1 (858) 832-8381
Email: David@Belenzon.com
Email: INFO@BELENZON.com
Website: http://www.belenzon.com

Represents: Artists/Bands; Variety Artists

Genres: Contemporary; Pop; Rock; R&B

Contact: David Belenzon

Management company based in Rancho Santa Fe, California, representing artists, variety artists, plus theatrical and production shows.

Dawn Elder Management
Email: deworldmusic@aol.com
Website: https://
dawnelderworldentertainment.com
Website: https://www.facebook.com/
DawnElderWorldEntertainment/

Represents: Artists/Bands

Genres: Classical; Jazz; Pop; Rock; Roots; Traditional; World

Have managed, represented and organised international tours for some of the most highly regarded international artists today.

DCA Productions
302A 12th Street, # 330
New York, NY 10014
Fax: +1 (609) 259-8260
Email: info@dcaproductions.com
Website: https://dcaproductions.com
Website: https://www.facebook.com/
dcaproductionsplus/

Represents: Artists/Bands; Comedians; Variety Artists

Genres: Pop; Rock; Folk

Contact: Daniel C. Abrahmsen, President; Gerri Abrahamsen, Vice President

Management company founded in 1983, specialising in variety performers, comedians, musical performers, theatre productions, and producing live events.

DDB Productions
Email: ddbprods@gmail.com
Website: https://www.ddbprods.com/
Website: http://www.deedeebridgewater.com

Represents: Artists/Bands; Lyricists; Producers; Songwriters; Studio Vocalists

Genres: Jazz; World; Alternative

Contact: Dee Dee Bridgewater

A boutique record label, music production company and talent management firm, based in Los Angeles, CA and New Orleans, LA. Founded by triple Grammy and Tony award winning Jazz artist.

Claim your free access to www.musicsocket.com: See p.211

Deep South Artist Management
RALEIGH
PO Box 17737
Raleigh, NC 27619

NASHVILLE
PO Box 121975
Nashville, TN 37212
Email: Hello@ DeepSouthEntertainment.com
Website: http://www. deepsouthentertainment.com
Website: https://www.facebook.com/deepsouthent

Represents: Artists/Bands

Genres: Alternative; Country; Pop; Rock; Americana; Christian

Record label, artist management firm, talent agency, and concert production company based in Raleigh, North Carolina, with offices in both Raleigh and Nashville, Tennessee.

Def Ro Inc.
33 Prospect Street, Suite 1r
Bloomfield, NJ 07003
Email: defroinc@msn.com
Website: http://sirro.tripod.com/index.html
Website: http://defroinc.blogspot.co.uk

Represents: Artists/Bands

Genres: Hip-Hop; Pop; R&B

Contact: Will Strickland

Management company based in Bloomfield, New Jersey. Send up to three tracks by mail only.

Delta Groove Music, Inc.
16501 Sherman Way Suite 215
Van Nuys, CA 91406
Fax: +1 (818) 907-1620
Email: info@deltagroovemusic.com
Website: http://www. deltagrooveproductions.com

Represents: Artists/Bands; Film / TV Composers; Lyricists; Producers; Songwriters; Sound Engineers; Studio Musicians; Studio Technicians; Studio Vocalists; Supervisors

Genres: Blues; Roots

Management company based in Van Nuys, California.

Direct Management Group (DMG)
8332 Melrose Ave, Top Floor
Los Angeles, CA 90069
Website: https://directmanagement.com

Represents: Artists/Bands

Genres: Pop

Contact: Martin Kirkup; Bradford Cobb; Steven Jensen

Management company based in West Hollywood, California. Founded in April 1985. Describes itself as an internationally oriented entertainment company with broad-based success in the representation of musical artists.

Dog & Pony Industries
Email: info@dogandponyindustries.com
Website: http://www. dogandponyindustries.com

Represents: Artists/Bands

Genres: All types of music

Specializing in talent management and the coordinating of concert tours and special projects in the Music, TV & Film industries. Contact by email.

Domo Music Group Management
11340 West Olympic Boulevard, Suite 270
Los Angeles, CA 90064
Fax: +1 (310) 966-4420
Email: domo@domo.com
Email: dino@domo.com
Website: https://www.domomusicgroup.com/management/
Website: https://www.facebook.com/officialdomomusicgroup

Access more listings online at www.musicsocket.com

Represents: Artists/Bands; DJs; Film / TV Composers; Producers; Songwriters; Studio Musicians

Genres: Contemporary; Classical; Folk; Indie; New Age; Pop; Rock; Singer-Songwriter; World; Ethnic

Contact: Eiichi Naito; Dino Malito (A&R)

Management company based in Los Angeles, California, handling Japanese artists. Prefers links to music online by email or via submission form on website, or send CD by post marked for the attention of A&R.

East Coast Entertainment (ECE)
Email: info@bookece.com
Website: https://www.bookece.com
Website: https://www.facebook.com/EastCoastEntertainment/

Represents: Artists/Bands; Comedians; DJs

Genres: All types of music

Describes itself as the largest full-service entertainment agency in the country.

Elevation Group Inc.
Email: kent@elevationgroup.net
Website: https://www.elevationgroup.net

Represents: Artists/Bands

Genres: All types of music

Contact: Kent Sorrell

Management company based in California.

Emcee Artist Management
Email: liz@emceeartist.com
Email: mfair@emceeartist.com
Website: https://www.emceeartist.com

Represents: Artists/Bands

Genres: Jazz; Blues; Rock

Contact: Liz Penta; Meagan Fair

Management company representing jazz, blues, and rock artists. No hip-hop.

Enlight Entertainment, Inc.
Website: http://www.enlight-ent.com
Website: https://www.facebook.com/tashia.l.stafford

Represents: Artists/Bands; Producers; Songwriters

Genres: R&B; Gospel; Rap

Contact: Tashia Stafford

Offers the following services:

- Producer and Personal Management
- Independent Publishing Company Consulting
- Administrative Assistant Services
- A & R Consulting and Administration
- Personal Assistants
- Song Writing Clinics

Entertainment Services International
1819 South Harlan Circle
Lakewood, CO 80232
Fax: +1 (303) 936-0069
Email: randy@esientertainment.com
Website: http://www.esientertainment.com

Represents: Artists/Bands

Genres: Rock; Classic Rock

Contact: Randy Erwin

Manager based in Lakewood, Colorado.

Entourage Talent Associates, Ltd
150 West 28th Street, Suite 1503
New York, NY 10001
Fax: +1 (212) 633-1818
Email: info@entouragetalent.com
Website: http://www.entouragetalent.com
Website: https://www.facebook.com/EntourageTalentAssociates

Represents: Artists/Bands

Genres: Pop; Rock; Singer-Songwriter; Jazz

Not currently seeking new acts for representation. However, you can submit your music and information for consideration for support/packaging with one of the existing clients for an upcoming tour. Send submissions by post or by email, or via form on website.

Fat City Artists
1906 Chet Atkins Place, Suite 502 Nashville, TN 37212
Fax: +1 (615) 321-5382
Website: http://fatcityartists.com

Represents: Artists/Bands

Genres: Acoustic; Blues; R&B; Celtic; Country; Folk; Funk; Gospel; Jazz; Pop; Reggae; Rockabilly; Rock and Roll; Ska; Swing; World

Artists management based in Nashville, Tennessee. Not signing new artists as at July 2020.

Fire Tower Entertainment
Los Angeles, CA
Email: artists@firetowerent.com
Email: info@firetowerent.com
Website: https://firetowerent.com
Website: https://www.facebook.com/firetowerent

Represents: Artists/Bands

Genres: Indie; Pop; Singer-Songwriter

Entertainment startup located in Los Angeles focused on artist management and A&R services.

First Access Entertainment
Website: https://www.facebook.com/firstaccessent

Represents: Artists/Bands

Genres: Pop; Rap; R&B; Hip-Hop

Management Company, Record Label, Music Publisher.

First Artists Management
4764 Park Granada, Suite 110
Calabasas, CA 91302
Fax: +1 (818) 377-7760
Email: info@firstartistsmgmt.com
Website: https://www.firstartistsmanagement.com

Represents: Film / TV Composers; Supervisors

Genres: Soundtracks

Management company based in Calabasas, California, specialising in the representation of composers, music supervisors, and music editors for film and television.

5B Artist Management
220 36th St, Suite B442
Brooklyn, NY 11232

LOS ANGELES:
12021 Jefferson Blvd,
Culver City, CA 90230
Email: info@5bam.com
Website: http://5bam.com

Represents: Artists/Bands

Genres: Alternative; Metal; Rock

Management company with offices in New York, Los Angeles and Birmingham (UK).

Fleming Artists
PO Box 1568
Ann Arbor, MI 48106
Email: jim@flemingartists.com
Email: cynthia@flemingartists.com
Website: https://www.flemingartists.com
Website: https://www.facebook.com/flemingartists/

Represents: Artists/Bands

Genres: Contemporary Roots Rock; Blues; Folk; Pop; Rock

Management company with a mission to "represent a high quality, diverse roster of performing artists by providing them with a unique, thoughtful and individualized approach to concert booking."

Fresh Flava Entertainment
2705 12th Street NE
Washington, DC 20018
Email: freshflava17@gmail.com
Website: http://www.freshflava.com

Represents: Artists/Bands

Genres: Hip-Hop; Jazz; Gospel; R&B; Rock

Management company based in Washington DC.

Funzalo Records
PO Box 571567
Tarzana, CA 91357
Email: funzalorecords@gmail.com
Email: dan@mikesmanagement.com
Website: https://funzalorecords.com
Website: https://www.facebook.com/funzalorecords

Represents: Artists/Bands; Producers

Genres: All types of music

Contact: Mike Lembo; Dan Agnew

Send submission through form on website, with short bio and links to songs online.

Gary Stamler Management
PO Box 34575
Los Angeles, CA 90034
Email: garystamler@me.com
Email: nancysefton@gsmgmt.net
Website: https://www.gsmgmt.net

Represents: Artists/Bands; Producers

Genres: All types of music

Contact: Gary Stamler; Nancy Sefton

Management company based in Los Angeles.

Gayle Enterprises, Inc.
51 Music Square East
Nashville, TN 37203
Email: info@crystalgayle.com
Website: https://crystalgayle.com
Website: https://www.facebook.com/236343614779

Represents: Artists/Bands

Genres: All types of music

Contact: Bill Gatzimos

Management company based in Nashville, Tennessee, dedicated to representing one artist only. No submissions or queries.

Gold Mountain Entertainment
LOS ANGELES

12400 Ventura Blvd., Suite 444
Studio City, CA 91604

NASHVILLE

11 Music Square East, Suite 103
Nashville, TN 37203
Fax: +1 (615) 255-9001
Email: info@gmemusic.com
Website: http://www.gmemusic.com

Represents: Artists/Bands

Genres: Contemporary; Blues; Folk; Indie; Pop; Punk; Reggae; Rock; Singer-Songwriter; World

Management company with offices in Los Angeles, Nasville, and Montreal.

Good Guy Entertainment
Email: aa@goodguyent.com
Website: https://www.facebook.com/GoodGuyEntertainment

Represents: Artists/Bands

Genres: Pop; Urban

Management company specialising in artist and project development, mass media marketing and promotion, independent record promotion, and television production.

The Gorfaine/Schwartz Agency, Inc.
4111 West Alameda Avenue, Suite 509
Burbank, CA 91505
Website: https://www.gsamusic.com
Website: https://www.facebook.com/gorfaineschwartz

Represents: Artists/Bands; Producers

Genres: All types of music

Management agency based in Burbank, California.

Grassy Hill Entertainment
303 West 42nd Street, Suite 614
New York, NY 10036

US Managers

Fax: +1 (212) 977-1069
Email: managers@grassyhill.net
Email: margo.parks@grassyhillentertainment.com
Website: http://www.grassyhillentertainment.com

Represents: Artists/Bands

Genres: Roots; Americana; Folk; Singer-Songwriter

Contact: Margo Parks; Julia Reinhart

A full service management company based in New York, describing itself as a "talent incubator" for independent artists in the roots / americana genres.

Hard Head Management
PO Box 651
New York, NY 10014
Fax: +1 (212) 337-0708
Email: info@hardhead.com
Website: https://www.hardhead.com

Represents: Artists/Bands

Genres: Americana; Electronic; Rock

Contact: Stefani Scamardo

Management company based in New York.

Hardin Entertainment
Email: info@hardinentertainment.com
Website: http://www.hardinentertainment.com
Website: https://www.facebook.com/hardinbourke/

Represents: Artists/Bands; Film / TV Composers; Lyricists; Producers; Songwriters; Studio Vocalists; Supervisors

Genres: Contemporary; Alternative; Americana; Blues; Christian; Country; Dance; Electronic; Folk; Hardcore; Indie; Latin; Pop; Rock; Roots; Singer-Songwriter; World

Management company with offices in Los Angeles and New York.

HardKnockLife Entertainment
Website: https://hardknocklifeent.com
Website: https://www.instagram.com/hardknocklifeent/

Represents: Artists/Bands

Genres: Acoustic; Hip-Hop; Pop; R&B; Rap

Contact via form on website, including links to your music online.

Harmony Artists
3575 Cahuenga Blvd. W, #560
Los Angeles, CA 90068
Fax: +1 (323) 655-5154
Email: contact_us@harmonyartists.com
Website: https://www.harmonyartists.com
Website: https://www.facebook.com/HarmonyArtistsLA/

Represents: Artists/Bands; Tribute Acts

Genres: Blues; Latin; Jazz; Swing

Specialises in providing top national headline and regional entertainment for venues throughout the world.

Hello! Booking, Inc.
PO Box 18717
Minneapolis, MN 55418
Fax: +1 (763) 463-1264
Email: eric@hellobooking.com
Website: https://www.hellobooking.com
Website: https://www.facebook.com/hellobookingusa

Represents: Artists/Bands

Genres: Country; Folk; Indie; Jazz; Hip-Hop; Acoustic; Rockabilly; Rock; Pop

Contact: Eric Roberts

Show booking company based in Minneapolis.

Hornblow Group USA, Inc.
Email: info@hornblowgroup.com
Website: https://www.hornblowgroup.com
Website: https://www.facebook.com/hornblowmusic/

Represents: Artists/Bands; Film / TV Composers; Lyricists; Producers; Songwriters; Studio Musicians

Genres: Indie; Pop; Rock; Alternative; Singer-Songwriter

Full-service artist management firm, independent record label, purveyors of cool t-shirts and bumper stickers.

Howard Rosen Promotion, Inc.
Email: info@howiewood.com
Email: Howie@howiewood.com
Website: https://howiewood.com/
Website: https://myspace.com/howardrosen

Represents: Artists/Bands

Genres: All types of music

Contact: Howard Rosen; Alex Louton

Full service radio promotion company based in Ojai, California. Submit music using online submissions system on website.

IMC Entertainment Group
Website: http://www.imcentertainment.com

Represents: Artists/Bands

Genres: Pop; R&B

Entertainment company based in Porter Ranch, California, providing entertainment and production services worldwide. Specialises in music performance, production, publishing and supervision services.

IMG Artists
Pleiades House
7 West 54th Street
New York, NY 10019
Fax: +1 (212) 994-3550
Email: artistsny@imgartists.com
Website: https://imgartists.com

Represents: Artists/Bands

Genres: Classic; Folk; Gospel; Jazz; World; Latin; Singer-Songwriter

Contact: Elizabeth Sobol, Senior Vice President, Managing Director; Steve Linder, Senior Vice President and Director, Attractions Division

Describes itself as the global leader in the arts management business, with offices in New York, London, Paris, Hanover, and Seoul.

Impact Artist Management
Kingston, NY 12401
Email: info@impactartist.com
Website: http://www.impactartist.com
Website: https://www.facebook.com/impactartistmanagement

Represents: Artists/Bands; Film / TV Composers; Songwriters; Supervisors

Genres: Contemporary; Blues; Folk; Indie; Jazz; Latin; R&B; Rock; Roots; Singer-Songwriter; World; Alternative; Alternative Country

Management company based in Kingston, New York.

In De Goot Entertainment
119 West 23rd Street, Suite 609
New York, NY 10011
Fax: +1 (212) 924-3242
Website: https://www.indegoot.com
Website: https://www.facebook.com/Indegoot/

Represents: Artists/Bands

Genres: Indie; Metal; Pop; Rock; Underground

Contact: Michael Iurato

Management company based in New York. Send unsolicited submissions by post.

In Touch Entertainment
309 W 55th St
New York, NY 10019
Email: info@intouchent.com
Website: https://intouchent.com
Website: https://www.facebook.com/intouchentertainment

Represents: Artists/Bands

Genres: All types of music

A worldwide entertainment organisation that manages both established and up-and-coming recording artists, books talent into venues, oversees music recording, and promotes and produces concerts and films. Send electronic press kit by email, including bio, audio, video, tour history, and contact info. Response only if interested.

Ina Dittke & Associates
6538 Collins Avenue, Suite 345,
Miami Beach, FL 33141
Email: ina@inadittke.com
Email: gina@inadittke.com
Website: https://inadittke.com
Website: https://www.facebook.com/inadittkeassociates/

Represents: Artists/Bands

Genres: Jazz; Latin; World

Music agency based in Miami, Florida, representing a varied and international roster of artists.

International Creative Management (ICM) Partners
LOS ANGELES
10250 Constellation Boulevard
Los Angeles, CA 90067

NEW YORK
65 East 55th Street
New York, NY 10022
Email: icmcorporatecommunications@icmpartners.com
Website: https://www.icmpartners.com/
Website: https://www.facebook.com/ICMPartners/

Represents: Artists/Bands; Comedians

Genres: All types of music

Concerts and live appearances department represents artists in all musical genres, including pop, rock, R&B, hip-hop, indie and adult contemporary. Arranges global engagements and tours in a wide variety of settings and venues.

Intrigue Music
Email: staff@intriguegroup.net
Website: https://www.intriguemusic.com
Website: https://www.facebook.com/intriguemusic

Represents: Artists/Bands

Genres: Pop; Rock

Full-service entertainment company based in New Haven, CT. Specialises in worldwide artist management, music publishing, and intellectual property rights management.

Invasion Group, Ltd
333 E 75th St #4A
New York, NY 10021
Fax: +1 (212) 414-0525
Email: info@invasiongroup.com
Website: http://www.invasiongroup.com
Website: https://facebook.com/invasiongroupltd

Represents: Artists/Bands; Film / TV Composers; Lyricists; Producers; Songwriters; Sound Engineers; Studio Musicians; Studio Technicians; Studio Vocalists; Supervisors

Genres: All types of music

Contact: Steven Saporta; Peter Casperson; Steve Dalmer

Management company based in New York.

James Joseph Music Management LA
3229 Rambla Pacifico Street
Malibu, CA 90265
Email: jj3@jamesjoseph.co.uk
Website: http://www.jamesjoseph.co.uk

Represents: Artists/Bands

Genres: All types of music

Management company with offices in Los Angeles, California, and London, UK.

Jampol Artist Management
8033 W. Sunset Blvd., Suite 3250
West Hollywood, CA 90046
Email: assistant@jamincla.com

Website: https://wemanagelegends.com
Website: https://www.facebook.com/jjampol

Represents: Artists/Bands

Genres: All types of music

Manages great legacy artists. Dedicated to the re-introduction of timeless art through modern means, and helps iconic artist legacies make the transition to the digital age with integrity. Does not manage new artists. If you are a legacy artist looking to extend your reach, use new technologies, or place your legacy in a modern context, send query by email.

Jay Anthony's Next Level Booking and Entertainment Agency, LLC
Las Vegas, NV
Email: Jayanthony@nextlevelbookingandentertainment.com
Email: Nextlevelbookingagency@gmail.com
Website: https://www.nextlevelbookingandentertainment.com
Website: https://www.facebook.com/JayAnthonysnextlevel/

Represents: Artists/Bands; Tribute Acts

Genres: All types of music

Always looking for exceptional talent to add to their roster. Looking for: experienced artists that believe in perfecting their craft; acts with great EPK's (no demo sites); and tributes acts that sound and look like the original act.

Jeff Roberts & Associates
Hendersonville, TN 37075
Fax: +1 (615) 851-7023
Website: https://jeffroberts.com
Website: https://www.facebook.com/jrabooking

Represents: Artists/Bands

Genres: Christian

Christina music booking agency, based in Tennessee.

Kari Estrin Management & Consulting
PO Box 60232
Nashville, TN 37206
Email: kari@kariestrin.com
Website: https://www.kariestrin.com
Website: https://www.facebook.com/kariestrinmanagement/

Represents: Artists/Bands

Genres: Americana; Folk; Roots; Acoustic

Based in Nashville, Tennessee. Offers artist management and consulting.

KBH Entertainment
Los Angeles, CA
Email: support@kbhentertainment.com
Website: https://kbhentertainment.com
Website: https://www.facebook.com/KBHEntertainment

Represents: Artists/Bands; Film / TV Composers; Producers; Studio Musicians; Studio Vocalists

Genres: All types of music

Contact: Brent Harvey

A full service entertainment consulting, booking, event production, management and marketing company, based in Los Angeles, California.

Kraft-Engel Management
3349 Cahuenga Blvd. West
Los Angeles, CA 90068
Email: info@Kraft-Engel.com
Website: https://kraft-engel.com

Represents: Film / TV Composers; Songwriters; Supervisors

Genres: Soundtracks

Management company based in Sherman Oaks, California, specialising in representing film and theatre composers, songwriters and music supervisors.

Kuper Personal Management
515 Bomar Street
Houston, TX 77006

Email: info@kupergroup.com
Website: http://www.kupergroup.com

Represents: Artists/Bands

Genres: Alternative; Americana; Folk; Roots Rock

Management company based in Houston, Texas.

The Kurland Agency
173 Brighton Avenue
Boston, MA 02134-2003
Email: agents@thekurlandagency.com
Website: https://www.thekurlandagency.com

Represents: Artists/Bands

Genres: Jazz; Blues

Contact: Ted Kurland

Management company based in Boston, best known for representing jazz artists.

LA Personal Development
Email: Glebe99@yahoo.com
Website: https://www.lapersdev.com
Website: https://www.facebook.com/lapersonaldevelopment/

Represents: Artists/Bands

Genres: All types of music

Contact: Mike Gormley

A management/consulting company started in 1983.

Larro Media
Email: steven@larromedia.com
Website: https://larromedia.com
Website: https://www.facebook.com/steven.rosen.969

Represents: Artists/Bands

Genres: All types of music

Contact: Steven Rosen

A full-service music, film and TV, and talent development company specializing in artist synch representation, music supervision and music clearance, talent/brand management, and TV and film production.

Leonard Business Management
5777 W. Century Blvd, Suite 1600
Los Angeles, CA 90045
Fax: +1 (310) 458-8862
Email: info@lbmgt.com
Website: http://leonardbusinessmanagement.com
Website: https://www.facebook.com/pages/Leonard-Business-Management/665044716881370

Represents: Artists/Bands

Genres: All types of music

Provides business management services to the entertainment industry, including business management, tour accounting, royalty services, etc.

Lippman Entertainment
Fax: +1 (805) 686-5866
Email: music@lippmanent.com
Email: info@lippmanent.com
Website: http://www.lippmanent.com
Website: https://www.facebook.com/lippmanent
Website: http://www.myspace.com/lippmanentertainment

Represents: Artists/Bands; Film / TV Composers; Producers; Sound Engineers; Studio Technicians

Genres: Pop; R&B; Rap; Hip-Hop; Rock; Singer-Songwriter; Urban

Contact: Michael Lippman; Nick Lippman

Management company based in California. Not accepting submissions as at September 2019.

Loggins Promotion
Nashville, TN
Email: staff@logginspromotion.com
Website: https://logginspromotion.com
Website: https://www.facebook.com/logginspromotion

Represents: Artists/Bands

Genres: R&B; Urban; Rap; Hip-Hop; Dance; Alternative; Rock; Americana; Jazz; Country; Pop

Full service promotion firm based in Nashville, Tennessee. Submit music using online form, or send email for permission to submit by post.

Lupo Entertainment
Email: steve@lupomusic.com
Website: http://www.lupomusic.com

Represents: Artists/Bands

Genres: Country; Pop; R&B; Rock; Hip-Hop

Contact: Steve Corbin

Management company and consulting service founded in 2003.

Madison House Inc.
1401 Walnut St, Suite 500
Boulder, CO 80302
Email: info@madison-house.com
Website: https://madisonhouseinc.com
Website: https://www.facebook.com/MadisonHouseInc

Represents: Artists/Bands

Genres: All types of music

Management company based in Boulder, Colorado.

Magus Entertainment Inc.
268 Water St
New York, NY 10038
Fax: +1 (212) 925-4007
Email: info@magusentertainment.com
Website: https://magusentertainment.com
Website: https://www.facebook.com/MagusEntertainment/

Represents: Artists/Bands; Lyricists; Producers; Songwriters; Sound Engineers; Studio Musicians; Studio Technicians; Studio Vocalists

Genres: Contemporary; Electronic; Indie; Latin; Pop; Punk; R&B; Rap; Hip-Hop; Rock; Urban; Singer-Songwriter

A New-York-based, full-service management company, representing both high profile recording artists and a number of mixers and producers.

Maine Road Management
PO Box 1412
Woodstock, NY 12498
Email: mailbox@maineroadmanagement.com
Website: https://maineroadmanagement.com
Website: https://www.facebook.com/maineroadmanagement

Represents: Artists/Bands; Producers

Genres: Country; Folk; Indie; Jazz; Rock

Contact: David Whitehead

New York-based management company.

Major Bob Music, Inc.
Website: https://www.majorbob.com
Website: https://www.facebook.com/majorbobmusic

Represents: Songwriters

Genres: Country; R&B; Soul; Pop

Contact: Bob Doyle; Tina Crawford

Management and publishing company based in Nashville, Tennessee.

The Major Group
33117 Woodward Ave., Suite 331,
Birmingham, MI 48009
Email: contact@themajorgroup.com
Website: http://www.themajorgroup.com
Website: https://www.facebook.com/tmgmajorproductions

Represents: Artists/Bands

Genres: Jazz; Rap; Techno; Rock; Pop; R&B

Contact: Brian Major

Management company based in Michigan. Accepts unsolicited material. Submit via online form.

The Management Ark, Inc.
Edward C. Arrendell, II
3 Bethesda Metro Center, Suite 700
Bethesda, MD 20814

Vernon H. Hammond III, CFP

124 US Managers

116 Villiage Boulevard, Suite 200
Princeton, NJ 08540
Email: ed@managementark.pro
Email: vernon@managementark.com
Website: http://www.managementark.com

Represents: Artists/Bands

Genres: Jazz

Contact: Edward C. Arrendell, II; Vernon H. Hammond III, CFP

Jazz management company with offices in Bethesda, Maryland, and Princeton, New Jersey.

Mars Jazz Booking
1006 Ashby Place
Charlottesville, VA 22901-4006
Fax: +1 (434) 979-6179
Email: reggie@marsjazz.com
Website: https://marsjazz.com

Represents: Artists/Bands

Genres: Jazz

Contact: Reggie Marshall

Jazz booking agency. Not currently accepting new clients or press kits, but happy to receive CDs and contact details and may contact further down the line if interested.

Mascioli Entertainment
Website: https://masciolientertainment.com

Represents: Artists/Bands

Genres: Country; Jazz; R&B; Swing; Rock

Contact: Paul Mascioli

Full-service entertainment company based in Orlando, Florida, offering artists management and booking for conventions, casinos, arenas, theaters, night clubs, fairs, festivals, and special events.

Mauldin Brand Agency
Email: info@mauldinbrand.com
Website: https://www.mauldinbrandinc.com

Represents: Artists/Bands; Producers; Songwriters

Genres: Hip-Hop; R&B; Rap; Pop

Contact: Michael Mauldin

Your Black American Entertainment Connection with more than 40 years experience in music leadership, management, branding, and marketing. Creates partnerships and enhances branded assets within the consumer marketplace with special focus on teens, young adults, legacy, and the future.

Max Bernard Management
Email: myron@maxbernard.com
Website: http://www.maxbernard.com
Website: https://www.facebook.com/maxbernardmanagement/

Represents: Artists/Bands; Producers; Songwriters; Studio Musicians; Studio Vocalists

Genres: Urban Indie Jazz R&B Soul Singer-Songwriter; Soundtracks Blues Mainstream Soulful

Contact: Myron Bernard

We, pride ourselves on this blueprint that we specialize in creating a backdrop of musical ambiance featuring the world's finest and unique talent while servicing your entertainment needs.

We actively commit to find quality entertainment and entertainer's that suit your local and international demographic areas and taste.

Offers personal consulting services in all areas of artist development, live entertainment and social media and online network marketing.

Media/PR services are outsourced additions provided to clients. Special event(s) implementation and tour management services are available upon request.

MBK Entertainment
519 8th Ave, 19th Floor
New York, NY 10018
Fax: +1 (212) 629-0035

Access more listings online at www.musicsocket.com

Email: info@mbkentertainment.com
Website: https://www.mbkentertainment.com

Represents: Artists/Bands; Film / TV Composers; Lyricists; Producers; Songwriters; Studio Musicians; Studio Vocalists

Genres: Contemporary; Gospel; Pop; R&B; Rap; Hip-Hop; Reggae; Urban

Contact: Jeff Robinson

Management company based in New York.

McDonough Management LLC
Email: frank@mcdman.com
Website: http://www.mcdman.com
Website: https://www.facebook.com/mcdmanagement

Represents: Producers; Songwriters; Sound Engineers

Genres: Rock

Contact: Frank McDonough

Management company representing record producers, engineers and mixers.

McGhee Entertainment
Fax: +1 (310) 358-9299
Email: info@mcgheela.com
Website: http://www.mcgheela.com
Website: https://www.facebook.com/McGheeEntertainment

Represents: Artists/Bands; Songwriters

Genres: Country; Metal; Rock; Singer-Songwriter; World

Contact: Don McGhee; Scott McGhee

Management company with offices in Los Angeles and Nashville.

Media Five Entertainment
PO BOX 21300
Lehigh Valley, PA 18002
Email: david.sestak@mediafiveent.com
Email: kayla.vaught@mediafiveent.com
Website: http://www.mediafiveent.com

Represents: Artists/Bands; Sound Engineers; Studio Musicians; Studio Technicians

Genres: Indie; Punk; Rock

Contact: David Sestak; Lyn Carey

Musicians/artists and technicians wanted – see website for info on submitting your details. If you are a band seeking representation visit the website and submit the appropriate form. After submitting the form online, you can post a bio, demo, CD/DVD etc. or other promotional material to the address below.

The MGMT Company
6906 Hollywood Blvd
Hollywood, CA 90028
Email: inquiries@themgmtcompany.com
Website: http://www.themgmtcompany.com

Represents: Artists/Bands

Genres: All types of music

Management company based in Hollywood, California.

Michael Anthony's Electric Events
Post Office Box 280848
Lakewood, CO 80228
Email: info2@electricevents.com
Website: http://www.electricevents.com

Represents: Artists/Bands

Genres: Country; Pop; Dance; Classic Rock

Contact: Michael A Tolerico

Music entertainment booking agency based in Lakewood, Colorado.

Michael Hausman Artist Management Inc.
17A Stuyvesant Oval
New York, NY 10009
Email: info@michaelhausman.com
Website: https://michaelhausman.com

Represents: Artists/Bands

Genres: Contemporary; Pop; Rock; Singer-Songwriter

Contact: Michael Hausman

US Managers

Management company based in New York.

Mike's Artist Management
PO Box 571567
Tarzana, CA 91357
Email: dan@mikesmanagement.com
Website: https://funzalorecords.com/mikes-artist-management/
Website: https://www.facebook.com/funzalorecords

Represents: Artists/Bands

Genres: Americana; Pop; Rock; Indie; Folk

Contact: Mike Lembo; Dan Agnew

Record label and artist management based in Tarzana, California. Send submissions via contact form on website, including links to music online.

Million Dollar Artists
12 Lake Forest Court West
St. Charles, MO 63301-4540
Fax: +1 (636) 724-1325
Email: info@americaneaglerecordings.com
Email: americaneaglerecordings@earthlink.net
Website: http://www.milliondollarartists.net
Website: https://americaneaglerecordings.com

Represents: Artists/Bands

Genres: All types of music

Contact: Dr. Charles Max E. Million

Management company based in St. Charles, Missouri. Send demos on CD only, with lyrics, bio, and photos / press coverage. Download and complete Preliminary Questionnaire from website. No submissions of MP3s or links by email – these will be ignored.

MM Music Agency
11 Island Avenue, Suite 1711
Miami, FL 33139
Fax: +1 (305) 831-4472
Email: info@mmmusicagency.com
Website: http://www.mmmusicagency.com
Website: https://www.facebook.com/mmmusicagency

Represents: Artists/Bands

Genres: Jazz; Regional; Contemporary

Contact: Maurice Montoya

Music agency based in Florida, handling jazz, Afro-Caribbean, Brazilian and contemporary music.

MOB Agency
6404 Wilshire Blvd
Los Angeles, CA 90048
Fax: +1 (323) 653-0428
Email: Mitch@mobagency.com
Email: joy@mobagency.com
Website: http://www.mobagency.com
Website: https://www.yellowpages.com/los-angeles-ca/mip/mob-agency-471004016

Represents: Artists/Bands

Genres: Alternative; Rock

Agency based in Los Angeles.

Modern Management
Email: info@modmgmt.com
Website: https://www.modmgmt.com
Website: https://www.facebook.com/modernmgmt

Represents: Artists/Bands

Genres: Country

Country management company.

Moksha Entertainment and Music Management (US)
Los Angeles
Email: MyInfoAtMoksha@gmail.com
Email: MokshaMusicManagement@gmail.com
Website: https://www.mokshaentertainment.com/

Represents: Artists/Bands

Genres: Pop; Punk Rock; Psychedelic Punk; Rock

Entertainment, Film, Music Management, Tour Services, and Recording Company, with offices in LA and London. Strives to

Access more listings online at www.musicsocket.com

Monotone, Inc.
820 Seward Street
Los Angeles, CA 90038
Email: info@monotoneinc.com
Website: https://www.monotoneinc.com

Represents: Artists/Bands

Genres: All types of music

Contact: Ian Montone

Music management company based in Los Angeles, California.

Monqui Presents
PO Box 5908
Portland, OR 97228
Email: monquipresents@gmail.com
Email: web@monqui.com
Website: https://monqui.com
Website: https://www.facebook.com/monquipresents

Represents: Artists/Bands

Genres: Alternative; Indie; Rock; Country; Pop

"Importers of fine live music", serving the Northwest since 1983. Send questions or comments by email and press kits by post.

Morris Higham Management
2001 Blair Blvd
Nashville, TN 37212
Website: https://morrishigham.com
Website: https://www.facebook.com/morrishighammanagement/

Represents: Artists/Bands

Genres: Country

Management company based in Nashville. Does not accept unsolicited material.

MSH Management
Email: mshmgmt@yahoo.com
Website: https://mshmgmt.wixsite.com/music-management

embolden and embody the human spirit through entertainment, music and film.

Represents: Artists/Bands

Genres: All types of music

Contact: Marney Hansen

Expertise and relationships in label management, artist development, retail sales, touring, digital sales and marketing, festival development, publicity, radio promotion, and more.

Murphy to Manteo (MTM) Music Management
Email: MarkZenow@MTMfirm.com
Website: http://www.mtmfirm.com

Represents: Artists/Bands; Producers; Songwriters

Genres: All types of music

Management company with its roots in Columbia, South Carolina. Contact by phone or by email.

Music + Art Management
15 W. Walnut St. Suite 202
Asheville, NC 28801
Website: https://musicandart.net
Website: https://www.facebook.com/Music-and-Art-Management-163558147005567/

Represents: Artists/Bands

Genres: Electronic; World; Experimental; Rock; Jazz

Full service management and production company specialising in the careers of performing and recording artists. Based in Asheville, North Carolina.

Music City Artists
7104 Peach Ct.
Brentwood, TN 37027
Fax: +1 (615) 266-6223
Email: cray@musiccityartists.com
Website: http://musiccityartists.com
Website: https://www.facebook.com/MusicCityArtists/

Represents: Artists/Bands

Genres: All types of music

Contact: Charles Ray, President / Agent

Full service booking agency representing nationally known artists for performing arts centers, casinos, and corporate entertainment.

Music Gallery International
Email: musicgallerymanagement@gmail.com
Website: http://musicgalleryinternational.com
Website: https://www.facebook.com/musicgalleryinternational

Represents: Artists/Bands; Studio Musicians

Genres: Alternative Hard Heavy Industrial Mainstream Power Americana Emo Garage Gothic Hardcore Metal Punk Rock

Contact: Jamie Moore

Offers management and consulting for a fixed fee (not a percentage).

Music World Entertainment
5120 Woodway Drive
Houston, Texas 77056
Website: http://musicworldent.com

Represents: Artists/Bands; Producers

Genres: Gospel; Pop; R&B; Urban

Management company based in Houston, Texas.

Myriad Artists
PO BOX 550
Carrboro, NC 27510
Email: trish@myriadartists.com
Email: booking@myriadartists.com
Website: https://www.myriadartists.com
Website: https://www.facebook.com/myriadartists/

Represents: Artists/Bands

Genres: Blues; Folk; Jazz; Americana

Contact: Trish Galfano

Management company based in Carrboro, North Carolina.

Nashville Records, LLC
Nashville, TN
Email: music@nashvillerecordsusa.com
Website: https://nashvillerecordsusa.com

Represents: Artists/Bands; Songwriters

Genres: Christian Acoustic Americana Country Pop Gospel; Americana

Contact: Lincoln Plowman

A full-service Artist Management and Record Label company. If you are serious about your career, so are we.

Females and minorities encouraged to apply.

Nettwerk Management
3900 West Alameda Ave, Suite 850
Burbank, CA 91505

NEW YORK
263 S. 4th St. P.O. Box 110649 Brooklyn, NY 11211
Fax: +1 (747) 477-1093
Website: https://nettwerk.com
Website: https://www.facebook.com/nettwerkmusicgroup

Represents: Artists/Bands; Film / TV Composers; Producers; Songwriters; Sound Engineers; Studio Technicians

Genres: Contemporary; Christian; Electronic; Folk; Indie; Latin; Pop; Punk; Rap; Rock; Hip-Hop; Dance; Singer-Songwriter; World

Media company with offices in New York, London, Vancouver, and Germany. Also label and music publishing company.

New Heights Entertainment
Email: info@newheightsent.com
Website: http://www.newheightsent.com

Represents: Artists/Bands; Producers; Songwriters

Genres: All types of music

Contact: Alan Melina

Privately held personal management and consulting firm, with its core business focusing on Music Producers, Songwriters,

Record Label Management, Music Publishing, Brand Development and Strategic Guidance for Entertainment Content and IP Creators. No unsolicited materials.

Nexus Artist Management
Email: info@nexusartists.com
Website: https://www.nexusartists.com
Website: https://www.facebook.com/Nexus.Artist.Management/

Represents: Artists/Bands; DJs

Genres: Hip-Hop; Funk; Reggae; Dubstep; Electronic; House; Techno; Progressive; Break Beat

US management company handling electronic artists.

Nice Management
Email: steve@nicemgmt.com
Website: https://nicemgmt.com
Website: https://www.facebook.com/nicemgmt/

Represents: Artists/Bands; Film / TV Composers; Producers; Songwriters

Genres: Rock

Contact: Steve Nice

Management company representing bands, composers, producers, songwriters, and mixers.

NSI Management
PO Box 959
Newburyport, MA 01950
Email: contact@newsoundmgmt.com
Website: https://www.newsoundmgmt.com
Website: http://facebook.com/danrussellmusic

Represents: Artists/Bands

Genres: Folk; Indie; Rock; Singer-Songwriter

Contact: Dan Russell

Management company based in Newburyport, Massachusetts.

Once 11 Entertainment
Email: javier@once11ent.com
Website: https://www.once11ent.com
Website: https://www.facebook.com/Once11Ent/

Represents: Artists/Bands

Genres: Latin; World

Arts and entertainment consulting and personal management firm representing all kinds of Latin and World music.

Open All Nite Entertainment
9636 McLennan Avenue
Northridge, CA 91413
Email: info@openallnite.com
Website: https://www.openallnite.com
Website: https://www.facebook.com/openallnite

Represents: Artists/Bands

Genres: All types of music

Contact: Steve Belkin

Consultant for indie/emerging artists and labels in development of all aspects of career and business.

Opus 3 Artists
470 Park Avenue South
9th Floor North
New York, NY 10016
Email: info@opus3artists.com
Website: https://www.opus3artists.com
Website: https://www.facebook.com/opus3artists

Represents: Artists/Bands

Genres: Classical; Jazz

Represents classical and jazz performing artists. Offices in New York and Berlin.

Outrider Music, LLC
Charlottesville, VA
Email: anne@outridermusic.com
Website: http://www.outridermusic.com
Website: https://www.facebook.com/Outridermusic/

US Managers

Represents: Artists/Bands; Lyricists; Songwriters

Genres: Post Rock; Progressive Rock; Post Metal; Hard Rock; Heavy Rock; Melodic Hardcore; Rock; Punk; Pop Rock; Pop Punk; Electronic Rock; Atmospheric Rock; Alternative; Alternative Rock; Acoustic Rock; Instrumental; Indie; Hardcore; Indie Rock; Ambient; Ambient Rock; Emo; Post Emo

Contact: Anne McGinnis-Townsend

I was born and raised in Charlottesville, and I became obsessed with music at an early age. I spent my early teenage years playing guitar in various pop-punk and alternative rock bands, but it soon became clear to me that I enjoyed the behind-the-scenes work just as much, if not more, than actually playing. After graduating from Charlottesville High School, I got my degree in Music Business from New York University. While at NYU, I spent two semesters interning for Warner Music Group and I had the opportunity to meet and learn from some incredible people. I realized that what I really wanted to do was to help upcoming artists navigate the early stages of their careers. Growing up in Charlottesville, I saw too many of our "hometown heroes" get signed to bad record deals and wash out, and I wanted to help prevent that. I started Outrider Music because I wanted to be an advocate for local bands, to help them navigate both the fun stuff (branding, marketing, touring, booking) and the not-so-fun stuff (contracts, PROs, insurance, taxes). I want to be a part of your team.

Pacific Talent

Email: andy@pacifictalent.com
Website: http://www.pacifictalent.com
Website: https://www.instagram.com/pacifictalentpdx/

Represents: Artists/Bands

Genres: All types of music

Contact: Andy Gilbert

Management company based in Oregon.

Paradigm Talent Agency

8942 Wilshire Boulevard
Beverly Hills, CA 90211
Fax: +1 (310) 288-2000
Website: https://www.paradigmagency.com

Represents: Artists/Bands

Genres: All types of music

Talent agency with offices in Los Angeles, New York, and London.

Paradise Artists

108 E Matilija St.
Ojai, CA 93023
Email: info@paradiseartists.com
Website: http://www.paradiseartists.com

Represents: Artists/Bands

Genres: Rock; Rock and Roll; Pop

Contact: Howie Silverman

Management company with offices in New York and California.

Pathfinder Management

30 Music Sq. W. Suite 201
Nashville, TN 37205

20 Delaware Ave. Suite 223
Delaware Water Gap, PA 18327

PO Box #100
Saylorsburg, PA 18353
Email: jim@pathfindermanagement.com
Website: https://www.pathfindermanagement.com
Website: http://thepressoffice.com

Represents: Artists/Bands

Genres: Country; Folk; Rock

Contact: Jim Della Croce

Management company based in Water Gap, Pennsylvania. Owner has represented such acts as The Beach Boys, Martina McBride, Bad Company, The Power Station/Robert Palmer and Andy Taylor of Duran, Duran, among others.

Patriot Management
Email: hello@patriotmanagement.com
Website: http://www.patriotmanagement.com
Website: https://www.instagram.com/patriotmgmt/

Represents: Artists/Bands; Producers; Songwriters

Genres: Pop; R&B; Rock

Management company representing over 45 artists, songwriters, and producers.

Persistent Management
Los Angeles, CA
Email: pm@persistentmanagement.com
Website: https://www.persistentmanagement.com
Website: https://www.facebook.com/persistentmanagement

Represents: Artists/Bands; Producers

Genres: All types of music

Management company based in Los Angeles. Submit your details through online Artist Submissions form, including links to music online. No postal submissions or phone calls.

Platinum Star Management
Beverly Hills, CA
Website: https://platinumstarmgmt.com
Website: https://www.facebook.com/platinumstarmanagement

Represents: Artists/Bands

Genres: All types of music

Been in the music and entertainment industry for over twenty years, whether it was working for Madonna's record label, Maverick Records (now part of Warner Bros Records) or slogging it out working for larger management firms, entertainment and digital marketing companies or movie studios like Sony Pictures. If you truly believe you or your band has the songs, the drive, the fans and magic to make it to the top then send a query by email.

Position Music
P.O. Box 25907
Los Angeles, CA 90025
Email: management@positionmusic.com
Email: contact@positionmusic.com
Website: https://www.positionmusic.com
Website: https://soundcloud.com/position_music

Represents: Artists/Bands; Film / TV Composers

Genres: Rap; Hip-Hop; Rock; Alternative; Dance; Electronic; Hardcore; Metal; Pop; R&B; Singer-Songwriter; Urban; World

Send web links or elecronic press kits by email. Do not chase by phone. Follow up by email only.

PRA [Patrick Rains & Associates]
Email: pra@prarecords.com
Website: https://www.prarecords.com
Website: https://twitter.com/prarecords

Represents: Artists/Bands

Genres: Jazz; Pop; Rock

Contact: Patrick Rains; Stephanie Pappas

Management company based in New York. No unsolicited material.

Pretty Lights
Email: contact@prettylightsmusic.com
Website: http://prettylightsmusic.com
Website: https://soundcloud.com/prettylights

Represents: Artists/Bands

Genres: All types of music

Submit demos using online form, available via website.

Primary Wave
NEW YORK
116 East 16th Street, 9th Floor
New York, NY 10003

LOS ANGELES
10850 Wilshire Blvd., Suite #600
Los Angeles, CA 90024

Email: info@primarywave.com
Website: https://primarywave.com
Website: https://www.facebook.com/PrimaryWave/

Represents: Artists/Bands; Producers; Songwriters

Genres: All types of music

Offers talent management, music publishing, television and film production, and brand marketing.

Prodigal Son Entertainment
Website: https://www.prodigalson-entertainment.com
Website: https://www.facebook.com/ScottWilliamsPSE
Website: https://myspace.com/prodigalsonentertainment

Represents: Artists/Bands

Genres: Alternative; Country; Christian; Instrumental; Rock; Hard Rock

Contact: Scott Williams

Artist management and career consultancy services.

Progressive Global Agency (PGA)
PO Box 50294
Nashville, TN 37205
Fax: +1 (615) 354-9101
Email: info@pgamusic.com
Website: https://pgamusic.com
Website: https://www.facebook.com/progressiveglobalagency

Represents: Artists/Bands

Genres: Pop; Rock; World

Contact: Buck Williams

Management company based in Nashville, Tennessee.

Proper Management
PO Box 68
Franklin, TN 37065
Website: http://www.propermgmt.com

Represents: Artists/Bands

Genres: Christian

Christian music management company based in Nashville, Tennessee. Not accepting submissions as at January 2021. Check website for current status.

Purple Rhino Music
Email: contact@purplerhinomusic.com
Website: http://www.purplerhinomusic.com

Represents: Artists/Bands; Lyricists; Producers; Studio Musicians

Genres: Acoustic Alternative Celtic Contemporary Commercial Electronic Experimental Extreme Funky Hard Glam Heavy Horror Industrial Mainstream Modern Melodic New Wave Power Post Progressive Soulful Thrash Tribal Twisted Underground Urban Black Metal Americana Black Origin Blue Beat Chill Classical Club Country Dance Deep Funk Emo Ethnic Fusion Funk Garage Gothic Grime Grind Guitar based Hardcore Hip-Hop Indie Instrumental Jazz Metal Melodicore Noise Core Nostalgia Pop Psychebilly Punk R&B Ragga Rap Reggae Reggaeton Rock Rock and Roll Rockabilly Roots Rhythm and Blues Singer-Songwriter Ska Soundtracks Spoken Word Swing Surf Synthpop Techno Trip Hop World

An international music management and promotions company. We currently operate in Houston, TX, London and Dublin.

We began operations in 2000 and represent a number of artists from numerous different genres.

If you are interested in our services, please feel free to visit our website or contact us directly.

Pyramid Entertainment Group
377 Rector Place, Suite 21A
New York, NY 10280
Fax: +1 (212) 242-6932
Website: https://pyramid-ent.com

Represents: Artists/Bands

Genres: Gospel; Jazz; Funk; Hip-Hop; R&B; Urban

US Managers

Contact: Sal Michaels

Management company based in New York.

Q Management
Fax: +1 (615) 599-1235
Website: https://qmanagementgroup.com

Represents: Artists/Bands

Genres: Rock

Rock manager based in Franklin, Tennessee.

Q Prime Management, Inc.
Email: newyork@qprime.com
Email: nashville@qprime.com
Website: https://qprime.com

Represents: Artists/Bands; Producers

Genres: Blues; Folk; Metal; Pop; Rock; Alternative; Singer-Songwriter

Contact: Cliff Burnstein; Peter Mensch

Management company with offices in New York, Nashville and London.

Rainmaker Artists
PO Box 342229
Austin, TX 78734
Fax: +1 (512) 843-7250
Website: https://www.rainmakerartists.com
Website: https://open.spotify.com/playlist/6bgMwK0DD5mlJStc3MaKBo

Represents: Artists/Bands

Genres: Pop; Rock

Management company based in Austin, Texas.

Red Entertainment Agency
505 8th Avenue Suite 1004
New York, NY 10018
Email: info@redentertainment.com
Email: carloskeyes@redentertainment.com
Website: http://www.redentertainment.com
Website: https://www.facebook.com/RedEntertainmentAgencyGroup

Represents: Artists/Bands

Genres: Funk; Jazz; Gospel; Latin; Hip-Hop; Pop; Rock; R&B; Urban

Contact: Carlos Keyes

Since its founding in 2002, has established itself as a leading entertainment talent agency, guiding the careers of an elite roster of musical artists. Under the leadership of agency President, has carved out a distinctive niche in the entertainment landscape and earned a reputation for putting artists' interests above all else. With a select group of professional agents working side by side, the agency credo is one of team work and availability that translates into successful relationships for all clients.

The select yet diverse client list allows it to effectively compete with other large agencies while guaranteeing personalized attention to every client. With offices in New York City, provides representation to clients across its music, motion picture, television and personal appearances worldwide.

Red Light Management (RLM)
Charlottesville; New York; Nashville; Los Angeles; Atlanta; Seattle
Website: https://www.redlightmanagement.com
Website: http://twitter.com/redlightmgmt

Represents: Artists/Bands; Film / TV Composers; Songwriters; Studio Musicians

Genres: Blues; Christian; Country; Dance; Electronic; Hardcore; Indie; Latin; Metal; Pop; Rap; Hip-Hop; Rock; Singer-Songwriter; World

Management company with offices in Charlottesville, New York, Nashville, Los Angeles, London, Bristol, Atlanta, and Seattle.

Regime Seventy-Two
Email: info@regimeinc.com
Website: https://www.regime72.com

Represents: Artists/Bands

Genres: All types of music

A company based in Art, Music, Fashion and Business.

Claim your free access to www.musicsocket.com: See p.211

Rick Alter Management (RAM)
PO Box 1864
Brentwood, TN 37024
Email: rickalter@aol.com
Website: http://www.rickalter.com

Represents: Artists/Bands

Genres: Country; Folk

Contact: Rick Alter

Country and folk manager based in Brentwood, Tennessee.

Riot Artists
Email: staff@riotartists.com
Website: https://www.riotartists.com
Website: https://www.facebook.com/RiotArtists

Represents: Artists/Bands

Genres: World; Traditional; Contemporary

Management company specialising in World music reflecting traditional culture, and incorporating contemporary sounds to varying degrees. Books artists from around the world, with an emphasis on Canada, the US, Mexico, Brazil, and Europe.

Riot Squad
Email: main@riotsquad.com
Website: http://riotsquad.com/

Represents: Artists/Bands

Genres: All types of music

An artist management company.

Ron Rainey Management Inc.
8500 Wilshire Boulevard, Suite 525
Beverly Hills, CA 90211
Fax: +1 (310) 557-8421
Website: http://www.ronrainey.com

Represents: Artists/Bands

Genres: Contemporary; Blues; Pop; Country; Rock

Management company based in Beverly Hills, California.

RPM Music Productions
420 West 14th Street, Suite 6NW
New York, NY 10014
Email: info@rpm-productions.com
Website: http://rpm-productions.com

Represents: Artists/Bands

Genres: Jazz; Pop

Contact: Danny Bennett

Management company based in New York.

Russell Carter Artist Management
Website: https://www.facebook.com/pages/Russell-Carter-Artist-Management/174050332290?pnref=about.overview
Website: https://twitter.com/RCAM_mgnt
Website: https://myspace.com/rcam

Represents: Artists/Bands

Genres: Contemporary; Alternative; Americana; Blues; Folk; Indie; Jazz; Singer-Songwriter; Pop; Rock

Management company based in Atlanta, Georgia.

Selak Entertainment, Inc.
466 Foothill Blvd. #184
La Canada, CA 91011
Fax: +1 (626)584-8122
Email: steve@selakentertainment.com
Website: https://selakentertainment.com
Website: https://www.facebook.com/selakentertainment/

Represents: Artists/Bands; Comedians; Tribute Acts

Genres: All types of music

Management company based in La Canada, California.

Semaphore Mgmt & Consulting
Website: https://www.semaphoremgmt.com
Website: https://www.instagram.com/semaphoremgmt

Represents: Artists/Bands

Genres: Alternative Atmospheric Avant-Garde Electronic Experimental Glam Industrial Heavy Hard Kraut Leftfield New Wave Non-Commercial Post Psychedelic Thrash Underground

Full scale artist management and consulting agency. We offer a la carte consulting and retainer services to bands and labels alike.

September Management (US)
New York / Los Angeles
Email: info@septembermanagement.com
Website: https://septembermanagement.com

Represents: Artists/Bands; Producers; Sound Engineers

Genres: All types of music

Represents a roster of internationally renowned recording artists, producers and mix engineers who have collectively amassed 44 Grammys, 12 Brit Awards, 2 Oscars, 2 Golden Globes and sold over 100 million albums worldwide. The company has offices in London, New York and Los Angeles.

Sherrod Artist Management
Morehead City, NC
Email: infosherrodartistmanagement@mail.com
Email: sherrodimprove79@gmail.com
Website: http://www.sherrodartistmanagement.com
Website: https://www.facebook.com/sherrodartistmanagement/

Represents: Artists/Bands

Genres: All types of music

Artist Management / Consultant / Artist Development / Music Manager / A&R. Charges $25 to submit.

Silva Artist Management (SAM)
Email: info@sammusicbiz.com
Website: http://www.sammusicbiz.com

Represents: Artists/Bands

Genres: Alternative; Indie; Metal; Pop; Punk; Rock

Management company managing major international rock/indie bands.

Singerman Entertainment
Los Angeles, CA
Email: info@SingermanEnt.com
Website: https://singermanent.com

Represents: Artists/Bands

Genres: Heavy Metal; Thrash; Rock; Hardcore; Rock and Roll

Management company with offices in Los Angeles, California, and Toronto, Ontario. No unsolicited materials.

SKH Music
540 President Street
Brooklyn, NY 11215
Email: skaras@skhmusic.com
Website: https://skhmusic.com

Represents: Artists/Bands; Lyricists; Producers

Genres: All types of music

Contact: Steve Karas

Management company formed in June 2009.

SMC Artists
Website: https://www.smcartists.com

Represents: Film / TV Composers; Songwriters

Genres: All types of music

Management company representing film and TV composers and songwriters.

Solid Music Company
Email: david@solidmusic.net
Website: http://www.solidmusic.net

Represents: Artists/Bands; DJs; Film / TV Composers; Lyricists; Producers; Songwriters; Sound Engineers; Studio Musicians; Studio Technicians

Genres: All types of music

Contact: David Surnow

A management company for artist, record producers, song writers, engineers, mixers and composers. We are located in Los Angeles and have been in business since 1990.

Sound Management, Inc.
1525 South Winchester Boulevard
San Jose, California 95128
Fax: +1 (408) 741-5824
Email: robert@soundmgt.com
Email: ron@soundmgt.com
Website: https://www.soundmgt.com/

Represents: Artists/Bands

Genres: Pop; Rock

Full-Service Artist Management Company based in San Jose, California, navigating the careers of a diverse roster including Multi-Platinum, Grammy Nominated, and Internationally Acclaimed Artists.

Soundtrack Music Associates (SMA)
1601 North Sepulveda Boulevard #579
Manhattan Beach, CA 90266
Email: info@soundtrk.com
Website: https://soundtrk.com

Represents: Film / TV Composers; Supervisors

Genres: Soundtracks

Contact: John Tempereau; Koyo Sonae; Isabel Pappani

Represents award-winning composers, music supervisors and music editors for film, television and all media.

Spectrum Talent Agency
1650 Broadway
New York, NY 10019
Email: chris@spectrumtalentagency.com
Email: jan@spectrumtalentagency.com
Website: https://www.spectrumtalentagency.com
Website: https://www.facebook.com/SpectrumTalentAgency

Represents: Artists/Bands

Genres: Dance; Hip-Hop; Pop; R&B; House

Full service global booking agency.

Spot Light Entertainment, Inc.
PO Box 1949
Lawrenceville, GA 30046
Email: info@spotlightentertainment.com
Website: http://www.spotlightentertainment.com

Represents: Artists/Bands; Comedians; Producers; Songwriters

Genres: Contemporary; Gospel; Hip-Hop; Pop; R&B; Rap

Management company based in Lawrenceville, Georgia.

Starkravin' Management
McLane & Wong
11135 Weddington Street, Suite #424
North Hollywood, CA 91601
Fax: +1 (818) 587-6802
Email: bcmclane@aol.com
Website: http://www.benmclane.com

Represents: Artists/Bands; Producers; Songwriters

Genres: Pop; R&B; Rock

Contact: Ben McLane

Management and entertainment law company based in North Hollywood. Provides personal management and legal services.

Sterling Artist Management
Email: mark@sterlingartist.com
Website: http://www.sterlingartist.com

Represents: Artists/Bands; Producers; Songwriters; Studio Musicians

Genres: Blues; Jazz; Singer-Songwriter

Contact: Mark Sterling

Devoted to managing artists whose talent, dedication and drive position them for success in today's music industry.

US Managers

Steven Scharf Entertainment (SSE)
Website: http://www.stevenscharf.com

Represents: Artists/Bands; Film / TV Composers; Producers; Songwriters; Supervisors

Genres: Alternative; Americana; Blues; Folk; Indie; Jazz; Metal; Pop; Rap; Hip-Hop; Rock; Roots; Singer-Songwriter; World; Soundtracks

Contact: Steven Scharf

Management company handling artists, composers, and producers.

Stiefel Entertainment
21650 Oxnard St # 1925
Woodland Hills, CA 91364
Email: contact@StiefelEnt.com
Website: http://www.stiefelent.com
Website: https://www.linkedin.com/company/stiefel-entertainment

Represents: Artists/Bands

Genres: Contemporary; Dance; Indie; Pop; Rock; Singer-Songwriter

Contact: Arnold Stiefel

Management company based in Woodland Hills, California.

Stiletto Entertainment
Website: https://www.stilettoentertainment.com
Website: https://www.facebook.com/stilettoentertainment

Represents: Artists/Bands; Producers; Songwriters

Genres: All types of music

Broadcasting and media production company.

Street Smart Management
Los Angeles, CA
Website: https://www.facebook.com/streetsmartmanagement
Website: https://twitter.com/streetsmartmgmt

Represents: Artists/Bands

Genres: Indie; Rock; Metal; Pop

Management company based in Los Angeles, California.

Strike up the Brand
Email: bradgelfond@strike-up-the-brand.com
Website: https://www.strike-up-the-brand.com
Website: https://www.linkedin.com/in/bradgelfond

Represents: Artists/Bands

Genres: Alternative

Contact: Brad Gelfond

Management company based in Los Angeles, California.

Suncoast Music Management
Email: suncoastbooking@aol.com
Email: suncoastoh@hotmail.com
Website: http://www.suncoastentertainment.biz

Represents: Artists/Bands; Tribute Acts

Genres: Disco; Classic Rock; Rock

Contact: Al Spohn; Quinton Coontz; Andy Bowman; Daniel Nathan

Management company specialising in tribute acts.

TAC Music Management
Website: https://tacmusicmanagement.com

Represents: Artists/Bands; Songwriters; Studio Musicians; Tribute Acts

Genres: Acoustic; Classic; Hard; Traditional; Regional; Soulful; Heavy; Funky; Commercial; Alternative; Americana; Blues; Country; Folk; Fusion; Funk; Guitar based; Indie; Jazz; Metal; R&B; Rock; Rock and Roll; Roots; Rhythm and Blues; Singer-Songwriter; Rockabilly

Contact: Tracey Chirhart

US Managers

Services include artist management, booking, promotion and marketing to both local and national artists. Genres include blues, rock, Americana, bluegrass, folk, country, and tributes.

Take Out Management
Email: AlexTakeOutManagement@gmail.com
Website: https://howiewood.com/take-out-management/
Website: https://www.facebook.com/HowardRosenPromotion/

Represents: Artists/Bands; Producers

Genres: All types of music

Contact: Howard Rosen

Has managed independent acts as well as acts signed to Columbia, Curb, Atlantic, etc. Currently focused on working with producers for upcoming major and independent releases. Contact by phone or by email.

Talent Source
The Mill at Nyack
15 North Mill Street
Nyack, NY 10960
Fax: +1 (845) 359-4609
Email: info@talentsourcemanagement.com
Website: http://www.talentsourcemanagement.com

Represents: Artists/Bands; Variety Artists

Genres: All types of music

Contact: Margo Lewis; Faith Fusillo

Management company based in Nyack, New York.

Tenth Street Entertainment
113 North San Vicente Blvd, 2nd Floor, Suite 241
Beverly Hills, CA 90211

1115 Broadway, 12th Floor
New York, NY 10010
Email: info@10thst.com
Website: http://www.10thst.com

Represents: Artists/Bands; Producers

Genres: All types of music

International company with offices in LA, London, and New York.

That's Entertainment International Inc. (TEI Entertainment)
3820 E. La Palma Ave
Anaheim, CA 92807
Email: thomas@teientertainment.com
Email: jmcentee@teientertainment.com
Website: http://www.teientertainment.com

Represents: Artists/Bands

Genres: All types of music

Contact: John D. McEntee, President

Celebrity Entertainment Resource Company based in Anaheim, California.

Third Coast Talent
PO Box 170
Chapmansboro, TN 37035
Fax: +1 (615) 685-3332
Email: carrie@thirdcoasttalent.com
Website: https://www.thirdcoasttalent.com

Represents: Artists/Bands

Genres: Country

Contact: Carrie Moore-Reed

Management company based in Kingston Springs, Tennessee.

Thirty Tigers
611 Merritt Avenue
Nashville, TN 37203
Website: https://www.thirtytigers.com/
Website: https://www.facebook.com/thirtytigers/

Represents: Artists/Bands

Genres: Indie; Rock; Urban

Contact: David Macias

Management company based in Nashville, Tennessee, with offices in Los Angeles, New York, North Carolina and London.

This Day And Age Management
301 South Perimeter Drive
Nashville, TN 37211
Website: https://www.thisdayandagemanagement.com
Website: https://www.instagram.com/thisdayandagemanagement/

Represents: Artists/Bands

Genres: Pop R&B Rap

Contact: David Patrick Small

We are a management and artist development company located in Nashville, TN. We focus on label pitches, booking and sync licensing pitches.

Threee
Website: https://www.threee.com
Website: https://twitter.com/threee_ent

Represents: Film / TV Composers; Producers; Songwriters

Genres: All types of music

Management company based in Los Angeles, California, representing producers, mixers, songwriters, and composers.

TKO Artist Management
Website: http://www.tkoartistmanagement.com
Website: https://www.facebook.com/TKOArtistMgmt/

Represents: Artists/Bands

Genres: Country

Management company based in Nashville Tennessee.

Tom Callahan & Associates (TCA)
Email: tc@tomcallahan.com
Website: https://www.tomcallahan.com
Website: https://www.linkedin.com/in/tom-callahan-771294/

Represents: Artists/Bands

Genres: All types of music

Full service music consulting company based in Boulder, Colorado, offering record promotion, publicity, internet marketing, production, and more.

Tractor Beam Managing & Consulting
Website: http://www.tractor-beam.com

Represents: Artists/Bands

Genres: Folk; Indie; Jazz; Pop; Punk; Rock; Roots

Contact: Dan Efram

Long term client roster is full, so only currently offering career coaching and advice services.

A Train Entertainment
PO Box 29242
Oakland, CA 94604
Email: postmaster@a-train.com
Website: http://a-train.com
Website: https://soundcloud.com/a-train-entertainment

Represents: Artists/Bands

Genres: All types of music

Entertainment services, including publishing administration, artist management, physical and digital distribution, international sales and more.

True Talent Entertainment
Email: TRUETALENTENTER@GMAIL.com
Website: http://www.truetalenter.com
Website: https://www.youtube.com/channel/UCXh-_1hDdqY1y92TorFfu7A

Represents: Artists/Bands; Film / TV Composers; Lyricists; Producers

Genres: R&B

Management, promotion, and production company. No unsolicited submissions.

Trunk Bass Entertainment
Email: info@trunkbassent.com
Website: https://www.trunkbassent.com

US Managers

Website: https://www.facebook.com/TrunkBASSent/

Represents: Artists/Bands

Genres: Alternative; Hip-Hop; Pop; R&B

Offers a range of services, including Podcast Editing, Artist Booking, Music Consultancy, Artist Development, Music Supervision, EPK Building, Campaign Management, Video Production, Tour Management, and Content Creation.

Tsunami Entertainment
Los Angeles / Las Vegas
Email: Info@tsunamient.com
Website: http://www.tsunamient.com

Represents: Artists/Bands; Producers

Genres: All types of music

Contact: Bruce Kirkland; Toni Young; Pip Moore

A creative and business solutions Company operating in the music, entertainment and media space, providing brand strategy, business development, marketing services, operational support systems and financial management.

Tuscan Sun Music
Nashville, TN
Email: mgmt@angelica.org
Website: http://www.tuscansunmusic.com
Website: http://www.angelica.org

Represents: Artists/Bands

Genres: Ambient; New Age; Pop

Management company based in Nashville, Tennessee.

Uncle Booking
5438 Winding Way Drive
Houston, TX 77091
Email: erik@unclebooking.com
Website: http://www.unclebooking.com

Represents: Artists/Bands

Genres: All types of music

Booking agency based in Texas.

Union Entertainment Group
Email: info@ueginc.com
Website: http://www.ueginc.com

Represents: Artists/Bands

Genres: Rock; Alternative; Blues; Country; Pop; Rap; Hip-Hop

Music management company.

United Talent Agency
9336 Civic Center Drive
Beverly Hills, CA 90210
Website: https://www.unitedtalent.com
Website: https://www.facebook.com/UnitedTalent/

Represents: Artists/Bands

Genres: All types of music

International talent agency with offices in London, Los Angeles, New York, and Nashville.

Universal Attractions Agency
NEW YORK
15 West 36th Street, 8th Floor
New York, NY 10018

LOS ANGELES
22025 Ventura Boulevard, #305
Los Angeles, CA 91364

Fax: +1 (212) 333-4508 / +1 (646) 304-5178
Email: info@universalattractions.com
Website: http://universalattractions.com
Website: https://www.facebook.com/UAAtalent/

Represents: Artists/Bands

Genres: All types of music

Talent agency with offices in New York and Los Angeles.

Universal Tone Management
PO Box 10348
San Rafael, CA 94912
Email: fanclub@santana.com
Email: merch@santana.com
Website: http://www.santana.com

Access more listings online at www.musicsocket.com

Represents: Artists/Bands; Songwriters

Genres: Blues; Latin; Pop; Rock

Management company based in San Rafael, California.

Val's Artist Management (VAM)
Email: info@vamnation.com
Website: http://www.vamnation.com
Website: https://www.facebook.com/VAMNation-Entertainment-108496975907793/

Represents: Artists/Bands

Genres: Contemporary; Blues; Classical; Country; Dance; Folk; Indie; Jazz; Latin; Pop; Punk; R&B; Rap; Hip-Hop; Rock; Roots; Urban; World

Contact: Valerie Wilson Morris

Aims to identify and cultivate the most elite talent in the entertainment industry. Describes itself as having "a keen understanding of the many facets of the industry gleaned through personal experience and proven professional success".

Variety Artists International
Email: John@varietyart.com
Email: Lloyd@varietyart.com
Website: https://varietyart.com

Represents: Artists/Bands

Genres: Folk; Jazz; Pop; Rap; Rock

Management company providing tour booking services.

Vector Management
PO Box 120479
Nashville, TN 37212

430 W. 15th Street
New York, NY 10011

LOS ANGELES
9350 Civic Center Drive
Beverly Hills, CA 90210
Website: http://www.vectormgmt.com

Represents: Artists/Bands; Songwriters

Genres: Contemporary; Alternative; Americana; Country; Folk; Gospel; Metal; Pop; Rock; Singer-Songwriter

Management company with offices in Nashville, New York, and Los Angeles.

Velvet Hammer Music & Management Group
Website: https://velvethammer.net
Website: https://www.facebook.com/velvethammermusicandmanagementgroup

Represents: Artists/Bands

Genres: All types of music

Contact: David Benveniste (Beno); Mark Wakefield; Samantha Waterman; Taryn Mazza; Kristin Van Trieste; Sara Pacheco; Samantha Surtida; Lauren Horne; Max Kane

Prides itself on identifying quality talent. Submit demos through online submission system.

Walker Entertainment Group
PO Box 7926
Houston, TX 77270
Website: http://www.walkerentertainmentgroup.com
Website: https://facebook.com/walkerentertainmentgrouptx

Represents: Artists/Bands

Genres: All types of music

Global provider of event management, production, and entertainment services.

Waxploitation
Email: artists@waxploitation.com
Website: http://www.waxploitation.com
Website: https://www.facebook.com/WaxploitationRecords/

Represents: Artists/Bands

Genres: Electronic; Indie; Hip-Hop; Rap; Reggae; Rock

Management company based in Los Angeles, California.

US Managers

Westwood Music Group
2740 Kalsted Street, Suite 200
North Port, FL 34288
Email: vkaply@westwoodmusicgroup.com
Website: https://www.westwoodmusicgroup.com

Represents: Artists/Bands; Film / TV Composers; Songwriters

Genres: Pop; Rock; Country; Blues; Jazz; R&B; Latin; Gospel; Instrumental

Contact: Victor Kaply; Steve Willoughby; George San Roman

Established in 1985, and currently based in North Port, Florida.

Whiplash PR and Management
398 Columbus Ave,
PMB #183,
Boston, MA 02116
Email: Rockergirl363@aol.com
Website: https://www.whiplashprandmanagement.com

Represents: Artists/Bands

Genres: All types of music

An independent PR, brand and marketing agency that services bands, musicians, indie labels and music service companies internationally. Send music by email.

Wolfson Entertainment, Inc.
2659 Townsgate Road, Suite 119
Westlake Village, CA 91361
Website: https://www.wolfsonent.com/
Website: https://www.facebook.com/wolfsonentinc

Represents: Artists/Bands

Genres: All types of music

Contact: Jonathan Wolfson

Management company based in Westlake Village, California.

Worlds End Management
Fax: +1 (323) 965-1547
Email: info@worldsend.com
Website: https://worldsend.com
Website: https://www.facebook.com/WorldsEndMgmt/

Represents: Artists/Bands; Film / TV Composers; Producers; Songwriters; Sound Engineers; Studio Technicians; Supervisors

Genres: All types of music

Contact: Sandy Roberton

Management company founded in London in 1980, before moving to the US in 1985.

Worldsound, LLC
Seattle, WA 98148
Website: https://www.worldsound.com
Website: https://www.facebook.com/worldsoundllc

Represents: Artists/Bands

Genres: Celtic; Folk; Pop; Rock; World; Rock and Roll

Management company founded in Southern California in 1992, now based in Seattle, Washington.

Wright Entertainment Group (WEG)
Website: http://www.wegmusic.com
Website: https://www.facebook.com/wegmusic

Represents: Artists/Bands

Genres: Hip-Hop; Pop; R&B; Rap; Rock; Singer-Songwriter

Contact: Johnny Wright

Artist management company. Develops and assembles aspiring musical talent and also represents a roster of veteran entertainers.

Access more listings online at www.musicsocket.com

UK Managers

For the most up-to-date listings of these and hundreds of other managers, visit https://www.musicsocket.com/managers

To claim your free access to the site, please see the back of this book.

!K7
217 Chester House
Kennington Park
1-3 Brixton Road
London
SW9 6DE
Email: artist-mgmt@k7.com
Website: http://k7.com
Website: https://twitter.com/K7MusicHQ

Represents: Artists/Bands

Genres: All types of music

Represents a varied roster of artists from a wide range of genres.

2-Tone Entertainment (2TE)
91 Peterborough Road
London
SW6 3BU
Email: info@2tone-entertainment.com
Website: https://www.instagram.com/2tone_ent/
Website: https://www.facebook.com/2tone.entertainment

Represents: Artists/Bands

Genres: Dance; Urban; Pop

Record label and talent management based in London.

360 Artist Development
42 Western Avenue
Birstall
WF17 0PF
Email: info@360artistdevelopment.com
Website: https://www.360artistdevelopment.com
Website: https://www.facebook.com/360artistdevelopment

Represents: Artists/Bands

Genres: All types of music

Management / consultancy company based in Wakefield. Submit demos via contact form on website.

4 Tunes Ltd
8 Whitehall Park Road
London
W4 3NE
Fax: +44 (0) 20 8442 7561
Email: andy@4-tunes.com
Website: http://4-tunes.com

Represents: Artists/Bands

Genres: All types of music

Contact: Andy Murray

Management company based in London.

Claim your free access to www.musicsocket.com: See p.211

UK Managers

7pm Management
Email: seven@7pmmanagement.com
Email: wolfie@7pmmanagement.com
Website: https://7pmmanagement.com/
Website: https://twitter.com/
7pmmanagement

Represents: Artists/Bands; DJs; Producers

Genres: All types of music

Works with music but is not genre specific. In simplest terms if we love it and if we can help make it as a business make money then we work with it.

Also acts as a consultant to top companies within the global industry.

A&R Factory
Email: info@anrfactory.com
Website: https://www.anrfactory.com/
Website: https://www.facebook.com/anrfactory

Represents: Artists/Bands

Genres: All types of music

Independent music blog that also offers an artist development program. Send demos through online submission form on website.

A2E – Artists 2 Events
PO Box 64
Ammanford
Carmarthenshire
SA18 9AB
Email: mike@artists2events.co.uk
Email: rob@artists2events.co.uk
Website: http://www.artists2events.co.uk

Represents: Artists/Bands

Genres: Acoustic; Blues; Celtic

Contact: Mike / Rob

Management company based in Ammanford, Carmarthenshire.

ADSRecords
2 Trinity Court
Newsom Place
Manor Road
St Albans
Hertfordshire
AL1 3FT
Email: music@adsrecords.co.uk
Email: podcast@adsrecords.co.uk
Website: https://www.adsrecords.co.uk
Website: https://soundcloud.com/adsrecordsuk

Represents: Artists/Bands

Genres: Acoustic; Alternative; Indie; Pop; Singer-Songwriter

Contact: Alex Dale-Staples

Artist management and composition services. To be considered for Artist Management send query by email, with "Artist Management" in the subject line, links to your music, and a 50-word description.

Aguia Music
Email: luana@aguiamusic.com
Website: https://www.facebook.com/AguiaMusic
Website: https://linktr.ee/aguiamusic

Represents: Artists/Bands

Genres: Americana; Country; Folk; Hip-Hop; R&B; Rap

All about the Vision – we understand the importance of having a coherent plan and supporting our artists in their professional and personal lives, always with the creative vision and approach making sure that every step counts to our future.

AirMTM
Shepherds Building West
Rockley Road
Shepherds Bush
London
W14 0DA
Email: info@airmtm.com
Website: http://www.airmtm.com

Represents: Artists/Bands

Genres: All types of music

Management company based in Shepherd's Bush, London.

Access more listings online at www.musicsocket.com

AJM
Email: juste@ajmofficial.co.uk
Website: https://www.ajmofficial.co.uk
Website: https://www.facebook.com/ajm.mgmt

Represents: Artists/Bands

Genres: Electronic; Pop

Send query by email with links to music online, bio, links to press shots (Dropbox or similar), your biggest achievements so far, and your goals and ambitions for the next 12 months.

Amber Artists
Email: management@amberartists.com
Email: info@amberartists.com
Website: http://www.amberartists.com

Represents: Artists/Bands

Genres: All types of music

Provides PR and management.

American Artiste (UK)
Cambridge
Email: information@americanartiste.com
Website: https://www.americanartiste.com
Website: https://www.facebook.com/americanartisteltd

Represents: Artists/Bands

Genres: All types of music

Management company with offices in Cambridge, UK, and Hollywood, USA. Send links to music online through online contact form.

Amour:Music
London
Email: info@amourmusic.co.uk
Website: https://amourmusic.co.uk
Website: https://www.facebook.com/AmourMusicUK/

Represents: Artists/Bands

Genres: All types of music

Artist Management and Career Guidance company based in London. Send query by email with links to music online. No downloads.

Amour:Music
Email: info@amourmusic.co.uk
Website: https://amourmusic.co.uk
Website: https://soundclock.com/amourmusicuk

Represents: Artists/Bands

Genres: Contemporary; Singer-Songwriter

Send query by email with links to streaming music online. No attachments or download links.

Anger Management
Email: info@anger-management.co
Website: https://www.anger-management.co
Website: https://www.facebook.com/AngerManagement100

Represents: Artists/Bands

Genres: All types of music

Provides artist and tour management services.

The Animal Farm
4th Floor, Block A
The Biscuit Factory
100 Clements Road
London
SE16 4DG
Email: info@theanimalfarm.co.uk
Website: http://www.theanimalfarm.co.uk
Website: https://www.facebook.com/theanimalfarmmusic

Represents: Artists/Bands

Genres: All types of music

Send query by email or through online form giving link to website where you can be seen and your music heard. Include reason for approach. No MP3 attachments by email. Do not expect feedback.

AprilSeven Music
London
Email: mike@aprilsevenmusic.com

Email: mail@aprilsevenmusic.com
Website: https://www.aprilsevenmusic.com

Represents: Artists/Bands; Producers

Genres: Jazz; Electronic; Soul

Music consultancy based in London, with expertise in marketing, PR, international and local distribution, and management.

Arlon Music
Email: info@arlonmusic.com
Website: http://www.arlonmusic.com

Represents: Artists/Bands

Genres: Alternative; Pop; Singer-Songwriter

Contact: Jamie Arlon

Management company based in London, including publishing company and independent record label. Send query by email with links to music online. No MP3s.

Artistes International Representation (AIR) Ltd
AIR House
Spennymoor
County Durham
DL16 7SE
Fax: +44 (0) 1388 812445
Email: info@airagency.com
Website: http://www.airagency.com

Represents: Artists/Bands; Comedians; Tribute Acts

Genres: All types of music

Management company based in County Durham.

Askonas Holt Ltd
15 Fetter Lane
London
EC4A 1BW
Fax: +44 (0) 20 7400 1799
Email: info@askonasholt.co.uk
Website: https://www.askonasholt.com
Website: https://www.facebook.com/askonasholt/

Represents: Artists/Bands

Genres: Classical

Formed in 1998 through an amalgamation of two long-established artist management companies, both based in London but with international connections.

ASM Talent
Email: albert@asmtalent.co.uk
Email: assistant@asmtalent.co.uk
Website: https://www.asmtalent.com

Represents: Artists/Bands

Genres: All types of music

Contact: Albert Samuel

A well-established London-based talent agency with a combination of over 50 years of talent management experience.

Aspire Music Management
Email: mel@aspiremusicmanagement.co.uk
Website: https://www.aspiremusicmanagement.co.uk
Website: https://www.facebook.com/AspireMusicManagement.co.uk/

Represents: Artists/Bands; Songwriters

Genres: Melodic Rock; Pop Rock; Acoustic

Contact: Melanie Perrett

Management company based in northern England, representing unsigned and indie artists and songwriters. Handles a wide range of genres, but particularly interested in Melodic Rock, Pop Rock, and Acoustic. Will consider other genres, however.

Associated London Management
London
Email: martin@associatedlondonmanagement.com
Email: jason@associatedlondonmanagement.com
Website: http://www.associatedlondonmanagement.com
Website: https://facebook.com/ALMgmt

Represents: Artists/Bands

Genres: Alternative

Management company based in London.

ATC Management
The Hat Factory
166-168 Camden Street
London
NW1 9PT, UK
Email: info@atcmanagement.com
Website: http://www.atcmanagement.com
Website: https://www.facebook.com/atcmanagement/

Represents: Artists/Bands

Genres: All types of music

London based management company willing to consider artists in all genres. Send demo via website.

AuthorityMGMT
Second Floor
Unit 14 Tileyard Studios
Tileyard Road
London
N7 9AH
Website: https://www.authoritymgmt.com
Website: http://soundcloud.com/authoritymgmt

Represents: Artists/Bands; Songwriters

Genres: Dance; Pop; Singer-Songwriter

Music management company based in London, with a global outlook. Represents artists and songwriters at all levels. Extensive experience in management, A&R, records, publishing and brands deals.

Autonomy Music Group
6a Tileyard Studios
London
N7 9AH
Email: hi@autonomymusicgroup.com
Website: https://autonomymusicgroup.com

Represents: Artists/Bands; DJs; Producers

Genres: All types of music

Provides bespoke artist and campaign services to artists, bands, producers, record labels and DJs. Send query via email.

Avenoir Records
Email: martin@avenoir.org
Website: https://avenoir.org
Website: https://www.facebook.com/avenoirrecords

Represents: Artists/Bands

Genres: All types of music

Offers various music and entertainment industry consultancy packages that range from advice, simple online marketing and branding through to full musical production, development and managerial services at a cost to suit any budget.

AWA Entertainments
4a Queens Road
Sheffield
S2 4DG
Email: awagency@aol.com
Website: http://www.awaentertainments.co.uk
Website: https://www.facebook.com/AWAentertainments/

Represents: Artists/Bands; Comedians; Tribute Acts

Genres: All types of music

Management company based in Sheffield. Describes itself as one of the UK's leading entertainment agencies, providing top bands, duos, solos, tributes, comedians and more to the entertainment world, including Social Clubs, Corporate Functions, Weddings, Parties, Military Functions, Theatres etc.

B.H. Hopper Management Ltd.
Shepherds Building – Unit G7
Rockley Road
London
W14 0DA
Email: hopper@hopper-management.com
Website: http://www.hoppermanagement.com

Represents: Artists/Bands

Genres: Jazz

Management company based in London handling Jazz artists only.

Bad Apple Music Group
Email: hello@badapplemusic.group
Website: https://www.badapplemusic.group
Website: https://www.facebook.com/badapplemusicgroup

Represents: Artists/Bands

Genres: Alternative; Indie; Rock

With strong experience in the ever-changing industry, we are proud to offer artist management and development, release plan assistance, and more to help you to take the right next steps in your music career.

Bandzmedia
Email: info@bandzmedia.com
Website: http://www.bandzmedia.com
Website: https://www.facebook.com/Bandzmedia

Represents: Artists/Bands

Genres: Acoustic; Pop; Rock; Soul; R&B

Contact: Jude Bumby

Management company based in York. Not accepting demo submissions as at June 2021. Check website for current status.

Bear Music Management
Hampshire
Email: info@bearmusicmanagement.co.uk
Website: https://www.bearmusicmanagement.co.uk
Website: https://www.facebook.com/bearmusicmanagementuk/

Represents: Artists/Bands

Genres: Indie; Pop; Rock

An artist management company based in Hampshire, UK. Specialises in the indie, rock, americana and pop genres with acts from the UK, pushing their music internationally. Pride themselves on being an artist friendly company whose main focus is on providing our artists with a platform to develop their careers and assist them in reaching their goals.

Big Bear Music
PO BOX 944
EDGBASTON
BIRMINGHAM
B16 8UT
Email: admin@bigbearmusic.com
Website: http://www.bigbearmusic.com
Website: https://www.facebook.com/Bigbearmusic/

Represents: Artists/Bands

Genres: Blues; Jazz; Swing

Contact: Jim Simpson

Represents and tours jazz, blue and swing attractions of the highest quality, mostly those signed to the Record label. We also oranise events and jazz festivals, including a midlands jazz festival established in 1985.

Big Dipper Productions Ltd
Email: contact@wearebigdipper.com
Email: adrian@insideslashout.com
Website: https://wearebigdipper.com/
Website: https://www.instagram.com/bigdipperproductions/

Represents: Artists/Bands

Genres: Indie; Pop; Rock

Established in 2000 to manage an experimental band discovered in Iceland. Have since broadened their horizons, frequently discovering and supporting unsigned talent and guiding them towards the right partners in an ever-changing industry. The modern music business offers artists both unparalleled opportunities and previously unseen challenges. Prides itself in being able to navigate through the new landscape, via a professional lifetime of shared experience and contacts.

Big Hug Management
Email: jeff@bighugmanagement.com
Website: http://www.bighugmanagement.com
Website: https://www.facebook.com/bighugmanagement

Represents: Artists/Bands

Genres: All types of music

Contact: Jeff Powell

One-man music management company. Home to Artists, Songwriters and Creatives. It's about raw talent and the long haul. No quick fixes. Artist Integrity is at the forefront.

Big Life Management
67-69 Chalton Street
London
NW1 1HY
Email: reception@biglifemanagement.com
Website: https://www.biglifemanagement.com

Represents: Artists/Bands; Producers

Genres: All types of music

Management company based in London, representing bands, solo artists, and producers. Send query by email with links to music online.

BiGiAM Promotions & Management
Email: info@bigiam.co.uk
Website: https://bigiam.co.uk
Website: https://www.facebook.com/BiGiAMPR/

Represents: Artists/Bands

Genres: All types of music

We promote, advise and manage businesses, events and personal creativity linked to music and the arts. Our portfolio is relatively wide and relatively varied; we play a significant role in the development, project management, marketing/promotions and sponsorship of a number of Brighton area based events.

If you think we can help your company/band/event etc, please approach us for a no obligation chat; we may well be less expensive than you think. Our aim is to provide unrivalled value and excellence in everything we do.

Black Fox Management
Email: generalenquiries@blackfoxmanagement.com
Website: http://blackfoxmanagement.com
Website: https://twitter.com/pollyrocker5

Represents: Artists/Bands

Genres: All types of music

Management company based in London.

BLOCS
Email: info@blocshq.com
Website: https://blocshq.com
Website: https://www.facebook.com/BLOCSHQ/

Represents: Artists/Bands

Genres: All types of music

A new model new music company with bases in Cardiff, Carmarthen, Swansea and Wrexham, and working with artists across the areas of management, live, and releases, with each working relationship tailored to meet the particular needs of each artist project.

Blue Raincoat Music
Unit G2
1 Leonard Circus
64 Paul Street
EC2A 4DQ
Email: info@blueraincoatmusic.com
Email: artists@blueraincoatmusic.com
Website: https://www.blueraincoatmusic.com
Website: https://soundcloud.com/WeAreBRM

Represents: Artists/Bands

Genres: All types of music

Management company based in London. Send demos by email.

Bold Management
85 Bold Street
Liverpool
L1 4HF
Fax: +44 (0) 1517 091895
Email: martin@bold-management.com
Website: http://www.bold-management.com
Website: https://www.facebook.com/boldmanagement

UK Managers

Represents: Artists/Bands; Producers; Songwriters

Genres: Pop; Rock; Indie

Contact: Martin O'Shea

Management company based in Liverpool. Send demo with bio and photos by email only.

Brian Yeates Associates Ltd
Website: http://www.brianyeates.co.uk
Website: https://www.facebook.com/yeatesentertainment

Represents: Artists/Bands; Comedians; DJs; Tribute Acts

Genres: All types of music

Contact: Ashley Yeates

Management company based in Sutton Coldfield in the West Midlands, with 30 years experience representing a variety of acts.

Brighthelmstone Promotions
Email: brighthelmstonepromotions@gmail.com
Email: james@brighthelmstonepromotions.co.uk
Website: http://www.brighthelmstonepromotions.co.uk
Website: https://www.facebook.com/brighthelmstonepromotions/

Represents: Artists/Bands

Genres: Americana; Folk; Indie

Management company based in Brighton, specialising in Americana and Roots.

Bulldozer Media Ltd
Email: info@bulldozermedia.com
Website: https://www.bulldozermedia.com
Website: https://soundcloud.com/bulldozermedia

Represents: Artists/Bands; DJs

Genres: All types of music

Artist management agency and music publisher.

BUT! Management
Email: jamesie@butgroup.com
Email: Nick.lyp@gmail.com
Website: http://www.butgroup.com
Website: https://www.facebook.com/butmusic/

Represents: Artists/Bands; Producers; Songwriters

Genres: Alternative; Pop; Rock; Singer-Songwriter

Contact: Allan James; Nick Robinson

Management, label, and publishing company based in Brighton. Founded to promote and develop new UK talent both domestically and internationally. Has a policy of listening to and providing feedback on anything received.

Catalyst Management
Website: https://www.facebook.com/officalcatalystmanagment/
Website: https://instagram.com/catalyst.management

Represents: Artists/Bands; Producers

Genres: All types of music

Management and marketing for UK artists aiming for mainstream success.

Chaos & Bedlam Management
Email: liza@chaosandbedlam.com
Website: https://www.musicglue.com/chaos-and-bedlam-consultancy/
Website: https://www.facebook.com/chaosandbedlam/

Represents: Artists/Bands

Genres: Rock

Contact: Liza Buddy

Rock management and consultancy company.

Closer Artists Management & Publishing
Matrix Studios
91 Peterborough Road
London

SW6 3BU
Email: info@closerartists.com
Website: https://www.closerartists.co.uk
Website: https://soundcloud.com/closer-artists

Represents: Artists/Bands

Genres: All types of music

Contact: Paul McDonald; Ryan Lofthouse

Management, record label and publishing company based in London.

CMP Entertainment
Email: info@cmpentertainment.com
Website: http://www.cmpentertainment.com
Website: https://www.facebook.com/CMPEntertainment

Represents: Artists/Bands; Tribute Acts

Genres: All types of music

Contact: Chas Cole; Rob Stringer

Management company based in Liverpool. Will consider all types of music, but works mainly with pop acts.

Conchord
London
Email: cathy@conchordmanagement.com
Website: http://conchordmanagement.com
Website: https://twitter.com/conchordmgmt

Represents: Artists/Bands

Genres: All types of music

Management company based in London.

Consolidated Artists
PO Box 87
Tarporley
CW6 9FN
Fax: +44 (0) 1829 730499
Email: alecconsol@aol.com
Email: ross@consolidatedartists.co.uk
Website: http://www.consolidatedartists.co.uk

Represents: Artists/Bands

Genres: Pop; Rock

Contact: Alec Leslie

Management company based in Tarporley.

Covert Talent Management
Email: covertdemos@gmail.com
Email: simon@coverttalent.com
Website: http://www.coverttalent.com
Website: https://www.instagram.com/coverttalent

Represents: Artists/Bands; Producers; Songwriters

Genres: All types of music

Contact: Simon King

A music management and publishing company that focuses on the creative, strategic and brand development of its hand-picked roster of clients.

Craft Management
Email: enquiries@craftmgmt.com
Website: https://craftmgmt.com

Represents: Artists/Bands; Producers

Genres: Alternative

Represents alternative artists and producers.

Create Management
Email: info@createmanagement.com
Website: http://www.createmanagement.com
Website: http://www.thecreategroup.co.uk

Represents: Artists/Bands; Producers

Genres: Commercial; Pop; Singer-Songwriter

Management company representing primarily singer-songwriters.

Creative International Artist Management
Email: info@cruisin.co.uk
Website: http://www.cruisin.co.uk

Represents: Artists/Bands

Genres: Metal; Pop; Rock

152 UK Managers

Management company set in 250 acres of countryside on the Wiltshire/Somerset border.

Creative Sounds UK
Email: ariches2@hotmail.co.uk
Website: https://www.creativesoundsuk.com
Website: https://www.facebook.com/CSUK1/

Represents: Artists/Bands

Genres: All types of music

Send query by email with links to your music online, a bio / onesheet / press kit, and your full contact information.

Creeme Entertainments
First Floor
293 Darwen Road
Bromley Cross
Bolton
BL7 9BT
Email: anthony@creeme.co.uk
Website: https://creeme.co.uk
Website: https://www.facebook.com/creemeentertainmentsltd

Represents: Artists/Bands; Comedians; Other Entertainers; Tribute Acts

Genres: All types of music

Contact: Anthony Ivers

Manages acts including music, tribute acts, lookalikes, comedians, after-dinner speakers, etc. for corporate events, and the pub and club circuits.

Crockford Management
Email: info@crockfordmanagement.com
Website: http://www.crockfordmanagement.com
Website: https://www.facebook.com/crockfordmgmt/

Represents: Artists/Bands

Genres: All types of music

Manager with over 35 years of experience. His clients have sold over 250 million albums worldwide.

Crossfire
3rd Floor
207 Regent Street
London
W1B 3HH
Email: info@crossfiremanagement.com
Website: http://www.crossfiremanagement.com

Represents: Artists/Bands

Genres: Classical; Dance; Pop; House

Management company based in London, describing itself as "an award winning music, creative and media management firm".

Crown Talent & Media Group
The Townhouse
52-54 Davies Street
Mayfair
London
W1K 5JF
Email: info@crowntalentgroup.com
Website: https://www.crowntalentgroup.com
Website: https://www.facebook.com/CrownTalentMedia

Represents: Artists/Bands; Producers

Genres: Commercial; Pop; Indie

Management company with offices in London and Los Angeles, handling chart-topping acts.

dandomanagement
Northamptonshire
Website: https://twitter.com/managementdando
Website: https://www.facebook.com/introducing.dandomanagement

Represents: Artists/Bands

Genres: Indie Rock; Singer-Songwriter

Contact: Martin Dando

Management company based in Northamptonshire.

Access more listings online at www.musicsocket.com

UK Managers

Danny Brittain Band Management (DBBM)
5 Grand Parade
St Leonards on Sea
East Sussex
TN38 0DD
Email: danny@dbbm.co.uk
Website: http://www.dbbm.co.uk

Represents: Artists/Bands

Genres: All types of music

Contact: Danny Brittain

Management company based in St Leonards on Sea. Describes itself as "The premier live music booking agency for any occasion".

Darkspin Music Management
Email: info@darkspin.co
Website: https://www.darkspinmusic.com
Website: https://linktr.ee/darkspin.co

Represents: Artists/Bands

Genres: All types of music

Contact: Laura Mckay

Independent artist management and unsigned artist development.

Darren Adam
Email: darren.adam@lbc.co.uk
Website: http://www.darrenadam.com
Website: https://twitter.com/darrenadam

Represents: Artists/Bands

Genres: All types of music

Radio broadcaster, writer, voiceover artist, and music manager.

Dawson Breed Music
Website: http://www.dawsonbreedmusic.com
Website: https://twitter.com/DawsonBreed

Represents: Artists/Bands

Genres: Americana; Folk; Indie; Pop; Acoustic

Contact: Debra Downes

A live music agency, we work with emerging acts and established acts, but only acts we are passionate about.

DEF (Deutsch Englische Freundschaft)
Email: info@d-e-f.com
Website: https://d-e-f.com
Website: https://www.facebook.com/DEFallesistgut

Represents: Artists/Bands

Genres: Dance; Electronic

Concentrates on electronic dance, but willing to consider all types of music.

Defenders Ent
Email: music@defendersent.com
Website: https://www.defendersent.com
Website: https://www.facebook.com/DefendersEnt/

Represents: Artists/Bands

Genres: Dance; Reggae; R&B; Rap

Formed in 2001 as an independent record label, has since been involved in managing, releasing and consulting for many acts/brands.

Deltasonic Records
Liverpool
Email: annheston@live.com
Website: http://deltasonicrecords.co.uk
Website: https://soundcloud.com/deltasonic-records

Represents: Artists/Bands

Genres: All types of music

Management company based in Liverpool and France. Send query via online form on website, with soundcloud links.

Deluxxe Management
Email: info@deluxxe.co.uk
Website: https://www.deluxxe.co.uk/
Website: http://www.facebook.com/DeluxxeArtistManagement

Represents: Artists/Bands

Genres: All types of music

Happy to receive new artist submissions. Send email with link to four songs, and social media links. Include message about why you think this is the right time to work with a manager. Response not guaranteed.

Deuce Management & Promotion
Email: rob@deucemusic.com
Website: https://www.deucemusic.com
Website: https://www.facebook.com/deucepr/

Represents: Artists/Bands

Genres: All types of music

Contact: Rob Saunders

Has established itself as one of the leading companies to offer services to unsigned/newly signed bands and artists worldwide. With a growing reputation of being at the forefront of the best new music on the scene and with its idyllically placed office in London, they aim to ensure bands and artists are offered ways and means to get their music heard to a wider audience.

For a FREE evaluation on your music please send a link to your material by email.

DFJ Artists
Studio 114
17 Amhurst Terrace
London
E8 2BT
Website: http://www.dfjartists.com

Represents: Artists/Bands; Producers; Songwriters

Genres: Jazz

Music management and consultancy services across jazz and related music genres.

Discovering Arts Music Group (DAMG)
Email: discovering@damg.co.uk
Website: https://discoveringartsmusicgroup.com
Website: https://www.facebook.com/DAMGRECORDS

Represents: Artists/Bands

Genres: All types of music

A London-based company that believes in business at the front and Music is at the back, (whereby, we protect the artists and their music). Providing a single home for Artists, which is comprised of 8 core businesses: *Record Company, *Publishing, *Management, *Booking *Studios/Production, *Events, *Fashion/Merchandise, and *Distribution. We promote, develop and support the visions of our artists, nurturing their growth from zero to hero. We are determined not to be tied to one style or preconceived ideas, but instead to embrace exceptional music from across the spectrum.

Always on the lookout for new talents, so if you have the talent and the confidence don't hesitate to send your music through the online demo submission form on the website.

Dissention Records + Artist Management
Website: https://www.dissentionrecords.com

Represents: Artists/Bands; Film / TV Composers; Other Entertainers

Genres: Alternative; Punk

Contact: Matthew Harris

Record label and artist management company originally founded in the States but now based in the UK. Send query by email with files or links to music online.

DMF Music Ltd
51 Queen Street
Exeter
Devon
EX4 3SR
Email: info@dmfmusic.co.uk
Website: https://dmfmusic.co.uk
Website: https://www.facebook.com/DMFMusicTeam

Represents: Artists/Bands

Genres: All types of music

Contact: David & Laura Farrow

Independent agency, artist management, promoter, and festival organiser based in Exeter. Send query by email with links to music online.

Don't Try
Suffolk
Email: ben@donttryrecords.com
Website: https://www.donttrymusic.com
Website: https://www.facebook.com/donttryuk

Represents: Artists/Bands; Producers

Genres: Alternative; Indie; Rock

Music company based in Suffolk, managing artists and producers.

Down For Life
Email: info@downforlifemusic.co.uk
Website: https://www.downforlifemusic.co.uk
Website: https://www.facebook.com/downforlifemusic

Represents: Artists/Bands

Genres: Alternative; Hardcore; Metal; Rock

UK based artist and event management company.

Steve Draper Entertainments
Fax: +44 (0) 1254 679005
Email: stevedraperents1@gmail.com
Website: http://www.stevedraperentertainments.co.uk

Represents: Artists/Bands; Comedians; Other Entertainers; Tribute Acts

Genres: All types of music

Contact: Steve Draper

Management and entertainment agency established for over 35 years.

Dreamboat Management
Email: contact@dreamboatmanagement.com
Email: ben.baldwin@dreamboatmanagement.com
Website: https://www.dreamboatmanagement.com
Website: https://www.facebook.com/dreamboatmanagement

Represents: Artists/Bands

Genres: Alternative; Indie

Contact: Ben Baldwin; Dean Christesen

International artist management company with staff in Bristol, UK, and Richmond, Virginia.

Duroc Media
Beechurst
Farnham Park Lane
Farnham Royal
Buckinghamshire
SL2 3LP
Email: info@durocmedia.com
Website: http://www.durocmedia.com

Represents: Artists/Bands

Genres: All types of music

Management and public relations consultants.

East City
London
Email: demo@eastcitymanagement.com
Website: https://www.facebook.com/eastcitymanagement
Website: https://twitter.com/eastcityMGMT

Represents: Artists/Bands

Genres: Alternative; Dance; Indie

Manager based in London. Send query by email with links to streaming music online.

Elephant Management
Manchester
Email: elephantmgmt@outlook.com
Website: https://elephantmanagement.site123.me
Website: https://www.facebook.com/elephantmanagement/

Represents: Artists/Bands

Genres: Alternative; Psychedelic Rock; Shoegaze

Music management and promotion company based in Manchester.

Empire Artist Management
16 Tileyard Studios
Tileyard Road
London
N7 9AH
Fax: +44 (0) 20 8968 5999
Email: info@empire-management.co.uk
Website: http://www.empire-management.co.uk
Website: https://twitter.com/EmpireMGMT_

Represents: Artists/Bands; Producers; Songwriters

Genres: All types of music

Management company based in London, representing well-known artists, as well as producers and writers.

End of the Trail Creative
Email: kelly@endofthetrailcreative.co.uk
Website: https://www.endofthetrailcreative.co.uk
Website: https://www.facebook.com/endofthetrailcreative

Represents: Artists/Bands

Genres: All types of music

Management company and record label.

Enso Music Management
Email: submissions@ensomgmt.com
Email: info@ensomgmt.com
Website: https://ensomgmt.com
Website: https://www.facebook.com/ensomanagement/

Represents: Artists/Bands

Genres: Metal

Southwest based band management, booking and PR company. Specialises in Metal. Send query by email with links to music online.

Epic Venom
Email: sarah@epicVenom.com
Website: https://www.epicvenom.com
Website: https://www.facebook.com/EpicVenom/

Represents: Artists/Bands

Genres: Rock

Contact: Sarah Furbey

Rock band management including PR, bookings, travel management, event scheduling, and financial record keeping.

Equator Music
London
Website: http://www.equatormusic.com

Represents: Artists/Bands

Genres: Indie; Pop; Rock

London-based management company which has been managing the affairs of major artists and writers for over 35 years.

Everybody's Management Ltd
31 Corsica Street
Highbury
London
N5 1JT
Email: info@everybody-s.com
Website: https://www.everybody-s.com
Website: https://www.facebook.com/everybodysmgmt

Represents: Artists/Bands

Genres: All types of music

Management company based in London.

F&G Management
Unit D
63 Salusbury Road
London
NW6 6NJ
Email: gavino@fgmusica.com
Website: http://www.fgmusica.com
Website: https://www.facebook.com/fgdjtrade

Represents: Artists/Bands; DJs

Genres: Alternative; Dance; Electronic; Experimental; House; Techno

Contact: Gavino Prunas

Started as a DJ booking agency in the late eighties. Interested in music which is eclectic, different, or quirky. Send demo by email.

Fave Sounds
Email: hello@favesounds.com
Website: https://www.favesounds.com
Website: https://www.facebook.com/favesounds/

Represents: Artists/Bands

Genres: All types of music

A platform that features and connects music artists with their audience using effective branding, social media management, and artist management. Send submissions via contact form on website.

Feed Your Head
Website: https://www.fyhpresents.com

Represents: Artists/Bands

Genres: Alternative; Electronic; Dance; Indie

Management company founded in 2008.

Feraltone
Email: rene@feraltone.co.uk
Website: http://www.feraltone.co.uk

Represents: Artists/Bands

Genres: All types of music

Artist management, records, and consulting.

Ferocious Talent
Email: ferocioustalent@gmail.com
Website: http://www.ferocioustalent.com
Website: https://www.facebook.com/ferocioustalentlondon/

Represents: Artists/Bands

Genres: All types of music

Artist service company offering artist management, music consultancy, music business development, agency and rights management, label services, and in-house production.

Finger Lickin' Management
67-69 Chalton Street
Somers Town
London
NW1 1HY
Email: info@fingerlickin.co.uk
Email: amie@fingerlickin.co.uk
Website: http://www.fingerlickinmanagement.co.uk
Website: https://soundcloud.com/fingerlickinmanagement

Represents: Artists/Bands

Genres: Dance; Electronic; Hip-Hop; Break Beat

World recognised booking and artist management agency, currently managing a number of award winning artists and labels.

Flat Cap Music
Email: mike@flatcapmusic.com
Website: https://uk.linkedin.com/company/flat-cap-music
Website: https://twitter.com/mikeflatcap

Represents: Artists/Bands

Genres: All types of music

Independent manager based in London.

Flat50
Email: info@flat50.co.uk
Website: http://www.flat50.co.uk
Website: https://www.youtube.com/user/pmj83hatl/videos

Represents: Artists/Bands

Genres: Pop; Rock; Rap

Artist representation, promotion, and management company based in London. Send demos or queries by email.

Flow State Music
Edinburgh
Email: kyle@flowstatemusic.co.uk
Website: https://flowstatemusic.co.uk
Website: https://www.facebook.com/flowstateedinburgh/

Represents: Artists/Bands; DJs

Genres: Alternative Dance; Electronic

Music company based in Edinburgh, offering Event Production; Artist & Tour Management; Live Music Promotion; Music Programming; Digital Communications (Social Media / Direct Marketing). Send query by email with links to music online.

FP / Fantastic Plastic Music
Unit 6 Trident House
London
SE1 8QW
Email: info@fpmusic.org
Website: http://www.fpmusic.org
Website: http://soundcloud.com/fantasticplasticrecords

Represents: Artists/Bands

Genres: Alternative

Music company including record label, publishing, and management services.

Freaks R Us
Email: freaks@freaksrus.net
Website: https://www.facebook.com/freakartists
Website: https://twitter.com/freakartists

Represents: Artists/Bands

Genres: Alternative; Electronic; Experimental; Post Punk

Record label and management company.

Freedom Management
Website: http://www.frdm.co.uk

Represents: Artists/Bands; Producers; Songwriters

Genres: Indie; Pop; Commercial

Provide a broad range of skills and experience including artist / producer / writer management and development, online and audio / visual support, marketing and promotion, touring, publishing, business affairs & finance.

Friends Vs Music Ltd
London
Email: pip@friendsvsmusic.com
Website: https://www.friendsvsmusic.com
Website: https://twitter.com/pipvsrecords

Represents: Artists/Bands; Producers

Genres: All types of music

Artist and producer management company and music consultancy based in London. Approach via form on website.

From the Whitehouse
Email: bookings@fromthewhitehouse.com
Email: katie@fromthewhitehouse.com
Website: http://www.fromthewhitehouse.com
Website: https://www.facebook.com/fromtheWhiteHouse/

Represents: Artists/Bands

Genres: Electronic; Folk; Indie; Singer-Songwriter; World

An award-winning music management, artist development, booking and promotion agency, covering all aspects of strategic artist development for musicians.

Front Room Songs
Website: https://frontroomsongs.com
Website: https://twitter.com/Frontroomsongs

Represents: Artists/Bands

Genres: Folk; Pop; Roots; World

Provides artist and project management for a growing roster of emerging artists spanning the folk / roots / world and pop genres. Send query through online contact form with links to music online.

Fruition Music
Website: http://www.fruitionmusic.co.uk

Represents: Artists/Bands

Genres: Dance; Indie

Offers artist management and music and media PR.

Future Songs
London
Email: michael@futuresongs.co.uk
Website: https://www.facebook.com/futuresongspublishing
Website: https://soundcloud.com/future-songs

Represents: Artists/Bands; Producers; Songwriters; Sound Engineers

Genres: Pop; R&B; Singer-Songwriter

A music company specializing in management and music publishing. The company was founded in 2015 and represents a talented roster of clients which includes Grammy Nominated songwriters, producers and mix engineers.

Ganbei Records
Shelton Street
London
Email: info@ganbeirecords.com
Website: https://ganbeirecords.com
Website: https://www.facebook.com/ganbeirecords

Represents: Artists/Bands

Genres: Alternative; Folk; Post Punk; Psychedelic Rock

Record label and artist management company that aims to help musicians release and promote their music. Send query by email with links to music online.

Golden Arm
Email: louise@goldenarm.me
Email: milo@goldenarm.me
Website: http://www.goldenarm.me

Represents: Artists/Bands

Genres: Alternative; Indie; Pop; Rock

Management company based in London.

Goo Music Management Ltd
Email: contact@goomusic.net
Website: https://www.goomusic.net
Website: https://www.facebook.com/goomusic

Represents: Artists/Bands

Genres: Alternative; Indie; Rock

Contact: Ben Kirby

Built from a background of gig promotion, festival production and artist liaison. Has trusting relationships with many industry contacts including record labels, publishers, booking agents and tour managers.

Graphite Media
Email: info@graphitemedia.net
Email: ben@graphitemedia.net
Website: https://www.graphitemedia.net
Website: https://twitter.com/Graphite1

Represents: Artists/Bands; DJs; Producers

Genres: Dance; Electronic

Contact: Ben Turner

A music management and brand services company, based between London and Los Angeles.

Green Productions Ltd
104 Roehampton House
39 Academy Way
Dagenham
Essex
RM8 2FJ
Email: info@green-productions.net
Website: http://www.green-productions.net

Represents: Artists/Bands

Genres: Hip-Hop; R&B

Contact: Les Green

Music project management company based in Dagenham, Essex.

Grizzly Management
25 Newman Street
London
W1N 1NP

UK Managers

Email: info@grizzlymanagement.com
Email: andy@grizzlymanagement.com
Website: https://www.grizzlymanagement.com
Website: https://www.facebook.com/grizzlymanagement

Represents: Artists/Bands

Genres: All types of music

Contact: Andrew Viitalahde-Pountain

Artist management company with offices in London, Manchester, and Helsinki.

Guvnor Management
Email: info@guvnormanagement.co.uk
Website: https://www.guvnormanagement.co.uk
Website: https://www.facebook.com/GuvnorManagement/

Represents: Artists/Bands; Comedians; Other Entertainers; Tribute Acts

Genres: Pop; Rock

An Entertainments Agency established in 2006, covering all aspects of the entertainments business from, cabaret artists, tribute shows, function bands, comedians, sporting and after dinner speakers.

Hal Carter Organisation
41 Horsefair Green
Stony Stratford
Milton Keynes
Bucks
MK11 1JP
Email: artistes@halcarterorg.com
Website: https://www.halcarterorg.com
Website: https://www.facebook.com/halcarterorg/

Represents: Artists/Bands; Tribute Acts

Genres: All types of music

Management company based in Milton Keynes.

Hand in Hive Independent Records & Management
London
Email: contact@handinhive.com
Email: tristan@handinhive.com
Website: https://www.handinhive.com
Website: https://soundcloud.com/hand-in-hive

Represents: Artists/Bands

Genres: Indie; Pop; Rock

Independent music company, formed in 2014 by two friends with a shared love of music, specialising in records, management, publishing and sync.

Handshake Ltd.
2 Holly House
Mill Street,
Uppermill
Greater Manchester
OL3 6LZ
Fax: +44 (0) 1457 810052
Email: info@handshakegroup.com
Website: http://www.Handshakegroup.com
Website: https://www.facebook.com/handshakeltd/

Represents: Artists/Bands; Comedians; DJs; Tribute Acts; Variety Artists

Genres: Pop; Rock and Roll; Commercial

Contact: Stuart Littlewood

Artistes Representation, and Concert Promotion Company, touring shows and events in the UK.

Also offering certain productions on a worldwide basis.

Hannah Management
Matix Studio
91 Peterborough Road
Fulham
London
SW6 3BU
Email: info@hannahmanagement.co.uk
Website: http://www.hannahmanagement.co.uk
Website: https://soundcloud.com/hannahmanagement

Represents: Artists/Bands; Producers

Genres: All types of music

Contact: A&R

A London based artist and producer management company.

The founder has been successfully managing artists and working in music publishing since 1978. The management team manage record producers as well as up and coming bands.

They have purposely kept their roster small with the intention of working with the best talent and helping them develop all aspects of their career.

Happy House Management & Marketing Services
Email: happyhousemanagement@gmail.com
Email: dannydeathdisco@googlemail.com
Website: http://happyhousemanagement.weebly.com
Website: https://www.facebook.com/happyhousemgmt

Represents: Artists/Bands

Genres: All types of music

Contact: Danny Watson

Management, marketing and product management company.

Heard and Seen
Greens Court
West Street
Midhurst
West Sussex
GU29 9NQ
Email: enquiries@heardandseen.com
Website: http://www.heardandseen.com
Website: https://www.facebook.com/Heard-and-Seen-Ltd-197097010394361/

Represents: Artists/Bands

Genres: All types of music

Offers a range of services to artists, including management. See website for full details.

Heist or Hit
12 Hilton Street
Manchester
M1 1JF
Email: submissions@heistorhit.com
Email: team@heistorhit.com
Website: http://www.heistorhit.com
Website: https://www.facebook.com/heistorhit

Represents: Artists/Bands

Genres: Acoustic; Alternative; Indie

Management company based in Manchester. Send demos by email.

Holier than Thou (HTT) Music
Email: David@httmusic.co.uk
Website: http://www.holierthanthou.co.uk
Website: http://www.httmusic.co.uk

Represents: Artists/Bands; Tribute Acts

Genres: Rock; Metal; Electronic; Alternative; Melodic Metal; Progressive Metal; Gothic Metal; Melodic Thrash

Offers music management, digital distribution, new release promotions, and music publishing admin. Handles Rock, Metal, and sub-genres including Electronic Crossovers.

Hope Management
Unit 4.16 The Paintworks
Bath Road
Bristol
BS4 3EH
Email: info@hopemanagement.co.uk
Website: http://www.hopemanagement.co.uk

Represents: Artists/Bands

Genres: Alternative; Dance

Management company based in Bristol, with US offices in Los Angeles.

Hot Gem
Glasgow
Email: sync@hotgem.co.uk
Email: demos@hotgem.co.uk
Website: http://www.hotgem.co.uk
Website: https://soundcloud.com/hotgemtunes

Represents: Artists/Bands

Genres: Ambient; Dance; Electronic; Experimental; Pop

Musician management and label based in Glasgow. Accepts demos, but must have difference / unique sound. No indie guitar bands. Send demos by email as MP3 attachments, or via soundcloud.

On hiatus as per July 2020.

Hot House Music Ltd
C/O Abbey Road Studios
3 Abbey Road
London
NW8 9AY
Fax: +44 (0) 20 7446 7448
Email: info@hot-house-music.com
Website: http://www.hot-house-music.com
Website: http://www.facebook.com/pages/HotHouse-Music/128423608511

Represents: Film / TV Composers; Supervisors

Genres: All types of music

Management company based in London, representing film and TV composers / music supervisors / score co-ordinators.

Hot Vox
London
Email: info@hotvox.co.uk
Website: https://hotvox.co.uk
Website: https://www.facebook.com/hotvox

Represents: Artists/Bands

Genres: All types of music

We work hard to create events that showcase the talents of our acts across the full range of genres, creating a great atmosphere for both musician and fan alike.

We also specialise in management, video production and work as consultants for branding, advertising, TV and film.

House of Us
London
Email: us@houseofus.co.uk
Email: caspar@houseofus.co.uk
Website: http://www.houseofus.co.uk
Website: https://www.facebook.com/houseofusmanagement/

Represents: Artists/Bands

Genres: Dance; House; Indie; Pop

London-based music management, consultancy, and PR company. Send query by email with links to music online.

HQ Familia
38 Charles Street
Leicester
LE1 1FB
Email: yasin@hqrecording.co.uk
Email: yasinelashrafi1980@live.co.uk
Website: http://www.hqrecording.co.uk/hq-familia/
Website: http://soundcloud.com/hqrecording

Represents: Artists/Bands

Genres: Electronic; Urban

Contact: Yasin El Ashrafi

Collective of like minded artists with associated record label and recording studio.

Humans & Other Animals
Email: rich@humansandotheranimals.co.uk
Website: http://www.humansandotheranimals.co.uk

Represents: Artists/Bands

Genres: Indie; Rock; Folk; Electronic

Interested in hearing from alternative and/or experimental indie, rock, folk and electronic artists.

ie:music
111 Frithville Gardens
London
W12 7JQ
Email: info@iemusic.co.uk
Website: https://iemusic.co.uk
Website: https://www.facebook.com/iemusic-150700438296856

Represents: Artists/Bands

Genres: All types of music

Management company with offices in London, Los Angeles, and Sydney.

Ignition Management
London
Website: https://www.ignition.co.uk
Website: https://twitter.com/IgnitionMusicUK

Represents: Artists/Bands

Genres: Alternative; Indie; Pop; Rock

Management company with offices in London and LA. Approach via online contact form, including as many links to your social media as possible. Response not guaranteed.

Impact Management
Website: http://impactartist.com/#artist-management-banner
Website: https://www.facebook.com/impactartistmanagement

Represents: Artists/Bands

Genres: All types of music

Is a boutique music management company.

Incendia Music
Email: info@incendiamusic.co.uk
Website: https://www.incendiamusic.co.uk
Website: https://soundcloud.com/incendia-music-management

Represents: Artists/Bands; Songwriters

Genres: Metal; Rock; Progressive

Contact: Lulu Davis

Artist Management, Publicity, and Consultancy services for Rock, Prog and Metal bands and artists.

Indevine
Email: sean@indevine.com
Website: https://www.indevine.com
Website: https://twitter.com/indevine

Represents: Artists/Bands; Songwriters

Genres: All types of music

Manager of a songwriter and several bands.

Innate – Music Ltd
Email: nathan@soundvault.tv
Website: https://www.innate-music.com/

Represents: Artists/Bands

Genres: All types of music

Contact: Nathan Graves

Creative strategy, project management, marketing and media consultancy established in 2003.

Insomnia Music UK
Email: management@insomniamusic.co.uk
Website: http://insomniamusic.co.uk
Website: https://www.facebook.com/InsomniaMusicUK/

Represents: Artists/Bands

Genres: Commercial; Pop

Music management company specialising in pop and commercial.

Intertalent Rights Group
First Floor, Malvern House
15-16 Nassau Street
London
W1W 7AB
Website: https://intertalentgroup.com
Website: https://twitter.com/InterTalent

Represents: Artists/Bands

Genres: Classical; Pop

Represents a range of talent, including musicians.

Intune Addicts
Email: info@intuneaddicts.com
Website: https://www.intuneaddicts.com
Website: https://www.facebook.com/intuneaddicts

Represents: Artists/Bands

Genres: All types of music

Contact: Bob James; Mark Smutz Smith; Graham Peacock; Holly Glanvill

Send query by email, describing achievements to date.

Involved Management
London
Email: info@involvedmanagement.com
Website: https://involvedmanagement.com

Represents: Artists/Bands

Genres: Chill; Electronic; House; Trance; Progressive House

Management company with offices in London and Los Angeles.

JA Artist Management
Email: info@jaartistmanagement.com
Website: https://www.jaartistmanagement.com
Website: https://www.facebook.com/JAArtistManagement

Represents: Artists/Bands

Genres: All types of music

Artist Management for South Coast UK bands and solo artists.

James Joseph Music Management
85 Cicada Road
London
SW18 2PA
Email: jj3@jamesjoseph.co.uk
Website: http://www.jamesjoseph.co.uk

Represents: Artists/Bands

Genres: All types of music

Contact: James Joseph

Management company with offices in London, UK, and Los Angeles, California.

JBLS Management
Unit 13, The Tay Building
2A Wrentham Avenue
London
NW10 3HA
Email: louise@jblsmanagement.com
Email: jo@jblsmanagement.com
Website: http://www.jblsmanagement.com
Website: https://www.facebook.com/JBLSManagement/

Represents: Artists/Bands; Producers; Songwriters

Genres: Electronic; Alternative; Pop; Singer-Songwriter

Contact: Louise Smith

London management company representing artists, producers, remixers, mixers, and writers.

Jelli Records
Email: jellirecords@yahoo.co.uk
Website: https://www.jelli-records.com
Website: https://www.facebook.com/Jelli.Records/

Represents: Artists/Bands

Genres: Acoustic; Folk; Roots

Record label and entertainment agency offering stage management, open mic nights and songwriter evenings, and consultancy services, as well as hosting two radio shows every weeks.

Jude Street Management
Email: info@judestreet.com
Email: paul@judest.com
Website: https://judestreet.com
Website: https://twitter.com/judestreetmusic

Represents: Artists/Bands; Film / TV Composers; Producers

Genres: Alternative; Pop; Indie; Classical

Contact: Paul Devaney

Music services and management company based in East London and established in 2005. Provides professional representation for bands, artists, producers and composers/arrangers in the fields of Alt/Pop/Indie, Classical, Games, Film and TV. Send query by email and follow up with demos upon request.

Kaleidoscope
3-5 Stepney Bank
Newcastle upon Tyne
NE1 2PW
Email: info@kaleidoscope-music.co.uk
Website: https://www.kaleidoscope-

music.co.uk
Website: https://www.facebook.com/KaleidoscopeUK/

Represents: Artists/Bands

Genres: All types of music

An artist management company and record label established in 2015 and based in Newcastle upon Tyne, UK. Established a sister company in Bangkok, Thailand, in 2021.

Karma Artists Music LLP
Unit 31, Tileyard Studios
Tileyard Road
Kings Cross
London
N7 9AH
Email: info@karmaartists.co.uk
Website: https://www.karmaartists.co.uk
Website: https://www.facebook.com/karmaartistsuk

Represents: Artists/Bands; Producers; Songwriters

Genres: All types of music

Contact: Jordan Jay; Ross Gautreau; Jess Miller

Multi-faceted entertainment company based in London, representing a roster with combined sales of over 400 million units.

Key Music Management
Suite 403, Bonded Warehouse
18 Lower Byrom Street
Manchester
M3 4AP
Email: contact@kmmltd.com
Email: contact@keymusicmanagement.com
Website: https://www.keymusicmanagement.com
Website: https://www.facebook.com/keymusicmanagement

Represents: Artists/Bands

Genres: Alternative

Contact: Richard Jones; Ryan Terpstra; Will Hanson; Marcus Jones

Management company based in Manchester.

KMY (Keep Me Young)
Email: Dan@keepmeyoung.uk
Website: https://www.keepmeyoung.uk
Website: https://www.instagram.com/KeepMeYoungUK/

Represents: Artists/Bands

Genres: Pop

Send query by email with links to music online.

KRMB Management & Consultancy
Metropolis Studios
70 Chiswick High Road
London
W4 1SY
Email: kreynolds@krmbmanagement.com
Website: https://www.krmbmanagement.com
Website: https://www.facebook.com/krmbmanagement

Represents: Artists/Bands

Genres: All types of music

Contact: Kevin Reynolds

Management and consultancy company offering artist development, creative direction, talent management, corporate entertainment, and consultancy.

La Rock Entertainment
2 Tunstall Road
London
SW9 8DA
Website: http://larockent.com

Represents: Artists/Bands; Producers

Genres: Dance; Urban; Electronic; Pop

Full service entertainment and music management company based in London. Send CD by post or MP3 links via contact form on website.

Laissez Faire Club
London
Email: jeremy@laissezfaireclub.com
Website: https://laissezfaireclub.tumblr.com
Website: https://www.facebook.com/jilloyd

Represents: Artists/Bands

Genres: All types of music

Contact: Jeremy Lloyd

Originally a live promotions company, now focuses solely on artist management.

Lazy Daze
Email: studio@lazydaze.co.uk
Website: http://www.lazydaze.co.uk
Website: https://www.facebook.com/LazyDazeRecs

Represents: Artists/Bands

Genres: Indie; Rock; Rock and Roll

Provide music management and label services for up and coming bands.

Line-Up pmc
10 Matthew Close
Newcastle upon Tyne
NE6 1XD
Email: chrismurtagh@line-up.co.uk
Website: http://www.line-up.co.uk

Represents: Artists/Bands

Genres: World

Contact: Chris Murtagh

Promotions and marketing consultancy company with over 25 years of experience specialising in live arts performance, ethnic and World Music. May not necessarily offer representation, but may pass your demo on to relevant contacts if potential is seen.

Liquid Management
Email: david@liquidmanagement.net
Email: steve@Liquidmanagement.net
Website: https://www.musicglue.com/liquidmanagement
Website: https://twitter.com/liquidmgmnt

Represents: Artists/Bands; DJs; Producers

Genres: All types of music

Contact: David Manders; Steve Dix

Management company with 20 years of managing artists through all levels of the music industry.

Listen to This Management
Email: info@lttmusicmanagement.com
Email: grant@lttmusicmanagement.com
Website: https://lttmusicmanagement.com
Website: https://www.facebook.com/listentothisuk

Represents: Artists/Bands

Genres: Alternative; Alternative Country; Rock; Indie

Contact: Grant Tilbury; Charlotte Final

Artist and tour management company with offices in London and Nashville.

Lokation
Email: lokationcreativeproduction@gmail.com
Website: https://www.lokationco.com
Website: https://www.facebook.com/LokationCo/

Represents: Artists/Bands

Genres: Heavy Metal; R&B; Urban

Offers creative production and management.

Lonewolf Talent Management
Email: rob@theboywiththelionhead.co.uk
Website: https://www.lonewolftalentmanagement.com
Website: https://www.facebook.com/lonewolftalent

Represents: Artists/Bands

Genres: Alternative; Ambient; Indie; Post Punk; Punk; Punk Rock

An artist management company focused on developing and supporting new and emerging artists to achieve their goals and help them through the various stages of their career in the music industry. Contact through form on website. No reply unless interested.

UK Managers

The Lost Atlantis Records
Email: Thelostatlantisrecords@gmail.com
Website: https://www.
thelostatlantisrecords.com
Website: https://twitter.com/crystalchild01

Genres: Hip-Hop; House; Rap; Soul; Techno; Urban

Contact: Charlene Jones

Artist development and management. Send query by email with up to three MP3 attachments.

LSH Management
7 The Courtyard
50 Lynton Road
London
N8 8SL
Email: info@lshmanagement.com
Website: https://www.lshmanagement.com
Website: https://soundcloud.com/lshmanagement

Represents: Artists/Bands

Genres: Indie; Jazz; Pop

Management company based in London.

Lucky House Management
Bristol
Email: luckyhousemanagement@gmail.com
Website: https://www.luckyhousemanagement.com/
Website: https://www.facebook.com/luckyhousemanagement

Represents: Artists/Bands

Genres: Grime; Hip-Hop; Rap; Soul; Urban

Contact: Jade Fearon

Personalised artist management, booking and casting agency.

Lucky Number Music Limited
Suite 3
Second Floor
344 Kingsland Rd
London
E8 4DA
Email: contact@luckynumbermusic.com
Website: https://www.
luckynumbermusic.com/
Website: https://soundcloud.com/luckynumbermusic

Represents: Artists/Bands

Genres: Indie; Pop; Electronic

Provide management and producer services, and also operate a record label.

Lyricom
Website: https://lyricom.co.uk

Represents: Artists/Bands; Producers; Songwriters

Genres: Indie; Singer-Songwriter; Urban

Managing a roster that spans both independent and major label Recording Artists, Digital Talents, Producers and Writers.

Offering expertise across Production, Distribution, Digital, Promotion, Brand & Franchise Extensions, Live, Merch, Team Architecture and Administration.

M24 Management
Manchester
Email: mgmt@m24management.com
Website: https://www.m24management.com
Website: https://www.facebook.com/M24ManagementAgency

Represents: DJs

Genres: House

Management company based in Manchester, representing House DJs.

MaDa Music Entertainment
London
Email: Adam@Madamusic.com
Website: https://madamusic.com
Website: https://soundcloud.com/mada-music

Represents: Artists/Bands; Producers

Genres: All types of music

London based multi divisional entertainment company specialising in Artist and Producer Management, Events, PR and Consultancy.

Claim your free access to www.musicsocket.com: See p.211

168 UK Managers

Particularly interested in pop, indie, and rock, but will consider most genres.

Major Labl
Website: https://www.majorlabl.com
Website: https://www.facebook.com/MajorLabl/

Represents: Artists/Bands

Genres: All types of music

Offers marketing and management services for unsigned and independent artists. Apply through online form.

Manners McDade Artist Management
3rd floor, 12 Greenhill Rents
London
EC1M 6BN
Email: submissions@mannersmcdade.co.uk
Email: info@mannersmcdade.co.uk
Website: http://mannersmcdade.co.uk
Website: https://www.facebook.com/mannersmcdademusic/

Represents: Film / TV Composers

Genres: All types of music

Management company based in London, representing composers for film and TV. Send submissions by email. Response only if interested.

Manta Ray Music
7-7c Snuff Street
Devizes
Wiltshire
SN10 1DU
Website: http://www.mantaraymusic.co.uk

Represents: Artists/Bands

Genres: All types of music

Management company focusing on early-stage A&R, "seeking out innate talent and potential". Offices in London and Berlin.

MBM (Music Business Management Ltd)
Labrican
Healey Dell Nature Reserve
Rochdale
OL12 6BG
Email: anne@mbmcorporate.co.uk
Email: phil@mbmcorporate.co.uk
Website: https://www.mbmcorporate.co.uk
Website: https://www.facebook.com/MBMCorporate

Represents: Artists/Bands; DJs; Tribute Acts

Genres: All types of music

Contact: Anne Barrett; Phil Barrett

Entertainment consultancy and artiste management. Specialises in Tributes and Tribite shows.

Memphia Music Management
Bristol
Email: jp@memphia.com
Website: https://www.memphia.com
Website: https://www.facebook.com/MemphiaMM/

Represents: Artists/Bands

Genres: Indie; Rock

Management company based in Bristol. Query by email or via contact us page on website.

Metal Music Bookings
Fax: +44 (0) 20 7084 0323
Email: contact@metalmusicbookings.com
Website: http://www.metalmusicbookings.com
Website: https://www.facebook.com/MetalMusicBookings

Represents: Artists/Bands

Genres: Alternative; Metal; Rock

Contact: Denise Dale

Independent Booking Agency specialising in representing artists in the Heavy Metal and Rock genres, but willing to consider other genres. Offers self-management subscription services.

UK Managers

Miller Music Management
Fax: +44 (0) 20 8964 4965
Email: info@m-music-m.com
Website: http://www.m-music-m.com

Represents: Artists/Bands

Genres: Indie; Rock; Singer-Songwriter

Contact: Carrie Hustler

Management company with offices in London and Los Angeles.

MJM Agency
Email: demos@mjmagency.co.uk
Email: info@mjmagency.co.uk
Website: http://www.mjmagency.co.uk

Represents: Artists/Bands; DJs; Other Entertainers

Genres: All types of music

Contact: Mike Jones

Management agency run on a part-time basis. Handles musical entertainers and performing acts. Send demos and/or band details by email.

Modest! Management
The Matrix Complex
91 Peterborough Road
London
SW6 3BU
Email: info@modestmanagement.com
Website: https://www.modestmanagement.com
Website: https://www.facebook.com/modestmanagement

Represents: Artists/Bands

Genres: Pop

Contact: Will Bloomfield; Richard Griffiths; Harry Magee

Management company based in London, handling several X-Factor winners/finalists. Send demos by email.

Moksha Management
PO Box 102
London
E15 2HH
Email: info@moksha.co.uk
Website: https://www.moksha.co.uk
Website: https://twitter.com/mokshamgt

Represents: Artists/Bands

Genres: Alternative Electronic Fusion; Contemporary; Dance

Demos preferred as streaming weblinks.

Moneypenny
Fax: +44 (0) 7977 455882
Email: enquiry@moneypennymusic.co.uk
Website: https://moneypennymusic.co.uk

Represents: Artists/Bands

Genres: Acoustic; Americana; Country; Classic Rock

Contact: Nigel Morton; Liz Lenten

A boutique, hands-on style booking agency for acts of assorted genres, specializing in Acoustic, Americana / Country and classic rock.

Morningstar
Email: enquiries@morningstarpro.co.uk
Email: artists@morningstarpro.co.uk
Website: https://www.morningstarpro.co.uk
Website: https://www.facebook.com/Mstarliveevents

Represents: Artists/Bands

Genres: Indie; Rock

Management agency based on the key values of honesty and a more personal touch with everyone they choose to represent.

Mother Artist Management
Email: info@motherartists.com
Website: https://www.motherartists.com
Website: https://www.facebook.com/motherartistsltd/

Represents: Artists/Bands

Genres: All types of music

Artist management and live music agency.

Music by Design
27 Lexington Street
Soho
London
W1F 9AQ
Email: info@musicbydesign.co.uk
Website: http://www.musicbydesign.co.uk
Website: https://twitter.com/i/events/1281585300804755458

Represents: Artists/Bands

Genres: All types of music

Contact: Sarah Edwards

"Innovative out of the box thinkers required. Send us your idea, receive a song. Let's create something good together".

Music Media Events
Website: http://www.musicmediaevents.com
Website: https://twitter.com/musicmediasean

Represents: Artists/Bands

Genres: Pop; Acoustic; Alternative; Folk

We have booked artists in to arenas, clubs, art centres, theatres, colleges, stadiums, festivals, Christmas switch-ons, store openings, charity, private and corporate events.

N.O.W. Music Management
1st Floor
25 Commercial Street
Brighouse
HD6 1AF
Email: info@now-music.com
Website: https://www.now-music.com

Represents: Artists/Bands; Tribute Acts

Genres: Pop; Rock

A management company based in Brighouse, West Yorkshire, with strong connections in Europe and with a small independent record company.

Nettwerk Management UK
15 Adeline Place, Ground Floor
London
WC1B 3AJ
Fax: +44 (0) 20 7456 9501

Email: info@nettwerk.com
Website: http://www.nettwerk.com
Website: https://www.facebook.com/nettwerkmusicgroup

Represents: Artists/Bands

Genres: All types of music

Management company headquartered in Vancouver, with offices in London, Hamburg, LA, and New York.

New Champion Management
Oh Yeah Centre
Belfast
BT1 2LG
Email: newchampionmanagement@gmail.com
Website: https://www.facebook.com/newchampionmanagement/
Website: https://www.instagram.com/newchampionmanagement/

Represents: Artists/Bands

Genres: Electronic; Folk; Indie; Pop; Punk

Provides artist management, PR and music consultancy services. Based in Northern Ireland.

New Level Music Management
Oxford
Email: newlevelmgmt@gmail.com
Website: https://www.facebook.com/NewLevelMgmt
Website: https://twitter.com/NewLevelMgmt

Represents: Artists/Bands

Genres: All types of music

Music management based in Oxford, with contacts with UK and international record labels, publishers, promoters, and booking agents. Provides artist management, tour booking / management, professional guidance, PR, release campaigns, and contract negotiation.

New Outlaw
Email: clare@newoutlaw.co.uk
Website: https://www.outlaw-pr.co.uk
Website: https://www.facebook.com/newoutlawmusic/

Access more listings online at www.musicsocket.com

Represents: Artists/Bands

Genres: All types of music

Specialises in album release management, PR, graphics and merchandise development for music artists. Send query by email with links / social media.

NewLevel Management
Oxford
Email: newlevelmgmt@gmail.com
Website: https://www.facebook.com/NewLevelMgmt
Website: https://twitter.com/NewLevelMgmt

Represents: Artists/Bands

Genres: All types of music

Music management company based in Oxford. Offers artist management, tour booking, professional guidance, tour management, PR, label mailouts, release campaign co-ordination, and contract negotiation.

No Half Measures Ltd
1st Floor
5 Eagle Street
Glasgow
G4 9XA
Email: info@nohalfmeasures.com
Website: https://nohalfmeasures.com/
Website: https://www.facebook.com/nohalfmeasures

Represents: Artists/Bands

Genres: All types of music

A company registered in Scotland, U.K. and based in Glasgow. The firm has a general structure based on its artist management, music publishing, record label and photography divisions. Works with a diverse range of artists and operates in huge variety of areas. These include artist management; intellectual property and rights management; music composition and publishing; audio and audio visual recording, mixing, and mastering; design, manufacturing, distribution and sale of audio and audio visual products, merchandise, clothing, apparel, and printed products; photography; marketing, promotion and advertising of these goods; sponsorship and branding; live entertainment performances, presentations and touring; event logistics, consultancy, management and promotion; sale of tickets; training and education.

Northern Music Co. Ltd
5A Victoria Road
Saltaire
Shipley
West Yorkshire
BD18 3LA
Fax: +44 (0) 1274 593546
Email: demos@northernmusic.co.uk
Email: info@northernmusic.co.uk
Website: http://www.northernmusic.co.uk
Website: https://www.facebook.com/NMCLtd

Represents: Artists/Bands

Genres: Metal; Rock

Contact: Andy Farrow

Send query by email with your band/act's name in the subject line, with details on what you are looking for; links to stream your music; a brief bio of your band/act; links to your website / social media / videos; and any details of existing industry partners / releases / live dates, etc.

NSB Artist Management
Email: nsbartistmanagement@gmail.com
Website: https://www.facebook.com/nsbartistmanagement
Website: https://linktr.ee/nsbartistmanagement

Represents: Artists/Bands

Genres: Hip-Hop; Soul; Urban

Send query by email with EPK and links to music online.

Off the Chart Promotions
Email: tim@offthechart.co.uk
Website: https://www.offthechart.co.uk
Website: https://www.facebook.com/offthechartmanagement

Represents: Artists/Bands

UK Managers

Genres: Folk; Pop; Rock; Indie; Singer-Songwriter

Management company based in Cambridge. Works with artists from the East of England and London.

Offbeat Management
Fax: +44 (0) 1912 640601
Email: info@offbeat-management.co.uk
Website: http://www.offbeat-management.co.uk

Represents: Artists/Bands

Genres: Acoustic Alternative Heavy Power Progressive Psychedelic Thrash; Ambient Black Metal Blues Chill Doom Garage Guitar based Instrumental Metal R&B Rock Rhythm and Blues Singer-Songwriter; Hard

Management company representing one band.

OnDaBeat Talent Management
4 Wandsworth Plain
Church Row
London
SW18 1ES
Email: mgmt@odbentltd.com
Website: https://ondabeat.co.uk
Website: https://soundcloud.com/ondabeatmgmt

Represents: Artists/Bands

Genres: Drum and Bass; Electronic; House; Hip-Hop; Rap; Techno

Management company and record studios based in London.

One Fifteen
A&R
1 Globe House
Middle Lane Mews
London
N8 8PN
Fax: +44 (0) 20 8442 7561
Email: demos@onefifteen.com
Email: contact@onefifteen.com
Website: https://www.onefifteen.com

Represents: Artists/Bands

Genres: All types of music

If submitting by email prefers links to your SoundCloud, YouTube or Facebook page. If you insist on sending MP3s, send no more than two. Include short bio, photo, social media links, and upcoming gig listings. CDs cannot be returned. Aims to listen to everything, but response not guaranteed if not interested.

141a Management
Email: admin@art19.co.uk
Website: https://www.141amanagement.co.uk
Website: https://www.facebook.com/141amanagementcompany/?fref=ts

Represents: Artists/Bands

Genres: All types of music

Music management company representing artists from all music genres.

140dB Management Limited
London
Email: ros@140db.co.uk
Website: https://www.biglifemanagement.com/140db
Website: https://www.facebook.com/140dBManagement/

Represents: Artists/Bands; Producers

Genres: All types of music

Contact: Ros Earls

Management company based in London. Represents artists and producers.

Opre Roma
Email: info@opreroma.co.uk
Website: https://opreroma.co.uk
Website: https://www.facebook.com/OpreRomaSounds

Represents: Artists/Bands

Genres: Acoustic; Americana; Folk; Guitar based; Indie

Contact: Nayfe Slusjan

Aims to help artists build long-term stability into their music careers, with 24/7 access to business management services and global

Access more listings online at www.musicsocket.com

representation. Send links to your music through online submission form.

Orean Music Ltd
Email: adrian@oreanmusic.com
Email: ah@oreanmusic.com
Website: https://oreanmusic.com
Website: https://www.facebook.com/oreanmusic/

Represents: Artists/Bands

Genres: Alternative; Dance; Electronic; Indie; Pop

Artist management company dedicated to helping independent artists grow and succeed in the music industry.

Ornadel Management
Email: info@ornadel.com
Email: guy@ornadel.com
Website: http://www.ornadel.com
Website: https://www.facebook.com/OrnadelMGM/

Represents: Artists/Bands; DJs

Genres: Dance

Contact: Guy Ornadel

Mainly works with DJs.

Paper House Music
89 Borough High Street
London
SE1 1NL
Fax: +44 (0) 20 7357 9750
Email: doug@paperhousemusic.co.uk
Email: matt@paperhousemusic.co.uk
Website: http://www.ma2music.com

Represents: Artists/Bands

Genres: All types of music

Management and promotion company based in London.

Park Promotions
Website: http://www.parkrecords.com
Website: https://www.facebook.com/Park-Promotions-141933172641365/

Represents: Artists/Bands

Genres: Folk; Singer-Songwriter; Roots; Acoustic; Folk Rock

Music company including record label and management and PR services.

Perfect Havoc Ltd
Email: info@perfecthavoc.com
Email: Adam.Griffin@perfecthavoc.com
Website: https://perfecthavoc.com
Website: https://www.facebook.com/perfecthavocmusic/

Represents: Artists/Bands

Genres: Dance; Disco; House

London-based music entertainment management, record label, and events. Submit demos as soundcloud links using online form on website.

Petty Music Management
Email: hello@pettymanagement.com
Website: https://pettymanagement.com
Website: https://www.facebook.com/pettymanagement

Represents: Artists/Bands

Genres: All types of music

UK management company.

Pieces of 8 Music
London
Email: info@piecesof8music.com
Website: https://piecesof8music.com
Website: https://www.facebook.com/Piecesof8Music

Represents: Artists/Bands; Producers; Songwriters; Sound Engineers

Genres: All types of music

Boutique management company set up to represent artists, producers, engineers, mixers and songwriters on a professional level.

Pierce Entertainment
Pierce House
London Apollo Complex
Queen Caroline Street
London W6 9QH
Email: info@pierce-entertainment.com
Website: http://www.pierce-entertainment.com
Website: https://www.facebook.com/PierceEnt/

Represents: Artists/Bands

Genres: Pop; R&B

Call in first instance. Send demo on invitation only.

Pillar Artists
Newcastle upon Tyne
Email: pillar.artists@gmail.com
Website: https://www.musicglue.com/pillar-artists
Website: https://facebook.com/PillarArtists

Represents: Artists/Bands

Genres: Acoustic; Alternative; Guitar based; Indie

Management agency based in Newcastle Upon Tyne. Also involved with independent gig promotion, PR, and booking.

Plus Music
Hoxton
London
Email: info@plusmusic.co.uk
Website: http://www.plusmusic.co.uk

Represents: Artists/Bands

Genres: Funk; Pop; R&B; Soul

Contact: Desmond Chisholm

Looking for male or female singers aged 16-23. Send MP3 with recent photo(s) and social media links by email. See website for full details.

PMS Music Management
122 London Road
Rayleigh
Essex
SS6 9BN
Fax: +44 (0) 1268 784807
Email: pmsmusicmgt@yahoo.co.uk
Website: https://pmsmusicmanagement.weebly.com

Represents: Artists/Bands; Tribute Acts

Genres: All types of music

Contact: Peter Scott

Send demo by post or email. MP3 preferred but not essential. Currently managing Indie/pop/rock but open to all genres. 'If I like it, I can represent it!' Welcomes all submissions in the form of CD, MP3 or video on DVD together with a biography and links to your Website, and any other relevant links. Particularly keen to work with unsigned bands.

Program Music, Ltd
197 Queen's Crescent
London
NW5 4DS
Email: info@program-music.co.uk
Website: https://www.program-music.co.uk

Represents: Artists/Bands; DJs

Genres: All types of music

Contact: Pete Whelan

Specialises in the production of immersive video domes and 3D experiences, large-scale audiovisual work and interactive installations.

Prolifica Management
London
Email: info@prolifica.co.uk
Website: http://www.prolificamanagement.co.uk
Website: https://www.instagram.com/prolificamanagement/

Represents: Artists/Bands

Genres: All types of music

London-based Music Management and Production Company. Send demo by email.

Psycho Management Company
Email: patrick@psycho.co.uk
Website: https://www.psycho.co.uk/
Website: https://twitter.com/psychomanco

Represents: Artists/Bands; Comedians; DJs; Other Entertainers; Tribute Acts

Genres: All types of music

Management company representing circus acts, entertainment acts, lookalikes, music acts, name acts, and tribute acts.

Push Music Management
London
Email: info@pushmusicmanagement.com
Website: https://pushmusicmanagement.com
Website: https://twitter.com/pushmusicmgmt

Represents: Artists/Bands

Genres: All types of music

Management company based in London.

PVA Management Ltd
County House
St Mary Street
Worcester WR1 1HB

Email: md@pvmedia.co.uk
Website: http://pvmedia.co.uk/

Represents: Artists/Bands

Genres: Classical

Broadcasting and Media Consultants, PVA Payroll Services, PVA Training and PVA Music.

Quest Management
Email: quest@maverick.com
Website: http://www.quest-management.com
Website: https://www.instagram.com/questartistmgmt/

Represents: Artists/Bands

Genres: All types of music

A collective of experienced management executives, renowned for innovations in creating lasting revenue strategies for artists.

Radius Music Ltd
PO Box 46375
London
SW17 9WJ
Email: info@radiusmusic.co.uk
Website: https://www.radiusmusic.co.uk
Website: https://www.facebook.com/radiusmusic

Represents: Artists/Bands; Producers; Songwriters

Genres: All types of music

UK based music industry management representing Songwriters and Producers.

Raven Black Music
Email: info@ravenblackmusic.com
Website: https://www.facebook.com/ravenblackmusic

Represents: Artists/Bands

Genres: Rock

Contact: Dean G. Hill

UK-based record label. Contact by email. No physical submissions.

Raw Power Management
London
Website: https://rawpowermanagement.com/
Website: https://www.facebook.com/rawpowermanagement

Represents: Artists/Bands

Genres: Punk Rock; Alternative; Metal; Rock

Punk rock management company with offices in London and Los Angeles.

Reaction Management
Email: jay.burnett@reaction-management.com
Email: jedd.lefthander@reaction-management.com
Website: https://www.reaction-management.com
Website: https://www.facebook.com/ReactionManagement

Genres: Alternative; Guitar based; Indie; Metal; Pop Punk; Rock; Singer-Songwriter

Joining the roster isn't a fast track to success but what we will do will set you up for a professional career in music. There are no contracts and you can stay with us for as long or short a period of time as you feel necessary. We have great contacts across the industry and have built up solid relationships with bookers, promoters, venues, PR and media not only in the UK, but across the globe.

Real Media Music
Email: info@realmediamusic.co.uk
Website: https://www.realmediamusic.co.uk
Website: https://www.facebook.com/RealMediaMusic

Represents: Artists/Bands

Genres: All types of music

International artist booking and management.

Rebel Rebel Artists
Email: nick@rebelrebelartists.co.uk
Email: nickconnett@hotmail.co.uk
Website: https://rebelrebelartistsa.wixsite.com/rebelrebelartists
Website: https://www.facebook.com/rebelrebelartists

Represents: Artists/Bands

Genres: Alternative; Electronic; Indie; Pop

Bespoke artist management / PR / bookings / consultancy. Submit through Spotify playlist, or by email.

Reckless Yes
Email: pete@recklessyes.com
Email: sarah@recklessyes.com
Website: https://recklessyes.com/artist-management/
Website: https://www.facebook.com/RecklessYes/

Represents: Artists/Bands

Genres: Acoustic; Alternative; Guitar based; Indie

Contact: Pete; Sarah

Independent record label, management and live music agency. Closed to submissions as at July 2022.

Red Afternoon Music
Email: info@redafternoonmusic.co.uk
Email: lewis@redafternoonmusic.co.uk
Website: https://www.redafternoonmusic.co.uk
Website: https://www.facebook.com/RedAfternoonMusic/

Represents: Artists/Bands

Genres: All types of music

Contact: Lewis Forrest

An Independent Record Company based in Central Scotland and London, UK. Provides label services, distribution, music publishing, specialist consultancy, artist development, artist management and live/ touring services. All genres accepted, but with a particular background in indie/ alternative, pop, EDM/house, Americana, country, jazz and R&B.

Red Grape Music
82 Chestnut Grove
New Malden
Surrey
KT3 3JS
Email: info@redgrapemusic.com
Website: https://www.redgrapemusic.com

Represents: Artists/Bands

Genres: Acoustic; Folk; Pop; Singer-Songwriter

Management company and record label based in New Malden, Surrey. Not accepting submissions as at September 2021. Check website for current status.

Revolt Artist Management
Email: demos@revoltartists.com
Website: https://www.revoltartists.com

Represents: Artists/Bands; Film / TV Composers; Lyricists; Producers; Songwriters; Studio Musicians; Studio Vocalists

Genres: Emo; Garage; Guitar based; Hardcore; Indie; Metal; Nostalgia; Pop; Punk; Rock; Rock and Roll; Singer-Songwriter; Surf

Contact: Lisa Mckeown

Artist Management and Development company based in the UK, providing exclusive worldwide representation to musicians. We offer services in artist management, social media management and artist development.

We've worked with 80's legend 'Tiffany', known for the 1987 Billboard #1 'I Think We're Alone Now', as well as 'Cellar Door Moon Crow', 'The Last Internationale', 'GUN', 'The Graveltones' and 'Silverkord' (just to name a few!)

Our artists have played Download Festival, Lollapalooza, Hellfest, Nova Rock, BST Hyde Park, Venoge Festival, Rock Werchter, Pinkpop Festival, Let's Rock 80's Festival, Forever Young Festival, Impact Festival.

Our artists have supported KISS, Rage Against The Machine, Deep Purple, The Picturebooks, Skindred.

Our artists have had their music featured in Umbrella Academy, TED, The Tonight Show Featuring Jimmy Fallon, The Masked Singer, McDonald's adverts.

Our artists have made TV appearances across the world including I'm a Celebrity Get Me Out of Here!, Strictly Come Dancing: It Takes Two, Lorraine, Loose Women, Good Morning Britain, This Morning, The Morning Show, Celebrity Boot Camp, Wogan.

Please send your music and social links by email.

Rhythmic Records Management and Production

Email: info@rhythmic-records.co.uk
Website: https://www.rhythmic-records.co.uk
Website: https://www.facebook.com/rhythmicrecordsuk

Represents: Artists/Bands

Genres: Dance; Hip-Hop; House; Pop

Contact: Zac Bikhazi

Independent record label and management company based in London. Submit query with links to music online through form on website or by email.

Richard Lipman

Email: richardlipmanfilms@gmail.com
Website: https://www.richardlipman.co
Website: https://www.facebook.com/richardlipman.co

Represents: Artists/Bands

Genres: Classical; Pop; Rock; World

Freelance filmmaker, photographer, and music manager.

Rock Artist Management (RAM)

Email: colinrockartistmgmt@aol.com
Email: bandmgmt@aol.com
Website: http://www.rockartistmanagement.com
Website: https://www.facebook.com/RAMRockArtistManagement/

Represents: Artists/Bands

Genres: Classic Rock; Blues; Pop; Rock

Contact: Peter Barton; Colin Black; Peter Hughes

Management company formed in the late eighties, specialising in retro rock, blues, and pop.

Rock Hippie Management & Music

Website: https://www.facebook.com/rockhippiem/
Website: https://twitter.com/RockHippieM

Represents: Artists/Bands; Comedians; DJs; Songwriters; Tribute Acts

Genres: All types of music

Management company based in London.

Rock People Management (RPM)
Email: terri@rockpeoplemanagement.com
Email: heidi@rockpeoplemanagement.com
Website: https://www.rockpeoplemanagement.com
Website: https://www.facebook.com/rockpeoplemanagement/

Represents: Artists/Bands

Genres: Blues; Rock

Contact: Terri Chapman; Heidi Kerr

With almost 14 years of experience in the music industry and a hands on approach, we can offer a wealth of knowledge, skills and opportunities to todays artists and bands.

Over those 14 years we have amassed a wealth of invaluable industry contacts from Radio to Press, Festivals to Merch Design and everything in between. We take immense pride and care in what we do, and always put your needs and requirements first.

Get in touch today to see how we can help you.

Rockstar Management
Email: hello@rockstar.management
Website: http://www.rockstar.management
Website: https://twitter.com/RockstarMGMT

Represents: Artists/Bands

Genres: All types of music

As an artist-centric, full-service management firm, we offer always-on support to new talent and established stars alike. We build careers from the ground up, engaging with the best in the business to empower the full scope of our clients' creative vision, amplifying their art to a global audience.

Rollover Productions
29 Beethoven Street
London
W10 4LG
Fax: +44 (0) 20 8968 1047
Email: a-r@rollover.co.uk
Website: http://www.rollover.co.uk
Website: https://www.facebook.com/RolloverMusicLondon

Represents: Artists/Bands

Genres: All types of music

Contact: Phillip Jacobs

Specialises in four areas of the music industry: studios, production, management, and publishing.

Rollover
29 Beethoven Street
London
W10 4LG
Fax: +44 (0) 20 8968 1047
Website: http://www.rollover.co.uk

Represents: Artists/Bands

Genres: All types of music

Management company based in London.

Rosier Artist Management (RAM)
Website: https://twitter.com/steverosier

Represents: Artists/Bands

Genres: Americana; Rock

Contact: Steve Rosier

UK manager focusing on Rock and Americana.

Roundface Music Management
Scotland
Email: george@roundfacemusic.com
Website: https://www.roundfacemusic.com
Website: https://www.facebook.com/RFmusicmanagement/

Represents: Artists/Bands

Genres: All types of music

Contact: George Murray

Music management company based in Scotland.

Running Media Group Ltd
Isle of Man
Website: https://www.runningmedia.com

Represents: Artists/Bands

Genres: Singer-Songwriter

Contact: Bob Miller

Artist management company based in the Isle of Man.

S&B Creative
Email: info@snbcreative.com
Website: http://www.snbcreative.com
Website: https://www.facebook.com/SnBCreative/

Represents: Artists/Bands; Film / TV Composers; Producers; Songwriters

Genres: All types of music

Talent management, record label, brand consultancy, and scores for film and TV.

Saga Entertainment
35 Berkeley Square
Mayfair
London
W1J 5BF
Email: info@sagaentertainment.tv
Website: https://www.sagaentertainment.tv
Website: http://www.facebook.com/SagaMusicUK

Represents: Artists/Bands

Genres: Electronic; Pop; Rock

Operates a production company, publishing house and record label with offices in London, England. Specialising in music management, artist development and label services.

Salvation Records
Email: thesoundofsalvation@hotmail.co.uk
Website: https://www.facebook.com/thesoundofsalvationrecords
Website: https://soundcloud.com/salvationrecords

Represents: Artists/Bands

Genres: Electronic; Garage; Psychedelic Rock; Punk

A UK based record label, management company and publisher releasing physical product "in a world of digital noise".

SAS Entertainment
Email: serena@sas-ents.com
Email: steve@sas-ents.com
Website: https://www.sas-ents.com
Website: https://www.facebook.com/SASbackstage

Represents: Artists/Bands

Genres: Americana; Dance; Indie; Pop; Rock

Contact: Steve Hughes; Serena Catapano

Offers Artist Management, Tour Management, Music Consultancy, and Event / Festival Booking.

Saviour Management
London
Email: james@svrmgmt.com
Email: jay@svrmgmt.com
Website: https://www.svrmgmt.com
Website: https://www.facebook.com/saviourmanagement

Represents: Artists/Bands

Genres: Alternative; Metal; Pop Punk

Contact: James Illsley; Jay Harris

Management company based in London. Send query via form on website.

SB Management
Greenhouse Studios
8 Mackintosh Lane
London
E9 6AB
Email: info@sb-management.com
Website: https://www.sb-management.com/
Website: https://twitter.com/sbmanagement

Represents: Artists/Bands; Producers; Songwriters

Genres: All types of music

180 UK Managers

Management company based in London and Los Angeles.

Scope Music Management
Email: info@scopemusicmanagement.com
Website: http://www.scopemusicmanagement.com
Website: https://www.facebook.com/ScopeMusicMgmt/

Represents: Artists/Bands

Genres: All types of music

Management company founded in 2012, boasting an eclectic roster of artists and bands. Send query by email with SoundCloud or YouTube links.

September Management (UK)
London
Email: info@septembermanagement.com
Website: https://septembermanagement.com

Represents: Artists/Bands; Producers; Sound Engineers

Genres: All types of music

Represents a roster of internationally renowned recording artists, producers and mix engineers who have collectively amassed 44 Grammys, 12 Brit Awards, 2 Oscars, 2 Golden Globes and sold over 100 million albums worldwide. The company has offices in London, New York and Los Angeles.

Serious
51 Kingsway Place
Sans Walk
Clerkenwell
London
EC1R 0LU
Website: https://serious.org.uk
Website: http://www.facebook.com/seriouslivemusic

Represents: Artists/Bands

Genres: Jazz; World; Contemporary

Management company based in London producing jazz, international, and contemporary music, and offering management, music publishing and the production of concerts, tours and special events. Send query via form on website, including links to music online.

74 Promotions
94 Centurion Road
Brighton
BN1 3LN
Email: andy@74promotions.com
Website: http://www.74promotions.com
Website: https://www.facebook.com/74-Promotions-181204548583646/

Represents: Artists/Bands

Genres: All types of music

Contact: Andy Hollis

Management company based in Brighton. Send demo by email or by post.

SGM Music Group Ltd
Base Studios
Unit 14
Rufford Road Trading Estate
Stourbridge
West Midlands
DY9 7ND
Email: info@sgmmusicgroup.com
Website: https://www.sgmmusicgroup.com
Website: https://www.facebook.com/sgmmusicgroup/

Represents: Artists/Bands

Genres: Pop; Rock

Contact: Scott Garrett

Management company based in Stourbridge, West Midlands. Send demos by post or send query by email with links to music online.

SGO Ltd
PO Box 2015
Salisbury
SP2 7WU
Fax: +44 (0) 1747 870678
Email: sgomusic@sgomusic.com
Website: http://www.sgomusic.com
Website: http://www.facebook.com/SGOMusic

Represents: Artists/Bands

Genres: All types of music

Contact: Stuart Ongley

Management company based in Salisbury. Send query in first instance. No unsolicited demos.

Shaw Thing Management
20 Coverdale Road
London
N11 3FG
Email: info@shawthingmanagement.com
Website: https://www.shawthingmanagement.com
Website: https://www.facebook.com/Shaw-Thing-Management-2205412639509595/?modal=admin_todo_tour

Represents: Artists/Bands

Genres: Pop

Send demo as MP3 file by email, including any additional information, such as photos etc.

Sidewinder Management Ltd
Email: sdw@sidewindermgmt.com
Website: http://www.sidewindermgmt.com

Represents: Artists/Bands

Genres: All types of music

Contact: Simon Watson

An Artist management company with over twenty five years experience managing a broad range of bands and solo artists.

Silverword Music Group
Website: https://www.silverword.co.uk

Represents: Artists/Bands

Genres: Urban; Dance; Pop; Rock; Jazz; Soul; Classical; Country; Gospel; R&B

Part of music group incorporating record label, promotion, publishing, distribution, etc.

Solar Management
Unit 10 Union Wharf
23 Wenlock Road
London
N1 7SB
Email: info@solarmanagement.co.uk
Website: https://www.solarmanagement.co.uk
Website: https://www.facebook.com/solarmanagement/

Represents: Artists/Bands; Producers

Genres: All types of music

Eexperience in producer and artist development, recording, touring, budgeting and all producer and artist contracts.

Sound Consultancy
Resound Media
PO Box 1324
Cheltenham
GL50 9EU
Email: hey@soundconsultancy.co.uk
Website: https://www.soundconsultancy.co.uk
Website: https://www.facebook.com/soundconsultancy

Represents: Artists/Bands

Genres: All types of music

Cheltenham music company offering artist development, mentoring, and promotion packages. Considers all genres, but mainly acoustic, rock, and folk.

The Soundcheck Group
29 Wardour Street
London
W1D 6PS
Email: info@thesoundcheckgroup.com
Website: https://www.thesoundcheckgroup.com
Website: https://www.facebook.com/thesoundcheckgroup1

Represents: Artists/Bands

Genres: All types of music

Contact: Daniel Hinchliffe

Has grown from a purely music PR company to an all-round PR and Management company representing pop and theatre artists as well as projects in the world of events, literary and branding.

Sounds Like A Hit Ltd
Email: info@soundslikeahit.com
Website: http://www.slahit.com

Represents: Artists/Bands

Genres: Pop; Dance; Country

Contact: Steve Crosby

Has previously worked with artists such as Steps, Dixie Chicks, and Shania Twain.

South Star Music
PO BOX 1350
Southampton
SO15 5WX
Email: admin@southstarmusic.co.uk
Website: http://www.southstarmusic.co.uk

Represents: Artists/Bands

Genres: All types of music

Based in Southampton, offers artist management and promotion, songwriting services, and studio recording, mixing, and mastering facilities.

Steve Allen Entertainments
The Coach House
163 Broadway
Peterborough
PE1 4DH
Fax: +44 (0) 1733 561854
Email: sales@sallenent.co.uk
Website: https://steveallenentertainments.co.uk
Website: https://www.facebook.com/steveallenentertainments/

Represents: Artists/Bands; Comedians; Other Entertainers; Tribute Acts

Genres: All types of music

Contact: Steve Allen

Based in Peterborough, in Cambridgeshire. Supplies entertainers and entertainments for private events and corporate occasions. Client base includes many National companies as well as most of the major Hotel Chains.

Storm5 Management
Resound Media
Brincliffe House
59 Wostenholm Road
Sheffield
S7 1LE
Email: info@storm5management.com
Website: http://www.storm5management.com
Website: https://www.facebook.com/storm5management/

Represents: Artists/Bands

Genres: All types of music

Management company based in Sheffield.

Stormcraft Music
Email: info@stormcraftmusic.com
Website: https://www.stormcraftmusic.com
Website: https://www.facebook.com/stormcraftmusic

Represents: Artists/Bands

Genres: Alternative Pop; Singer-Songwriter; Guitar based

We specialise in the management and development of up and coming talented artists.

Covering a wide range of the musical spectrum we strive to develop the careers of the next generation of original musicians.

With over 10 years worth of industry experience we are able to closely work with each artist to help shape their career and be their gateway into both the music industry and into the public eye.

Sugar House Music
Email: info@sugarhousemusic.co.uk
Email: ros@140db.co.uk
Website: https://www.sugarhousemusic.co.uk
Website: https://www.facebook.com/sugarhousemusic/

Represents: Artists/Bands

Genres: Indie; New Wave; Pop; Rock

Contact: Lee McCarthy; Ady Hall

Record Making / Music Production / Songwriting / Artist Development / Taste Makers.

Tap Music
Email: info@tapmgmt.com
Website: https://tap-music.com
Website: https://www.facebook.com/tapmusicofficial/

Represents: Artists/Bands; Producers; Songwriters

Genres: All types of music

Music management company with offices in London, Berlin, LA and Sydney.

Tape
London
Email: dangarber@taperec.com
Website: http://www.taperec.com
Website: https://twitter.com/taperec

Represents: Artists/Bands

Genres: All types of music, except: Metal; Techno

Management company with offices in London and Barcelona. Contact through form on website.

Third Bar Artist Development
C/O Oh yeah Music Centre
15-21 Gordon Street
Belfast
BT1 2LG
Email: davy@thirdbar.co.uk
Email: candice@thirdbar.co.uk
Website: http://thirdbar.co.uk
Website: https://twitter.com/thirdbarbelfast

Represents: Artists/Bands

Genres: All types of music

Contact: Davy Matchett

Artist development business based in Belfast. Send music via online file transfer system (see website).

This Is Music Ltd
408 Brickfields
37 Cremer Street
London
E2 8HD
Email: simon@thisismusicltd.com
Website: http://thisismusicltd.com
Website: https://www.soundcloud.com/this-is-music

Represents: Artists/Bands; Producers

Genres: Electronic; Underground; Indie; Pop

Contact: Simon Gold

Music company based in London and Los Angeles. Provides management and label services for artists and producers.

Tone Management
Email: hello@tonemgmt.com
Website: http://tonemgmt.com
Website: https://www.instagram.com/tonemanagement/

Represents: Artists/Bands

Genres: Metal; Rock; Pop; Post Rock; Hardcore; Punk

Management company with offices in Leeds, London, Bristol, and New York. Contact by email.

Toonteen Industries: Management & Promotions
Bury St Edmunds
Suffolk
Email: demos@toonteen.co.uk
Email: joe@toonteen.co.uk
Website: https://www.toonteen.co.uk
Website: https://www.facebook.com/toonteenAM

Represents: Artists/Bands

Genres: Acoustic Alternative Heavy Progressive Ambient Emo Hardcore Indie Metal Pop Punk Rock

Contact: Joe Weaver

Management company based in Bury St Edmunds. Promotes shows with various bands in venues all over East Anglia, but

184   UK Managers

mainly focused within Bury St Edmunds. Also manages bands and solo artists. Send query by email with links to music online. No attachments. Response not guaranteed.

Top Draw Music Management
Email: james@tdmm.co.uk
Website: https://www.facebook.com/TopDrawMusicManagement

Represents: DJs; Producers

Genres: Dance; Electronic

Contact: James Hamilton

A creative, connected and multi-faceted agency. Works with artists in electronic music, along with brands, where music, fashion and technology intersect, providing consultancy and direction.

Trak Image Music Ltd
12 Hilton Street
Manchester
M1 1JF
Email: team@heistorhit.com
Email: mgmt@heistorhit.com
Website: http://www.heistorhit.com
Website: https://www.facebook.com/heistorhit

Represents: Artists/Bands

Genres: Shoegaze; Chill; Indie; Acoustic; Alternative

Music company based in Manchester. Sending demos by email is not ideal and will not guarantee a reply. Instead, write a URL (e.g. private Soundcloud playlist) on a postcard and send by post. Everything submitted in this way will be listened to.

Transcend Music Ltd
Email: info@transcendmusic.com
Website: http://transcendmusic.com

Represents: Artists/Bands

Genres: Metal; Rock

Rock and metal management company. Offers consultancy, management and bespoke solutions for the music and entertainment industry.

Travelled Music
Email: alan@travelledmusic.co.uk
Email: ian@travelledmusic.co.uk
Website: https://www.travelledmusic.co.uk
Website: https://twitter.com/travelledmusic

Represents: Artists/Bands

Genres: Alternative; Rock; Electronic; Indie

Contact: Alan Thompson; Ian Thompson

Music company offering artist and tour management, websites and social media, direct-to-fan marketing, bookings and promotions, event management.

Trinifold Management
12 Oval Road
London
NW1 7DH
Fax: +44 (0) 20 7419 4325
Website: https://www.trinifold.co.uk
Website: https://www.instagram.com/trinifold

Represents: Artists/Bands

Genres: All types of music

Submit demo via form on website.

Tsunami Music
20–22 Wenlock Road
London
N1 7GU
Email: demos@tsunamimusic.com
Email: hello@tsunamimusic.com
Website: http://www.tsunamimusic.com

Represents: Film / TV Composers; Supervisors

Genres: All types of music

Provides composed music for film, TV, video games, etc.

UAC Management
Email: hristo@uacmanagement.co.uk
Email: thrasher@uacmanagement.co.uk
Website: https://uacmanagement.co.uk
Website: https://www.facebook.com/uacmanagement/

Represents: Artists/Bands

Genres: All types of music

Contact: Hristo Penchev; Kevin Thrasher

Designed and projected to perform as a world class management and consulting agency and to establish strong capacity and potential to provide high-level of professional expertise in the different aspects of the entertainment industry.

Underplay
Email: chrisbellam@underplay.co.uk
Website: https://www.underplay.co.uk
Website: https://www.instagram.com/u_n_d_e_r_p_l_a_y/

Represents: Artists/Bands

Genres: All types of music

Contact: Chris Bellam

Artist management and promotion.

Up On Mars
Brighton
Email: hello@uponmars.com
Website: https://uponmars.com
Website: https://www.linkedin.com/company/up-on-mars/

Represents: Artists/Bands

Genres: Electronic; Pop

Artist management company based in Brighton. Send demos via form on website.

Uplifted Music Management
Manchester
M41
Website: https://www.upliftedmusicmanagement.co.uk

Represents: Artists/Bands; DJs

Genres: Dance; Electronic

Electronic / Dance artist management, based in Manchester.

Upside Management Ltd
18 Cherrington Gardens
Stourbridge
West Midlands
DY9 0QB
Email: denise@upsideuk.com
Email: simon@upsideuk.com
Website: https://www.upsideuk.com
Website: https://www.facebook.com/upsideuk

Represents: Artists/Bands

Genres: Dance; Pop

Contact: Denise Beighton; Simon Jones

Management company based in Stourbridge, West Midlands.

Various Artists Management
37 Lonsdale Road
London
NW6 6RA
Email: info@variousartistsmanagement.com
Website: https://variousartistsmanagement.com
Website: https://www.facebook.com/variousartistsmanagement

Represents: Artists/Bands; Producers

Genres: All types of music

Management company with offices in London, Los Angeles, and Hong Kong.

Verdigris Management
Email: info@verdigrismanagement.com
Website: https://www.verdigrismanagement.com

Represents: Artists/Bands; Producers; Sound Engineers

Genres: All types of music

A full service management company with a roster of Mercury and Grammy-nominated artists, producers and mixers.

Viral Music
Brunswick Mill
Manchester
M40 7EZ
Email: info@viralmusicuk.com
Website: https://www.viralmusicuk.com
Website: https://www.facebook.com/ViralMusicUK/

186 UK Managers

Represents: Artists/Bands; DJs

Genres: Dance; House; Commercial

Management company providing conservatoire-trained, professionally-accomplished musicians to the nightlife entertainment industry, as well as for a wide range of other events, including weddings and private/corporate functions.

Virtually Pop
VO2, 22 Jordan Street
Baltic Creative Quarter
Liverpool
Merseyside
L1 0BP
Email: info@virtuallypop.com
Website: https://www.virtuallypop.com/contact
Website: https://www.facebook.com/virtuallypopmusicgroup

Represents: Artists/Bands

Genres: Acoustic; Folk; Jazz; Pop; Rock

Music company based in Liverpool, offering Artist Management, Tour Promotion and Publishing.

We Like Oliver
London
Email: olly@welikeoliver.com
Website: https://welikeoliver.com
Website: https://www.facebook.com/welikeoliver

Represents: Artists/Bands

Genres: All types of music

Contact: Olly Andrews

Offers "Complete digital Marketing & IT Solutions for your creative business".

The Weird and the Wonderful
London
Email: info@theweirdandthewonderful.com
Website: https://theweirdandthewonderfulofficial.tumblr.com/
Website: https://www.facebook.com/theweirdandthewonderfulofficial

Represents: Artists/Bands

Genres: Electronic; Folk; House; Techno; Urban

An international multi-discipline music and arts talent consultancy and management company.

Wildlife Entertainment Ltd
Email: info@wildlife-entertainment.com
Website: https://www.wildlife-entertainment.com

Represents: Artists/Bands

Genres: Indie; Rock; R&B

Management company based in South West London. Send query by email and follow up with demo upon request.

XIX Entertainment Ltd
259a Pavilion Road
London
SW1X 0BP
Email: info@xixentertainment.com
Website: https://www.xixentertainment.com
Website: https://twitter.com/XIX_NEWS

Represents: Artists/Bands

Genres: All types of music

Management company responsible for such shows as American Idol and Little Britain USA. Has offices in London and Los Angeles.

XVII Music Group
Brighton
Email: info@xviimusic.com
Website: https://xviimusic.com
Website: https://soundcloud.com/xviimusicgroup

Represents: Artists/Bands

Genres: All types of music

Artists development and record label based in Brighton. Send demos by email.

Access more listings online at www.musicsocket.com

Yearone Management
Email: pharris@yearonesm.com
Website: https://www.yearonesm.com
Website: https://www.facebook.com/yearonesm/

Represents: Artists/Bands

Genres: All types of music

Looking for any sort of artist either up and coming or established for us to take to the next level. Contact via contact form on website.

Yellowbrick Music
Email: info@yellowbrickmusic.com
Email: meredith@yellowbrickmusic.com
Website: https://yellowbrickmusic.com
Website: https://twitter.com/YellBrickMusic

Represents: Artists/Bands

Genres: All types of music

Label service company based in London, offering artists a creative range of support and tools. Send query by email or via online contact form.

YMU Group
Clifton Works
23 Grove Park Terrace
Chiswick
London
W4 3QE

180 Great Portland Street
London
W1W 5QZ

3rd Floor Colwyn Chambers
19 York Street
Manchester
M2 3BA
Email: enquiries@ymugroup.com
Website: https://www.ymugroup.com

Represents: Artists/Bands; DJs; Producers; Songwriters

Genres: Alternative Rock; Dance; Electronic; Pop

Management company with offices in London, Manchester, Washington DC, California, and New York.

Young Guns
2 Princes Street
Mayfair
London
W1B 2LB
Email: hello@younggunsgroup.com
Website: https://www.younggunsgroup.com
Website: https://www.facebook.com/YoungGunsLtd

Represents: Artists/Bands; Producers; Studio Musicians

Genres: Classical; Jazz; Pop; Fusion

A music agency that creates acts and sources musicians from all genres for the events, record and TV industries.

Youthquake
Email: contact@youthquake.london
Website: https://youthquake.london/
Website: https://www.instagram.com/youthquakemgmt/

Represents: Artists/Bands

Genres: Alternative; Guitar based

Artist management company based in Isleworth.

Z Management
Email: alex@zman.co.uk
Website: http://www.zman.co.uk
Website: https://www.facebook.com/zmanagementuk

Represents: Artists/Bands; DJs; Producers; Songwriters

Genres: All types of music

Management company based in London, handling song writers, producers, mixers, remixers, and artists. Send demo by email.

Zero Myth
Website: https://www.zeromyth.co.uk
Website: https://twitter.com/ZeroMythUK

Represents: Artists/Bands

Genres: Alternative; Pop; Rock

A creative music management company, specialising in artist development and project management. Aims to create sustainable artist led campaigns by managing strategic development, distribution and partnerships. Offers fixed-fee consultation sessions.

Canadian Managers

For the most up-to-date listings of these and hundreds of other managers, visit https://www.musicsocket.com/managers

*To claim your **free** access to the site, please see the back of this book.*

Bedlam Music Management
290 Gerrard St East
Toronto, ON M5A 2G4

LOS ANGELES
4525 Russell Ave #1
Los Angeles CA 90027

NASHVILLE
1300 Clinton St, Suite 205
Nashville, TN 37203
Email: info@bedlammusicmgt.com
Website: http://www.bedlammusicmgt.com

Represents: Artists/Bands

Genres: All types of music

A full service artist management company based in Toronto, Canada, with offices in Los Angeles and Nashville.

Bruce Allen Talent
#500-425 Carrall Street
Vancouver, BC
V6B 6E3
Fax: +1 (604) 688-7118
Email: info@bruceallen.com
Website: https://www.bruceallen.com

Represents: Artists/Bands; Producers

Genres: All types of music

Contact: Bruce Allen

Talent agency based in Vancouver, British Columbia. Not accepting unsolicited material as at July 2021.

Coalition Music
1731 Lawrence Ave East
Toronto, Ontario, M1R 2X7
Fax: +1 (866) 206-6370
Email: info@coalitionmusic.com
Website: https://www.coalitionmusic.com
Website: https://www.facebook.com/CoalitionMUS

Represents: Artists/Bands

Genres: Contemporary; Indie; Pop; Rock; Singer-Songwriter; Alternative; Jazz; Punk; R&B; Rap; Hip-Hop

Send query and links to music online via submission form on website.

Feeling Productions, Inc.
1131A Leslie St
North York, ON, M3C 2J6
Website: https://www.celinedion.com

Represents: Artists/Bands

Genres: Pop

Management company based in Ontario.

Macklam Feldman Management
#200 – 1505 West 2nd Avenue
Vancouver, BC
V6H 3Y4
Email: info@mfmgt.com
Website: http://www.mfmgt.com
Website: https://twitter.com/MFMGT

Represents: Artists/Bands; Producers

Genres: Pop; Rock; Jazz; World; Alternative; Indie

Contact: Sam Feldman; Steve Macklam

Management company based in Vancouver, Canada. Send demos by email with links to music online (soundcloud, spotify, etc.).

Nettwerk Management
1675 West 2nd Ave, 2nd Floor
Vancouver, BC. V6J 1H3
Email: info@nettwerk.com
Website: http://www.nettwerk.com

Represents: Artists/Bands; Film / TV Composers; Producers; Songwriters; Sound Engineers; Studio Technicians

Genres: Contemporary; Christian; Electronic; Folk; Indie; Latin; Pop; Punk; Rap; Rock; Hip-Hop; Dance; Singer-Songwriter

Music company based in Vancouver, Canada (head office), with other offices in the US and Europe. Includes label, management, and publishing arms.

Talk's Cheap Management
Website: https://talks-cheap.com/contact
Website: https://www.facebook.com/Voivod

Represents: Artists/Bands

Genres: Metal; Punk; Hardcore; Rock; Roots

Management company based in Canada.

Managers Index

This section lists managers by their genres, with directions to the section of the book where the full listing can be found.

You can create your own customised lists of managers using different combinations of these subject areas, plus over a dozen other criteria, instantly online at https://www.musicsocket.com.

*To claim your **free** access to the site, please see the back of this book.*

All types of music
!K7 (*UK*)
360 Artist Development (*UK*)
4 Tunes Ltd (*UK*)
7pm Management (*UK*)
A&R Factory (*UK*)
ACA Music & Entertainment (*US*)
Aesthetic V (*US*)
AirMTM (*UK*)
Amber Artists (*UK*)
American Artiste (UK) (*UK*)
Amour:Music (*UK*)
AMW Group Inc. (*US*)
Anger Management (*UK*)
The Animal Farm (*UK*)
APA (Agency for the Performing Arts) (*US*)
Artistes International Representation (AIR) Ltd (*UK*)
ASM Talent (*UK*)
ATC Management (*UK*)
Autonomy Music Group (*UK*)
Avenoir Records (*UK*)
AWA Entertainments (*UK*)
Backer Entertainment (*US*)
Backstage Entertainment (*US*)
Bedlam Music Management (*Can*)
Big Hug Management (*UK*)
Big Life Management (*UK*)
Big Noise (*US*)
BiGiAM Promotions & Management (*UK*)
Bill Silva Management (*US*)
Black Fox Management (*UK*)
BLOCS (*UK*)
Blue Raincoat Music (*UK*)
Brian Yeates Associates Ltd (*UK*)
Bruce Allen Talent (*Can*)
Bsquared MGMT (*US*)
Bulldozer Media Ltd (*UK*)
C Management (*US*)
Catalyst Management (*UK*)
Celebrity Enterprises (CE) Inc. (*US*)
Century Artists Management Agency, LLC (*US*)
Closer Artists Management & Publishing (*UK*)
CMP Entertainment (*UK*)
Conchord (*UK*)
Covert Talent Management (*UK*)
Creative Artists Agency (CAA) (*US*)
Creative Sounds UK (*UK*)
Creeme Entertainments (*UK*)
Crockford Management (*UK*)
Crush Music Media Management (*US*)
Culler Talent Management (*US*)
Cumberland Music Collective (*US*)
Danny Brittain Band Management (DBBM) (*UK*)
Darkspin Music Management (*UK*)
Darren Adam (*UK*)

Claim your free access to www.musicsocket.com: See p.211

Managers Index

Deltasonic Records (*UK*)
Deluxxe Management (*UK*)
Deuce Management & Promotion (*UK*)
Discovering Arts Music Group (DAMG) (*UK*)
DMF Music Ltd (*UK*)
Dog & Pony Industries (*US*)
Steve Draper Entertainments (*UK*)
Duroc Media (*UK*)
East Coast Entertainment (ECE) (*US*)
Elevation Group Inc. (*US*)
Empire Artist Management (*UK*)
End of the Trail Creative (*UK*)
Everybody's Management Ltd (*UK*)
Fave Sounds (*UK*)
Feraltone (*UK*)
Ferocious Talent (*UK*)
Flat Cap Music (*UK*)
Friends Vs Music Ltd (*UK*)
Funzalo Records (*US*)
Gary Stamler Management (*US*)
Gayle Enterprises, Inc. (*US*)
The Gorfaine/Schwartz Agency, Inc. (*US*)
Grizzly Management (*UK*)
Hal Carter Organisation (*UK*)
Hannah Management (*UK*)
Happy House Management & Marketing Services (*UK*)
Heard and Seen (*UK*)
Hot House Music Ltd (*UK*)
Hot Vox (*UK*)
Howard Rosen Promotion, Inc. (*US*)
ie:music (*UK*)
Impact Management (*UK*)
In Touch Entertainment (*US*)
Indevine (*UK*)
Innate - Music Ltd (*UK*)
International Creative Management (ICM) Partners (*US*)
Intune Addicts (*UK*)
Invasion Group, Ltd (*US*)
JA Artist Management (*UK*)
James Joseph Music Management (*UK*)
James Joseph Music Management LA (*US*)
Jampol Artist Management (*US*)
Jay Anthony's Next Level Booking and Entertainment Agency, LLC (*US*)
Kaleidoscope (*UK*)
Karma Artists Music LLP (*UK*)
KBH Entertainment (*US*)
KRMB Management & Consultancy (*UK*)
LA Personal Development (*US*)
Laissez Faire Club (*UK*)
Larro Media (*US*)
Leonard Business Management (*US*)
Liquid Management (*UK*)
MaDa Music Entertainment (*UK*)
Madison House Inc. (*US*)
Major Labl (*UK*)
Manners McDade Artist Management (*UK*)
Manta Ray Music (*UK*)
MBM (Music Business Management Ltd) (*UK*)
The MGMT Company (*US*)
Million Dollar Artists (*US*)
MJM Agency (*UK*)
Monotone, Inc. (*US*)
Mother Artist Management (*UK*)
MSH Management (*US*)
Murphy to Manteo (MTM) Music Management (*US*)
Music by Design (*UK*)
Music City Artists (*US*)
Nettwerk Management UK (*UK*)
New Heights Entertainment (*US*)
New Level Music Management (*UK*)
New Outlaw (*UK*)
NewLevel Management (*UK*)
No Half Measures Ltd (*UK*)
One Fifteen (*UK*)
141a Management (*UK*)
140dB Management Limited (*UK*)
Open All Nite Entertainment (*US*)
Pacific Talent (*US*)
Paper House Music (*UK*)
Paradigm Talent Agency (*US*)
Persistent Management (*US*)
Petty Music Management (*UK*)
Pieces of 8 Music (*UK*)
Platinum Star Management (*US*)
PMS Music Management (*UK*)
Pretty Lights (*US*)
Primary Wave (*US*)
Program Music, Ltd (*UK*)
Prolifica Management (*UK*)
Psycho Management Company (*UK*)
Push Music Management (*UK*)
Quest Management (*UK*)
Radius Music Ltd (*UK*)
Real Media Music (*UK*)
Red Afternoon Music (*UK*)
Regime Seventy-Two (*US*)
Riot Squad (*US*)
Rock Hippie Management & Music (*UK*)
Rockstar Management (*UK*)
Rollover Productions (*UK*)
Rollover (*UK*)
Roundface Music Management (*UK*)

Access more listings online at www.musicsocket.com

Managers Index

S&B Creative (*UK*)
SB Management (*UK*)
Scope Music Management (*UK*)
Selak Entertainment, Inc. (*US*)
September Management (UK) (*UK*)
September Management (US) (*US*)
74 Promotions (*UK*)
SGO Ltd (*UK*)
Sherrod Artist Management (*US*)
Sidewinder Management Ltd (*UK*)
SKH Music (*US*)
SMC Artists (*US*)
Solar Management (*UK*)
Solid Music Company (*US*)
Sound Consultancy (*UK*)
The Soundcheck Group (*UK*)
South Star Music (*UK*)
Steve Allen Entertainments (*UK*)
Stiletto Entertainment (*US*)
Storm5 Management (*UK*)
Take Out Management (*US*)
Talent Source (*US*)
Tap Music (*UK*)
Tape (*UK*)
Tenth Street Entertainment (*US*)
That's Entertainment International Inc. (TEI Entertainment) (*US*)
Third Bar Artist Development (*UK*)
Threee (*US*)
Tom Callahan & Associates (TCA) (*US*)
A Train Entertainment (*US*)
Trinifold Management (*UK*)
Tsunami Entertainment (*US*)
Tsunami Music (*UK*)
UAC Management (*UK*)
Uncle Booking (*US*)
Underplay (*UK*)
United Talent Agency (*US*)
Universal Attractions Agency (*US*)
Various Artists Management (*UK*)
Velvet Hammer Music & Management Group (*US*)
Verdigris Management (*UK*)
Walker Entertainment Group (*US*)
We Like Oliver (*UK*)
Whiplash PR and Management (*US*)
Wolfson Entertainment, Inc. (*US*)
Worlds End Management (*US*)
XIX Entertainment Ltd (*UK*)
XVII Music Group (*UK*)
Yearone Management (*UK*)
Yellowbrick Music (*UK*)
Z Management (*UK*)

Acoustic
A2E - Artists 2 Events (*UK*)

ADSRecords (*UK*)
Aspire Music Management (*UK*)
Bandzmedia (*UK*)
Dawson Breed Music (*UK*)
Fat City Artists (*US*)
HardKnockLife Entertainment (*US*)
Heist or Hit (*UK*)
Hello! Booking, Inc. (*US*)
Jelli Records (*UK*)
Kari Estrin Management & Consulting (*US*)
Moneypenny (*UK*)
Music Media Events (*UK*)
Nashville Records, LLC (*US*)
Offbeat Management (*UK*)
Opre Roma (*UK*)
Outrider Music, LLC (*US*)
Park Promotions (*UK*)
Pillar Artists (*UK*)
Purple Rhino Music (*US*)
Reckless Yes (*UK*)
Red Grape Music (*UK*)
TAC Music Management (*US*)
Toonteen Industries: Management & Promotions (*UK*)
Trak Image Music Ltd (*UK*)
Virtually Pop (*UK*)

Alternative
ADSRecords (*UK*)
Advanced Alternative Media (AAM) (*US*)
Allure Media Entertainment Group (*US*)
Apex Talent Group (*US*)
Arlon Music (*UK*)
Associated London Management (*UK*)
Bad Apple Music Group (*UK*)
Big Hassle Management (*US*)
Bitchin' Entertainment (*US*)
Burgess World Co. (*US*)
BUT! Management (*UK*)
CEC Management (*US*)
Coalition Music (*Can*)
Craft Management (*UK*)
DDB Productions (*US*)
Deep South Artist Management (*US*)
Dissention Records + Artist Management (*UK*)
Don't Try (*UK*)
Down For Life (*UK*)
Dreamboat Management (*UK*)
East City (*UK*)
Elephant Management (*UK*)
F&G Management (*UK*)
Feed Your Head (*UK*)
5B Artist Management (*US*)
Flow State Music (*UK*)

Managers Index

FP / Fantastic Plastic Music (*UK*)
Freaks R Us (*UK*)
Ganbei Records (*UK*)
Golden Arm (*UK*)
Goo Music Management Ltd (*UK*)
Hardin Entertainment (*US*)
Heist or Hit (*UK*)
Holier than Thou (HTT) Music (*UK*)
Hope Management (*UK*)
Hornblow Group USA, Inc. (*US*)
Ignition Management (*UK*)
Impact Artist Management (*US*)
JBLS Management (*UK*)
Jude Street Management (*UK*)
Key Music Management (*UK*)
Kuper Personal Management (*US*)
Listen to This Management (*UK*)
Loggins Promotion (*US*)
Lonewolf Talent Management (*UK*)
Macklam Feldman Management (*Can*)
Metal Music Bookings (*UK*)
MOB Agency (*US*)
Moksha Management (*UK*)
Monqui Presents (*US*)
Music Gallery International (*US*)
Music Media Events (*UK*)
Offbeat Management (*UK*)
Orean Music Ltd (*UK*)
Outrider Music, LLC (*US*)
Pillar Artists (*UK*)
Position Music (*US*)
Prodigal Son Entertainment (*US*)
Purple Rhino Music (*US*)
Q Prime Management, Inc. (*US*)
Raw Power Management (*UK*)
Reaction Management (*UK*)
Rebel Rebel Artists (*UK*)
Reckless Yes (*UK*)
Russell Carter Artist Management (*US*)
Saviour Management (*UK*)
Semaphore Mgmt & Consulting (*US*)
Silva Artist Management (SAM) (*US*)
Steven Scharf Entertainment (SSE) (*US*)
Stormcraft Music (*UK*)
Strike up the Brand (*US*)
TAC Music Management (*US*)
Toonteen Industries: Management & Promotions (*UK*)
Trak Image Music Ltd (*UK*)
Travelled Music (*UK*)
Trunk Bass Entertainment (*US*)
Union Entertainment Group (*US*)
Vector Management (*US*)
YMU Group (*UK*)
Youthquake (*UK*)

Zero Myth (*UK*)
Ambient
Bitchin' Entertainment (*US*)
Hot Gem (*UK*)
Lonewolf Talent Management (*UK*)
Offbeat Management (*UK*)
Outrider Music, LLC (*US*)
Toonteen Industries: Management & Promotions (*UK*)
Tuscan Sun Music (*US*)
Americana
Aguia Music (*UK*)
Bitchin' Entertainment (*US*)
Brighthelmstone Promotions (*UK*)
Brilliant Productions (*US*)
CEC Management (*US*)
Dawson Breed Music (*UK*)
Deep South Artist Management (*US*)
Grassy Hill Entertainment (*US*)
Hard Head Management (*US*)
Hardin Entertainment (*US*)
Kari Estrin Management & Consulting (*US*)
Kuper Personal Management (*US*)
Loggins Promotion (*US*)
Mike's Artist Management (*US*)
Moneypenny (*UK*)
Music Gallery International (*US*)
Myriad Artists (*US*)
Nashville Records, LLC (*US*)
Opre Roma (*UK*)
Purple Rhino Music (*US*)
Rosier Artist Management (RAM) (*UK*)
Russell Carter Artist Management (*US*)
SAS Entertainment (*UK*)
Steven Scharf Entertainment (SSE) (*US*)
TAC Music Management (*US*)
Vector Management (*US*)
Atmospheric
Outrider Music, LLC (*US*)
Semaphore Mgmt & Consulting (*US*)
Avant-Garde
Semaphore Mgmt & Consulting (*US*)
Black Metal
Offbeat Management (*UK*)
Purple Rhino Music (*US*)
Black Origin
Purple Rhino Music (*US*)
Blue Beat
Purple Rhino Music (*US*)
Blues
A2E - Artists 2 Events (*UK*)
Act 1 Entertainment (*US*)
Artist Representation and Management (ARM) Entertainment (*US*)

Access more listings online at www.musicsocket.com

Big Bear Music (*UK*)
Bitchin' Entertainment (*US*)
Blind Ambition Management, Ltd (*US*)
Brilliant Productions (*US*)
Burgess World Co. (*US*)
Cantaloupe Music Productions, Inc. (*US*)
CEC Management (*US*)
Collin Artists (*US*)
Concerted Efforts (*US*)
Delta Groove Music, Inc. (*US*)
Emcee Artist Management (*US*)
Fat City Artists (*US*)
Fleming Artists (*US*)
Gold Mountain Entertainment (*US*)
Hardin Entertainment (*US*)
Harmony Artists (*US*)
Impact Artist Management (*US*)
The Kurland Agency (*US*)
Max Bernard Management (*US*)
Myriad Artists (*US*)
Offbeat Management (*UK*)
Q Prime Management, Inc. (*US*)
Red Light Management (RLM) (*US*)
Rock Artist Management (RAM) (*UK*)
Rock People Management (RPM) (*UK*)
Ron Rainey Management Inc. (*US*)
Russell Carter Artist Management (*US*)
Sterling Artist Management (*US*)
Steven Scharf Entertainment (SSE) (*US*)
TAC Music Management (*US*)
Union Entertainment Group (*US*)
Universal Tone Management (*US*)
Val's Artist Management (VAM) (*US*)
Westwood Music Group (*US*)

Break Beat
Finger Lickin' Management (*UK*)
Nexus Artist Management (*US*)

Celtic
A2E - Artists 2 Events (*UK*)
Fat City Artists (*US*)
Purple Rhino Music (*US*)
Worldsound, LLC (*US*)

Chill
Involved Management (*UK*)
Offbeat Management (*UK*)
Purple Rhino Music (*US*)
Trak Image Music Ltd (*UK*)

Christian
25 Artist Agency (*US*)
The Brokaw Company (*US*)
Deep South Artist Management (*US*)
Hardin Entertainment (*US*)
Jeff Roberts & Associates (*US*)
Nashville Records, LLC (*US*)
Nettwerk Management (*US*)

Nettwerk Management (*Can*)
Prodigal Son Entertainment (*US*)
Proper Management (*US*)
Red Light Management (RLM) (*US*)

Classic
Act 1 Entertainment (*US*)
Arslanian & Associates, Inc. (*US*)
Artist Representation and Management (ARM) Entertainment (*US*)
Big Beat Productions, Inc. (*US*)
Entertainment Services International (*US*)
IMG Artists (*US*)
Michael Anthony's Electric Events (*US*)
Moneypenny (*UK*)
Rock Artist Management (RAM) (*UK*)
Suncoast Music Management (*US*)
TAC Music Management (*US*)

Classical
American International Artists, Inc. (*US*)
Askonas Holt Ltd (*UK*)
BBA Management & Booking (*US*)
Bitchin' Entertainment (*US*)
Crossfire (*UK*)
Dawn Elder Management (*US*)
Domo Music Group Management (*US*)
Intertalent Rights Group (*UK*)
Jude Street Management (*UK*)
Opus 3 Artists (*US*)
Purple Rhino Music (*US*)
PVA Management Ltd (*UK*)
Richard Lipman (*UK*)
Silverword Music Group (*UK*)
Val's Artist Management (VAM) (*US*)
Young Guns (*UK*)

Club
Purple Rhino Music (*US*)

Commercial
Create Management (*UK*)
Crown Talent & Media Group (*UK*)
Freedom Management (*UK*)
Handshake Ltd. (*UK*)
Insomnia Music UK (*UK*)
Purple Rhino Music (*US*)
TAC Music Management (*US*)
Viral Music (*UK*)

Contemporary
Amour:Music (*UK*)
Big Beat Productions, Inc. (*US*)
Black Dot Management (*US*)
Booking Entertainment (*US*)
Chapman & Co. Management (*US*)
Coalition Music (*Can*)
Collin Artists (*US*)
David Belenzon Management, Inc. (*US*)
Domo Music Group Management (*US*)

Managers Index

Fleming Artists (US)
Gold Mountain Entertainment (US)
Hardin Entertainment (US)
Impact Artist Management (US)
Magus Entertainment Inc. (US)
MBK Entertainment (US)
Michael Hausman Artist Management Inc. (US)
MM Music Agency (US)
Moksha Management (UK)
Nettwerk Management (US)
Nettwerk Management (Can)
Purple Rhino Music (US)
Riot Artists (US)
Ron Rainey Management Inc. (US)
Russell Carter Artist Management (US)
Serious (UK)
Spot Light Entertainment, Inc. (US)
Stiefel Entertainment (US)
Val's Artist Management (VAM) (US)
Vector Management (US)

Country
Act 1 Entertainment (US)
Aguia Music (UK)
American Artists Entertainment Group (US)
Artist Representation and Management (ARM) Entertainment (US)
Big Beat Productions, Inc. (US)
Bitchin' Entertainment (US)
Brick Wall Management (US)
The Brokaw Company (US)
Bulletproof Artist Management (US)
Case Entertainment Group Inc. (US)
Deep South Artist Management (US)
Fat City Artists (US)
Hardin Entertainment (US)
Hello! Booking, Inc. (US)
Impact Artist Management (US)
Listen to This Management (UK)
Loggins Promotion (US)
Lupo Entertainment (US)
Maine Road Management (US)
Major Bob Music, Inc. (US)
Mascioli Entertainment (US)
McGhee Entertainment (US)
Michael Anthony's Electric Events (US)
Modern Management (US)
Moneypenny (UK)
Monqui Presents (US)
Morris Higham Management (US)
Nashville Records, LLC (US)
Pathfinder Management (US)
Prodigal Son Entertainment (US)
Purple Rhino Music (US)

Red Light Management (RLM) (US)
Rick Alter Management (RAM) (US)
Ron Rainey Management Inc. (US)
Silverword Music Group (UK)
Sounds Like A Hit Ltd (UK)
TAC Music Management (US)
Third Coast Talent (US)
TKO Artist Management (US)
Union Entertainment Group (US)
Val's Artist Management (VAM) (US)
Vector Management (US)
Westwood Music Group (US)

Dance
2-Tone Entertainment (2TE) (UK)
Apex Talent Group (US)
AuthorityMGMT (UK)
Celebrity Talent Agency Inc. (US)
Crossfire (UK)
DEF (Deutsch Englische Freundschaft) (UK)
Defenders Ent (UK)
East City (UK)
F&G Management (UK)
Feed Your Head (UK)
Finger Lickin' Management (UK)
Flow State Music (UK)
Fruition Music (UK)
Graphite Media (UK)
Hardin Entertainment (US)
Hope Management (UK)
Hot Gem (UK)
House of Us (UK)
La Rock Entertainment (UK)
Loggins Promotion (US)
Michael Anthony's Electric Events (US)
Moksha Management (UK)
Nettwerk Management (US)
Nettwerk Management (Can)
Orean Music Ltd (UK)
Ornadel Management (UK)
Perfect Havoc Ltd (UK)
Position Music (US)
Purple Rhino Music (US)
Red Light Management (RLM) (US)
Rhythmic Records Management and Production (UK)
SAS Entertainment (UK)
Silverword Music Group (UK)
Sounds Like A Hit Ltd (UK)
Spectrum Talent Agency (US)
Stiefel Entertainment (US)
Top Draw Music Management (UK)
Uplifted Music Management (UK)
Upside Management Ltd (UK)
Val's Artist Management (VAM) (US)

Access more listings online at www.musicsocket.com

Managers Index 197

Viral Music (*UK*)
YMU Group (*UK*)
Deep Funk
Purple Rhino Music (*US*)
Disco
Big Beat Productions, Inc. (*US*)
Perfect Havoc Ltd (*UK*)
Suncoast Music Management (*US*)
Doom
Offbeat Management (*UK*)
Drum and Bass
OnDaBeat Talent Management (*UK*)
Dubstep
Nexus Artist Management (*US*)
Electronic
AJM (*UK*)
Apex Talent Group (*US*)
AprilSeven Music (*UK*)
Bitchin' Entertainment (*US*)
CEC Management (*US*)
DEF (Deutsch Englische Freundschaft) (*UK*)
F&G Management (*UK*)
Feed Your Head (*UK*)
Finger Lickin' Management (*UK*)
Flow State Music (*UK*)
Freaks R Us (*UK*)
From the Whitehouse (*UK*)
Graphite Media (*UK*)
Hard Head Management (*US*)
Hardin Entertainment (*US*)
Holier than Thou (HTT) Music (*UK*)
Hot Gem (*UK*)
HQ Familia (*UK*)
Humans & Other Animals (*UK*)
Involved Management (*UK*)
JBLS Management (*UK*)
La Rock Entertainment (*UK*)
Lucky Number Music Limited (*UK*)
Magus Entertainment Inc. (*US*)
Moksha Management (*UK*)
Music + Art Management (*US*)
Nettwerk Management (*US*)
Nettwerk Management (*Can*)
New Champion Management (*UK*)
Nexus Artist Management (*US*)
OnDaBeat Talent Management (*UK*)
Orean Music Ltd (*UK*)
Outrider Music, LLC (*US*)
Position Music (*US*)
Purple Rhino Music (*US*)
Rebel Rebel Artists (*UK*)
Red Light Management (RLM) (*US*)
Saga Entertainment (*UK*)
Salvation Records (*UK*)

Semaphore Mgmt & Consulting (*US*)
This Is Music Ltd (*UK*)
Top Draw Music Management (*UK*)
Travelled Music (*UK*)
Up On Mars (*UK*)
Uplifted Music Management (*UK*)
Waxploitation (*US*)
The Weird and the Wonderful (*UK*)
YMU Group (*UK*)
Emo
Music Gallery International (*US*)
Outrider Music, LLC (*US*)
Purple Rhino Music (*US*)
Revolt Artist Management (*UK*)
Toonteen Industries: Management & Promotions (*UK*)
Ethnic
Domo Music Group Management (*US*)
Purple Rhino Music (*US*)
Experimental
Bitchin' Entertainment (*US*)
F&G Management (*UK*)
Freaks R Us (*UK*)
Hot Gem (*UK*)
Music + Art Management (*US*)
Purple Rhino Music (*US*)
Semaphore Mgmt & Consulting (*US*)
Extreme
Purple Rhino Music (*US*)
Folk
21st Century Artists, Inc. (*US*)
Aguia Music (*UK*)
Bitchin' Entertainment (*US*)
Blind Ambition Management, Ltd (*US*)
Brighthelmstone Promotions (*UK*)
Bulletproof Artist Management (*US*)
Case Entertainment Group Inc. (*US*)
Concerted Efforts (*US*)
Dawson Breed Music (*UK*)
DCA Productions (*US*)
Domo Music Group Management (*US*)
Fat City Artists (*US*)
Fleming Artists (*US*)
From the Whitehouse (*UK*)
Front Room Songs (*UK*)
Ganbei Records (*UK*)
Gold Mountain Entertainment (*US*)
Grassy Hill Entertainment (*US*)
Hardin Entertainment (*US*)
Hello! Booking, Inc. (*US*)
Humans & Other Animals (*UK*)
IMG Artists (*US*)
Impact Artist Management (*US*)
Jelli Records (*UK*)

Claim your free access to **www.musicsocket.com**: *See p.211*

Managers Index

Kari Estrin Management & Consulting (*US*)
Kuper Personal Management (*US*)
Maine Road Management (*US*)
Mike's Artist Management (*US*)
Music Media Events (*UK*)
Myriad Artists (*US*)
Nettwerk Management (*US*)
Nettwerk Management (*Can*)
New Champion Management (*UK*)
NSI Management (*US*)
Off the Chart Promotions (*UK*)
Opre Roma (*UK*)
Park Promotions (*UK*)
Pathfinder Management (*US*)
Q Prime Management, Inc. (*US*)
Red Grape Music (*UK*)
Rick Alter Management (RAM) (*US*)
Russell Carter Artist Management (*US*)
Steven Scharf Entertainment (SSE) (*US*)
TAC Music Management (*US*)
Tractor Beam Managing & Consulting (*US*)
Val's Artist Management (VAM) (*US*)
Variety Artists International (*US*)
Vector Management (*US*)
Virtually Pop (*UK*)
The Weird and the Wonderful (*UK*)
Worldsound, LLC (*US*)

Funk
Bitchin' Entertainment (*US*)
Fat City Artists (*US*)
Nexus Artist Management (*US*)
Plus Music (*UK*)
Purple Rhino Music (*US*)
Pyramid Entertainment Group (*US*)
Red Entertainment Agency (*US*)
TAC Music Management (*US*)

Funky
Purple Rhino Music (*US*)
TAC Music Management (*US*)

Fusion
Moksha Management (*UK*)
Purple Rhino Music (*US*)
TAC Music Management (*US*)
Young Guns (*UK*)

Garage
Music Gallery International (*US*)
Offbeat Management (*UK*)
Purple Rhino Music (*US*)
Revolt Artist Management (*UK*)
Salvation Records (*UK*)

Glam
Purple Rhino Music (*US*)
Semaphore Mgmt & Consulting (*US*)

Gospel
Blind Ambition Management, Ltd (*US*)
Celebrity Talent Agency Inc. (*US*)
Concerted Efforts (*US*)
Enlight Entertainment, Inc. (*US*)
Fat City Artists (*US*)
Fresh Flava Entertainment (*US*)
IMG Artists (*US*)
MBK Entertainment (*US*)
Music World Entertainment (*US*)
Nashville Records, LLC (*US*)
Pyramid Entertainment Group (*US*)
Red Entertainment Agency (*US*)
Silverword Music Group (*UK*)
Spot Light Entertainment, Inc. (*US*)
Vector Management (*US*)
Westwood Music Group (*US*)

Gothic
Bitchin' Entertainment (*US*)
Holier than Thou (HTT) Music (*UK*)
Music Gallery International (*US*)
Purple Rhino Music (*US*)

Grime
Lucky House Management (*UK*)
Purple Rhino Music (*US*)

Grind
Purple Rhino Music (*US*)

Guitar based
Offbeat Management (*UK*)
Opre Roma (*UK*)
Pillar Artists (*UK*)
Purple Rhino Music (*US*)
Reaction Management (*UK*)
Reckless Yes (*UK*)
Revolt Artist Management (*UK*)
Stormcraft Music (*UK*)
TAC Music Management (*US*)
Youthquake (*UK*)

Hard
Music Gallery International (*US*)
Offbeat Management (*UK*)
Outrider Music, LLC (*US*)
Prodigal Son Entertainment (*US*)
Purple Rhino Music (*US*)
Semaphore Mgmt & Consulting (*US*)
TAC Music Management (*US*)

Hardcore
Down For Life (*UK*)
Hardin Entertainment (*US*)
Music Gallery International (*US*)
Outrider Music, LLC (*US*)
Position Music (*US*)
Purple Rhino Music (*US*)
Red Light Management (RLM) (*US*)
Revolt Artist Management (*UK*)

Access more listings online at www.musicsocket.com

Managers Index 199

Singerman Entertainment (*US*)
Talk's Cheap Management (*Can*)
Tone Management (*UK*)
Toonteen Industries: Management & Promotions (*UK*)
Heavy
Lokation (*UK*)
Music Gallery International (*US*)
Offbeat Management (*UK*)
Outrider Music, LLC (*US*)
Purple Rhino Music (*US*)
Semaphore Mgmt & Consulting (*US*)
Singerman Entertainment (*US*)
TAC Music Management (*US*)
Toonteen Industries: Management & Promotions (*UK*)
Hip-Hop
Aguia Music (*UK*)
Allure Media Entertainment Group (*US*)
Bitchin' Entertainment (*US*)
The Brokaw Company (*US*)
Celebrity Talent Agency Inc. (*US*)
Coalition Music (*Can*)
DAS Communications Ltd (*US*)
Def Ro Inc. (*US*)
Finger Lickin' Management (*UK*)
First Access Entertainment (*US*)
Fresh Flava Entertainment (*US*)
Green Productions Ltd (*UK*)
HardKnockLife Entertainment (*US*)
Hello! Booking, Inc. (*US*)
Lippman Entertainment (*US*)
Loggins Promotion (*US*)
The Lost Atlantis Records (*UK*)
Lucky House Management (*UK*)
Lupo Entertainment (*US*)
Magus Entertainment Inc. (*US*)
Mauldin Brand Agency (*US*)
MBK Entertainment (*US*)
Nettwerk Management (*US*)
Nettwerk Management (*Can*)
Nexus Artist Management (*US*)
NSB Artist Management (*UK*)
OnDaBeat Talent Management (*UK*)
Position Music (*US*)
Purple Rhino Music (*US*)
Pyramid Entertainment Group (*US*)
Red Entertainment Agency (*US*)
Red Light Management (RLM) (*US*)
Rhythmic Records Management and Production (*UK*)
Spectrum Talent Agency (*US*)
Spot Light Entertainment, Inc. (*US*)
Steven Scharf Entertainment (SSE) (*US*)
Trunk Bass Entertainment (*US*)

Union Entertainment Group (*US*)
Val's Artist Management (VAM) (*US*)
Waxploitation (*US*)
Wright Entertainment Group (WEG) (*US*)
Horror
Purple Rhino Music (*US*)
House
Bitchin' Entertainment (*US*)
Crossfire (*UK*)
F&G Management (*UK*)
House of Us (*UK*)
Involved Management (*UK*)
The Lost Atlantis Records (*UK*)
M24 Management (*UK*)
Nexus Artist Management (*US*)
OnDaBeat Talent Management (*UK*)
Perfect Havoc Ltd (*UK*)
Rhythmic Records Management and Production (*UK*)
Spectrum Talent Agency (*US*)
Viral Music (*UK*)
The Weird and the Wonderful (*UK*)
House
Bitchin' Entertainment (*US*)
Crossfire (*UK*)
F&G Management (*UK*)
House of Us (*UK*)
Involved Management (*UK*)
The Lost Atlantis Records (*UK*)
M24 Management (*UK*)
Nexus Artist Management (*US*)
OnDaBeat Talent Management (*UK*)
Perfect Havoc Ltd (*UK*)
Rhythmic Records Management and Production (*UK*)
Spectrum Talent Agency (*US*)
Viral Music (*UK*)
The Weird and the Wonderful (*UK*)
Indie
ADSRecords (*UK*)
Advanced Alternative Media (AAM) (*US*)
Apex Talent Group (*US*)
Bad Apple Music Group (*UK*)
Bear Music Management (*UK*)
Big Dipper Productions Ltd (*UK*)
Big Hassle Management (*US*)
Bold Management (*UK*)
Brighthelmstone Promotions (*UK*)
Brilliant Corners Artist Management (*US*)
CEC Management (*US*)
Coalition Music (*Can*)
Crown Talent & Media Group (*UK*)
dandomanagement (*UK*)
Dawson Breed Music (*UK*)
Domo Music Group Management (*US*)

Claim your free access to www.musicsocket.com: *See p.211*

Managers Index

Don't Try (*UK*)
Dreamboat Management (*UK*)
East City (*UK*)
Equator Music (*UK*)
Feed Your Head (*UK*)
Fire Tower Entertainment (*US*)
Freedom Management (*UK*)
From the Whitehouse (*UK*)
Fruition Music (*UK*)
Gold Mountain Entertainment (*US*)
Golden Arm (*UK*)
Goo Music Management Ltd (*UK*)
Hand in Hive Independent Records & Management (*UK*)
Hardin Entertainment (*US*)
Heist or Hit (*UK*)
Hello! Booking, Inc. (*US*)
Hornblow Group USA, Inc. (*US*)
House of Us (*UK*)
Humans & Other Animals (*UK*)
Ignition Management (*UK*)
Impact Artist Management (*US*)
In De Goot Entertainment (*US*)
Jude Street Management (*UK*)
Lazy Daze (*UK*)
Listen to This Management (*UK*)
Lonewolf Talent Management (*UK*)
LSH Management (*UK*)
Lucky Number Music Limited (*UK*)
Lyricom (*UK*)
Macklam Feldman Management (*Can*)
Magus Entertainment Inc. (*US*)
Maine Road Management (*US*)
Max Bernard Management (*US*)
Media Five Entertainment (*US*)
Memphia Music Management (*UK*)
Mike's Artist Management (*US*)
Miller Music Management (*UK*)
Monqui Presents (*US*)
Morningstar (*UK*)
Nettwerk Management (*US*)
Nettwerk Management (*Can*)
New Champion Management (*UK*)
NSI Management (*US*)
Off the Chart Promotions (*UK*)
Opre Roma (*UK*)
Orean Music Ltd (*UK*)
Outrider Music, LLC (*US*)
Pillar Artists (*UK*)
Purple Rhino Music (*US*)
Reaction Management (*UK*)
Rebel Rebel Artists (*UK*)
Reckless Yes (*UK*)
Red Light Management (RLM) (*US*)
Revolt Artist Management (*UK*)
Russell Carter Artist Management (*US*)
SAS Entertainment (*UK*)
Silva Artist Management (SAM) (*US*)
Steven Scharf Entertainment (SSE) (*US*)
Stiefel Entertainment (*US*)
Street Smart Management (*US*)
Sugar House Music (*UK*)
TAC Music Management (*US*)
Thirty Tigers (*US*)
This Is Music Ltd (*UK*)
Toonteen Industries: Management & Promotions (*UK*)
Tractor Beam Managing & Consulting (*US*)
Trak Image Music Ltd (*UK*)
Travelled Music (*UK*)
Val's Artist Management (VAM) (*US*)
Waxploitation (*US*)
Wildlife Entertainment Ltd (*UK*)
Industrial
Music Gallery International (*US*)
Purple Rhino Music (*US*)
Semaphore Mgmt & Consulting (*US*)
Instrumental
Bitchin' Entertainment (*US*)
Collin Artists (*US*)
Offbeat Management (*UK*)
Outrider Music, LLC (*US*)
Prodigal Son Entertainment (*US*)
Purple Rhino Music (*US*)
Westwood Music Group (*US*)
Jazz
Act 1 Entertainment (*US*)
American International Artists, Inc. (*US*)
AprilSeven Music (*UK*)
B.H. Hopper Management Ltd. (*UK*)
BBA Management & Booking (*US*)
Big Bear Music (*UK*)
Big Beat Productions, Inc. (*US*)
Bitchin' Entertainment (*US*)
Black Dot Management (*US*)
Booking Entertainment (*US*)
Burgess World Co. (*US*)
Cantaloupe Music Productions, Inc. (*US*)
CEC Management (*US*)
Celebrity Talent Agency Inc. (*US*)
Chaney Gig Affairs (CGA) (*US*)
Chapman & Co. Management (*US*)
Coalition Music (*Can*)
Collin Artists (*US*)
Concerted Efforts (*US*)
Dawn Elder Management (*US*)
DDB Productions (*US*)
DFJ Artists (*UK*)
Emcee Artist Management (*US*)

Managers Index

Entourage Talent Associates, Ltd (*US*)
Fat City Artists (*US*)
Fresh Flava Entertainment (*US*)
Harmony Artists (*US*)
Hello! Booking, Inc. (*US*)
IMG Artists (*US*)
Impact Artist Management (*US*)
Ina Dittke & Associates (*US*)
The Kurland Agency (*US*)
Loggins Promotion (*US*)
LSH Management (*UK*)
Macklam Feldman Management (*Can*)
Maine Road Management (*US*)
The Major Group (*US*)
The Management Ark, Inc. (*US*)
Mars Jazz Booking (*US*)
Mascioli Entertainment (*US*)
Max Bernard Management (*US*)
MM Music Agency (*US*)
Music + Art Management (*US*)
Myriad Artists (*US*)
Opus 3 Artists (*US*)
PRA [Patrick Rains & Associates] (*US*)
Purple Rhino Music (*US*)
Pyramid Entertainment Group (*US*)
Red Entertainment Agency (*US*)
RPM Music Productions (*US*)
Russell Carter Artist Management (*US*)
Serious (*UK*)
Silverword Music Group (*UK*)
Sterling Artist Management (*US*)
Steven Scharf Entertainment (SSE) (*US*)
TAC Music Management (*US*)
Tractor Beam Managing & Consulting (*US*)
Val's Artist Management (VAM) (*US*)
Variety Artists International (*US*)
Virtually Pop (*UK*)
Westwood Music Group (*US*)
Young Guns (*UK*)

Kraut
Semaphore Mgmt & Consulting (*US*)

Latin
BBA Management & Booking (*US*)
Cantaloupe Music Productions, Inc. (*US*)
Celebrity Talent Agency Inc. (*US*)
Collin Artists (*US*)
Hardin Entertainment (*US*)
Harmony Artists (*US*)
IMG Artists (*US*)
Impact Artist Management (*US*)
Ina Dittke & Associates (*US*)
Magus Entertainment Inc. (*US*)
Nettwerk Management (*US*)
Nettwerk Management (*Can*)

Once 11 Entertainment (*US*)
Red Entertainment Agency (*US*)
Red Light Management (RLM) (*US*)
Universal Tone Management (*US*)
Val's Artist Management (VAM) (*US*)
Westwood Music Group (*US*)

Leftfield
Semaphore Mgmt & Consulting (*US*)

Mainstream
Max Bernard Management (*US*)
Music Gallery International (*US*)
Purple Rhino Music (*US*)

Melodic
Aspire Music Management (*UK*)
Holier than Thou (HTT) Music (*UK*)
Outrider Music, LLC (*US*)
Purple Rhino Music (*US*)

Melodicore
Purple Rhino Music (*US*)

Metal
Artist Representation and Management (ARM) Entertainment (*US*)
Bitchin' Entertainment (*US*)
Ciulla Management, Inc. (*US*)
Creative International Artist Management (*UK*)
Down For Life (*UK*)
Enso Music Management (*UK*)
5B Artist Management (*US*)
Holier than Thou (HTT) Music (*UK*)
In De Goot Entertainment (*US*)
Incendia Music (*UK*)
Lokation (*UK*)
McGhee Entertainment (*US*)
Metal Music Bookings (*UK*)
Music Gallery International (*US*)
Northern Music Co. Ltd (*UK*)
Offbeat Management (*UK*)
Outrider Music, LLC (*US*)
Position Music (*US*)
Purple Rhino Music (*US*)
Q Prime Management, Inc. (*US*)
Raw Power Management (*UK*)
Reaction Management (*UK*)
Red Light Management (RLM) (*US*)
Revolt Artist Management (*UK*)
Saviour Management (*UK*)
Silva Artist Management (SAM) (*US*)
Singerman Entertainment (*US*)
Steven Scharf Entertainment (SSE) (*US*)
Street Smart Management (*US*)
TAC Music Management (*US*)
Talk's Cheap Management (*Can*)
Tone Management (*UK*)

Toonteen Industries: Management & Promotions (*UK*)
Transcend Music Ltd (*UK*)
Vector Management (*US*)

Modern
Purple Rhino Music (*US*)

New Age
Domo Music Group Management (*US*)
Tuscan Sun Music (*US*)

New Wave
Purple Rhino Music (*US*)
Semaphore Mgmt & Consulting (*US*)
Sugar House Music (*UK*)

Noise Core
Purple Rhino Music (*US*)

Non-Commercial
Semaphore Mgmt & Consulting (*US*)

Nostalgia
Purple Rhino Music (*US*)
Revolt Artist Management (*UK*)

Pop
2-Tone Entertainment (2TE) (*UK*)
ADSRecords (*UK*)
Advanced Alternative Media (AAM) (*US*)
AJM (*UK*)
Allure Media Entertainment Group (*US*)
American Artists Entertainment Group (*US*)
Apex Talent Group (*US*)
Arlon Music (*UK*)
Aspire Music Management (*UK*)
AuthorityMGMT (*UK*)
Bandzmedia (*UK*)
Bear Music Management (*UK*)
Big Dipper Productions Ltd (*UK*)
Big Hassle Management (*US*)
Bitchin' Entertainment (*US*)
Bold Management (*UK*)
Booking Entertainment (*US*)
Brick Wall Management (*US*)
The Brokaw Company (*US*)
Bulletproof Artist Management (*US*)
BUT! Management (*UK*)
Career Artist Management (CAM) (*US*)
Case Entertainment Group Inc. (*US*)
CEC Management (*US*)
Coalition Music (*Can*)
Consolidated Artists (*UK*)
Create Management (*UK*)
Creative International Artist Management (*UK*)
Crossfire (*UK*)
Crown Talent & Media Group (*UK*)
D. Bailey Management, Inc. (*US*)
DAS Communications Ltd (*US*)

David Belenzon Management, Inc. (*US*)
Dawn Elder Management (*US*)
Dawson Breed Music (*UK*)
DCA Productions (*US*)
Deep South Artist Management (*US*)
Def Ro Inc. (*US*)
Direct Management Group (DMG) (*US*)
Domo Music Group Management (*US*)
Entourage Talent Associates, Ltd (*US*)
Equator Music (*UK*)
Fat City Artists (*US*)
Feeling Productions, Inc. (*Can*)
Fire Tower Entertainment (*US*)
First Access Entertainment (*US*)
Flat50 (*UK*)
Fleming Artists (*US*)
Freedom Management (*UK*)
Front Room Songs (*UK*)
Future Songs (*UK*)
Gold Mountain Entertainment (*US*)
Golden Arm (*UK*)
Good Guy Entertainment (*US*)
Guvnor Management (*UK*)
Hand in Hive Independent Records & Management (*UK*)
Handshake Ltd. (*UK*)
Hardin Entertainment (*US*)
HardKnockLife Entertainment (*US*)
Hello! Booking, Inc. (*US*)
Hornblow Group USA, Inc. (*US*)
Hot Gem (*UK*)
House of Us (*UK*)
Ignition Management (*UK*)
IMC Entertainment Group (*US*)
In De Goot Entertainment (*US*)
Insomnia Music UK (*UK*)
Intertalent Rights Group (*UK*)
Intrigue Music (*US*)
JBLS Management (*UK*)
Jude Street Management (*UK*)
KMY (Keep Me Young) (*UK*)
La Rock Entertainment (*UK*)
Lippman Entertainment (*US*)
Loggins Promotion (*US*)
LSH Management (*UK*)
Lucky Number Music Limited (*UK*)
Lupo Entertainment (*US*)
Macklam Feldman Management (*Can*)
Magus Entertainment Inc. (*US*)
Major Bob Music, Inc. (*US*)
The Major Group (*US*)
Mauldin Brand Agency (*US*)
MBK Entertainment (*US*)
Michael Anthony's Electric Events (*US*)

Managers Index

Michael Hausman Artist Management Inc. (*US*)
Mike's Artist Management (*US*)
Modest! Management (*UK*)
Moksha Entertainment and Music Management (US) (*US*)
Monqui Presents (*US*)
Music Media Events (*UK*)
Music World Entertainment (*US*)
N.O.W. Music Management (*UK*)
Nashville Records, LLC (*US*)
Nettwerk Management (*US*)
Nettwerk Management (*Can*)
New Champion Management (*UK*)
Off the Chart Promotions (*UK*)
Orean Music Ltd (*UK*)
Outrider Music, LLC (*US*)
Paradise Artists (*US*)
Patriot Management (*US*)
Pierce Entertainment (*UK*)
Plus Music (*UK*)
Position Music (*US*)
PRA [Patrick Rains & Associates] (*US*)
Progressive Global Agency (PGA) (*US*)
Purple Rhino Music (*US*)
Q Prime Management, Inc. (*US*)
Rainmaker Artists (*US*)
Reaction Management (*UK*)
Rebel Rebel Artists (*UK*)
Red Entertainment Agency (*US*)
Red Grape Music (*UK*)
Red Light Management (RLM) (*US*)
Revolt Artist Management (*UK*)
Rhythmic Records Management and Production (*UK*)
Richard Lipman (*UK*)
Rock Artist Management (RAM) (*UK*)
Ron Rainey Management Inc. (*US*)
RPM Music Productions (*US*)
Russell Carter Artist Management (*US*)
Saga Entertainment (*UK*)
SAS Entertainment (*UK*)
Saviour Management (*UK*)
SGM Music Group Ltd (*UK*)
Shaw Thing Management (*UK*)
Silva Artist Management (SAM) (*US*)
Silverword Music Group (*UK*)
Sound Management, Inc. (*US*)
Sounds Like A Hit Ltd (*UK*)
Spectrum Talent Agency (*US*)
Spot Light Entertainment, Inc. (*US*)
Starkravin' Management (*US*)
Steven Scharf Entertainment (SSE) (*US*)
Stiefel Entertainment (*US*)
Stormcraft Music (*UK*)
Street Smart Management (*US*)
Sugar House Music (*UK*)
This Day And Age Management (*US*)
This Is Music Ltd (*UK*)
Tone Management (*UK*)
Toonteen Industries: Management & Promotions (*UK*)
Tractor Beam Managing & Consulting (*US*)
Trunk Bass Entertainment (*US*)
Tuscan Sun Music (*US*)
Union Entertainment Group (*US*)
Universal Tone Management (*US*)
Up On Mars (*UK*)
Upside Management Ltd (*UK*)
Val's Artist Management (VAM) (*US*)
Variety Artists International (*US*)
Vector Management (*US*)
Virtually Pop (*UK*)
Westwood Music Group (*US*)
Worldsound, LLC (*US*)
Wright Entertainment Group (WEG) (*US*)
YMU Group (*UK*)
Young Guns (*UK*)
Zero Myth (*UK*)

Post
Freaks R Us (*UK*)
Ganbei Records (*UK*)
Lonewolf Talent Management (*UK*)
Outrider Music, LLC (*US*)
Purple Rhino Music (*US*)
Semaphore Mgmt & Consulting (*US*)
Tone Management (*UK*)

Power
Music Gallery International (*US*)
Offbeat Management (*UK*)
Purple Rhino Music (*US*)

Progressive
Holier than Thou (HTT) Music (*UK*)
Incendia Music (*UK*)
Involved Management (*UK*)
Nexus Artist Management (*US*)
Offbeat Management (*UK*)
Outrider Music, LLC (*US*)
Purple Rhino Music (*US*)
Toonteen Industries: Management & Promotions (*UK*)

Psychebilly
Purple Rhino Music (*US*)

Psychedelic
Elephant Management (*UK*)
Ganbei Records (*UK*)
Moksha Entertainment and Music Management (US) (*US*)
Offbeat Management (*UK*)

Managers Index

Salvation Records (*UK*)
Semaphore Mgmt & Consulting (*US*)
Punk
  Bitchin' Entertainment (*US*)
  Coalition Music (*Can*)
  Dissention Records + Artist Management (*UK*)
  Freaks R Us (*UK*)
  Ganbei Records (*UK*)
  Gold Mountain Entertainment (*US*)
  Lonewolf Talent Management (*UK*)
  Magus Entertainment Inc. (*US*)
  Media Five Entertainment (*US*)
  Moksha Entertainment and Music Management (US) (*US*)
  Music Gallery International (*US*)
  Nettwerk Management (*US*)
  Nettwerk Management (*Can*)
  New Champion Management (*UK*)
  Outrider Music, LLC (*US*)
  Purple Rhino Music (*US*)
  Raw Power Management (*UK*)
  Reaction Management (*UK*)
  Revolt Artist Management (*UK*)
  Salvation Records (*UK*)
  Saviour Management (*UK*)
  Silva Artist Management (SAM) (*US*)
  Talk's Cheap Management (*Can*)
  Tone Management (*UK*)
  Toonteen Industries: Management & Promotions (*UK*)
  Tractor Beam Managing & Consulting (*US*)
  Val's Artist Management (VAM) (*US*)
Ragga
  Purple Rhino Music (*US*)
RampB
  Act 1 Entertainment (*US*)
  Aguia Music (*UK*)
  Allure Media Entertainment Group (*US*)
  American Artists Entertainment Group (*US*)
  Bandzmedia (*UK*)
  Big Beat Productions, Inc. (*US*)
  Bitchin' Entertainment (*US*)
  Black Dot Management (*US*)
  Booking Entertainment (*US*)
  Case Entertainment Group Inc. (*US*)
  Celebrity Talent Agency Inc. (*US*)
  Chaney Gig Affairs (CGA) (*US*)
  Coalition Music (*Can*)
  Collin Artists (*US*)
  D. Bailey Management, Inc. (*US*)
  David Belenzon Management, Inc. (*US*)
  Def Ro Inc. (*US*)

Defenders Ent (*UK*)
Enlight Entertainment, Inc. (*US*)
Fat City Artists (*US*)
First Access Entertainment (*US*)
Fresh Flava Entertainment (*US*)
Future Songs (*UK*)
Green Productions Ltd (*UK*)
HardKnockLife Entertainment (*US*)
IMC Entertainment Group (*US*)
Impact Artist Management (*US*)
Lippman Entertainment (*US*)
Loggins Promotion (*US*)
Lokation (*UK*)
Lupo Entertainment (*US*)
Magus Entertainment Inc. (*US*)
Major Bob Music, Inc. (*US*)
The Major Group (*US*)
Mascioli Entertainment (*US*)
Mauldin Brand Agency (*US*)
Max Bernard Management (*US*)
MBK Entertainment (*US*)
Music World Entertainment (*US*)
Offbeat Management (*UK*)
Patriot Management (*US*)
Pierce Entertainment (*UK*)
Plus Music (*UK*)
Position Music (*US*)
Purple Rhino Music (*US*)
Pyramid Entertainment Group (*US*)
Red Entertainment Agency (*US*)
Silverword Music Group (*UK*)
Spectrum Talent Agency (*US*)
Spot Light Entertainment, Inc. (*US*)
Starkravin' Management (*US*)
TAC Music Management (*US*)
This Day And Age Management (*US*)
True Talent Entertainment (*US*)
Trunk Bass Entertainment (*US*)
Val's Artist Management (VAM) (*US*)
Westwood Music Group (*US*)
Wildlife Entertainment Ltd (*UK*)
Wright Entertainment Group (WEG) (*US*)
Rap
  Aguia Music (*UK*)
  Bitchin' Entertainment (*US*)
  Case Entertainment Group Inc. (*US*)
  Coalition Music (*Can*)
  Defenders Ent (*UK*)
  Enlight Entertainment, Inc. (*US*)
  First Access Entertainment (*US*)
  Flat50 (*UK*)
  HardKnockLife Entertainment (*US*)
  Lippman Entertainment (*US*)
  Loggins Promotion (*US*)
  The Lost Atlantis Records (*UK*)

Access more listings online at www.musicsocket.com

Managers Index

Lucky House Management (*UK*)
Magus Entertainment Inc. (*US*)
The Major Group (*US*)
Mauldin Brand Agency (*US*)
MBK Entertainment (*US*)
Nettwerk Management (*US*)
Nettwerk Management (*Can*)
OnDaBeat Talent Management (*UK*)
Position Music (*US*)
Purple Rhino Music (*US*)
Red Light Management (RLM) (*US*)
Spot Light Entertainment, Inc. (*US*)
Steven Scharf Entertainment (SSE) (*US*)
This Day And Age Management (*US*)
Union Entertainment Group (*US*)
Val's Artist Management (VAM) (*US*)
Variety Artists International (*US*)
Waxploitation (*US*)
Wright Entertainment Group (WEG) (*US*)

Reggae
Act 1 Entertainment (*US*)
Celebrity Talent Agency Inc. (*US*)
Defenders Ent (*UK*)
Fat City Artists (*US*)
Gold Mountain Entertainment (*US*)
MBK Entertainment (*US*)
Nexus Artist Management (*US*)
Purple Rhino Music (*US*)
Waxploitation (*US*)

Reggaeton
Purple Rhino Music (*US*)

Regional
Big Beat Productions, Inc. (*US*)
Brilliant Productions (*US*)
Cantaloupe Music Productions, Inc. (*US*)
MM Music Agency (*US*)
TAC Music Management (*US*)

Rhythm and Blues
Offbeat Management (*UK*)
Purple Rhino Music (*US*)
TAC Music Management (*US*)

Rock and Roll
Fat City Artists (*US*)
Handshake Ltd. (*UK*)
Lazy Daze (*UK*)
Paradise Artists (*US*)
Purple Rhino Music (*US*)
Revolt Artist Management (*UK*)
Singerman Entertainment (*US*)
TAC Music Management (*US*)
Worldsound, LLC (*US*)

Rock
21st Century Artists, Inc. (*US*)
Act 1 Entertainment (*US*)
Advanced Alternative Media (AAM) (*US*)

Allure Media Entertainment Group (*US*)
American Artists Entertainment Group (*US*)
Apex Talent Group (*US*)
Arslanian & Associates, Inc. (*US*)
Artist Representation and Management (ARM) Entertainment (*US*)
Aspire Music Management (*UK*)
Bad Apple Music Group (*UK*)
Bandzmedia (*UK*)
BBA Management & Booking (*US*)
Bear Music Management (*UK*)
Big Beat Productions, Inc. (*US*)
Big Dipper Productions Ltd (*UK*)
Big Hassle Management (*US*)
Bitchin' Entertainment (*US*)
Bold Management (*UK*)
Booking Entertainment (*US*)
Brick Wall Management (*US*)
Brilliant Corners Artist Management (*US*)
The Brokaw Company (*US*)
Bulletproof Artist Management (*US*)
Burgess World Co. (*US*)
BUT! Management (*UK*)
Career Artist Management (CAM) (*US*)
Case Entertainment Group Inc. (*US*)
CEC Management (*US*)
Chaos & Bedlam Management (*UK*)
Ciulla Management, Inc. (*US*)
Coalition Music (*Can*)
Concerted Efforts (*US*)
Consolidated Artists (*UK*)
Creative International Artist Management (*UK*)
D. Bailey Management, Inc. (*US*)
dandomanagement (*UK*)
DAS Communications Ltd (*US*)
Dave Kaplan Management (*US*)
David Belenzon Management, Inc. (*US*)
Dawn Elder Management (*US*)
DCA Productions (*US*)
Deep South Artist Management (*US*)
Domo Music Group Management (*US*)
Don't Try (*UK*)
Down For Life (*UK*)
Elephant Management (*UK*)
Emcee Artist Management (*US*)
Entertainment Services International (*US*)
Entourage Talent Associates, Ltd (*US*)
Epic Venom (*UK*)
Equator Music (*UK*)
5B Artist Management (*US*)
Flat50 (*UK*)
Fleming Artists (*US*)
Fresh Flava Entertainment (*US*)

Claim your free access to www.musicsocket.com: See p.211

Managers Index

Ganbei Records (UK)
Gold Mountain Entertainment (US)
Golden Arm (UK)
Goo Music Management Ltd (UK)
Guvnor Management (UK)
Hand in Hive Independent Records & Management (UK)
Hard Head Management (US)
Hardin Entertainment (US)
Hello! Booking, Inc. (US)
Holier than Thou (HTT) Music (UK)
Hornblow Group USA, Inc. (US)
Humans & Other Animals (UK)
Ignition Management (UK)
Impact Artist Management (US)
In De Goot Entertainment (US)
Incendia Music (UK)
Intrigue Music (US)
Kuper Personal Management (US)
Lazy Daze (UK)
Lippman Entertainment (US)
Listen to This Management (UK)
Loggins Promotion (US)
Lonewolf Talent Management (UK)
Lupo Entertainment (US)
Macklam Feldman Management (Can)
Magus Entertainment Inc. (US)
Maine Road Management (US)
The Major Group (US)
Mascioli Entertainment (US)
McDonough Management LLC (US)
McGhee Entertainment (US)
Media Five Entertainment (US)
Memphia Music Management (UK)
Metal Music Bookings (UK)
Michael Anthony's Electric Events (US)
Michael Hausman Artist Management Inc. (US)
Mike's Artist Management (US)
Miller Music Management (UK)
MOB Agency (US)
Moksha Entertainment and Music Management (US) (US)
Moneypenny (UK)
Monqui Presents (US)
Morningstar (UK)
Music + Art Management (US)
Music Gallery International (US)
N.O.W. Music Management (UK)
Nettwerk Management (US)
Nettwerk Management (Can)
Nice Management (US)
Northern Music Co. Ltd (UK)
NSI Management (US)
Off the Chart Promotions (UK)

Offbeat Management (UK)
Outrider Music, LLC (US)
Paradise Artists (US)
Park Promotions (UK)
Pathfinder Management (US)
Patriot Management (US)
Position Music (US)
PRA [Patrick Rains & Associates] (US)
Prodigal Son Entertainment (US)
Progressive Global Agency (PGA) (US)
Purple Rhino Music (US)
Q Management (US)
Q Prime Management, Inc. (US)
Rainmaker Artists (US)
Raven Black Music (UK)
Raw Power Management (UK)
Reaction Management (UK)
Red Entertainment Agency (US)
Red Light Management (RLM) (US)
Revolt Artist Management (UK)
Richard Lipman (UK)
Rock Artist Management (RAM) (UK)
Rock People Management (RPM) (UK)
Ron Rainey Management Inc. (US)
Rosier Artist Management (RAM) (UK)
Russell Carter Artist Management (US)
Saga Entertainment (UK)
Salvation Records (UK)
SAS Entertainment (UK)
SGM Music Group Ltd (UK)
Silva Artist Management (SAM) (US)
Silverword Music Group (UK)
Singerman Entertainment (US)
Sound Management, Inc. (US)
Starkravin' Management (US)
Steven Scharf Entertainment (SSE) (US)
Stiefel Entertainment (US)
Street Smart Management (US)
Sugar House Music (UK)
Suncoast Music Management (US)
TAC Music Management (US)
Talk's Cheap Management (Can)
Thirty Tigers (US)
Tone Management (UK)
Toonteen Industries: Management & Promotions (UK)
Tractor Beam Managing & Consulting (US)
Transcend Music Ltd (UK)
Travelled Music (UK)
Union Entertainment Group (US)
Universal Tone Management (US)
Val's Artist Management (VAM) (US)
Variety Artists International (US)
Vector Management (US)

Access more listings online at www.musicsocket.com

Virtually Pop (UK)
Waxploitation (US)
Westwood Music Group (US)
Wildlife Entertainment Ltd (UK)
Worldsound, LLC (US)
Wright Entertainment Group (WEG) (US)
YMU Group (UK)
Zero Myth (UK)
Rockabilly
　Act 1 Entertainment (US)
　Fat City Artists (US)
　Hello! Booking, Inc. (US)
　Purple Rhino Music (US)
　TAC Music Management (US)
Roots
　21st Century Artists, Inc. (US)
　Act 1 Entertainment (US)
　Blind Ambition Management, Ltd (US)
　Brilliant Productions (US)
　Dawn Elder Management (US)
　Delta Groove Music, Inc. (US)
　Fleming Artists (US)
　Front Room Songs (UK)
　Grassy Hill Entertainment (US)
　Hardin Entertainment (US)
　Impact Artist Management (US)
　Jelli Records (UK)
　Kari Estrin Management & Consulting (US)
　Kuper Personal Management (US)
　Park Promotions (UK)
　Purple Rhino Music (US)
　Steven Scharf Entertainment (SSE) (US)
　TAC Music Management (US)
　Talk's Cheap Management (Can)
　Tractor Beam Managing & Consulting (US)
　Val's Artist Management (VAM) (US)
Shoegaze
　Elephant Management (UK)
　Trak Image Music Ltd (UK)
Singer-Songwriter
　ADSRecords (UK)
　Amour:Music (UK)
　Apex Talent Group (US)
　Arlon Music (UK)
　AuthorityMGMT (UK)
　Bitchin' Entertainment (US)
　Blind Ambition Management, Ltd (US)
　Brick Wall Management (US)
　Brilliant Corners Artist Management (US)
　Burgess World Co. (US)
　BUT! Management (UK)
　Coalition Music (Can)
　Concerted Efforts (US)

Create Management (UK)
dandomanagement (UK)
Domo Music Group Management (US)
Entourage Talent Associates, Ltd (US)
Fire Tower Entertainment (US)
From the Whitehouse (UK)
Future Songs (UK)
Gold Mountain Entertainment (US)
Grassy Hill Entertainment (US)
Hardin Entertainment (US)
Hornblow Group USA, Inc. (US)
IMG Artists (US)
Impact Artist Management (US)
JBLS Management (UK)
Lippman Entertainment (US)
Lyricom (UK)
Magus Entertainment Inc. (US)
Max Bernard Management (US)
McGhee Entertainment (US)
Michael Hausman Artist Management Inc. (US)
Miller Music Management (UK)
Nettwerk Management (US)
Nettwerk Management (Can)
NSI Management (US)
Off the Chart Promotions (UK)
Offbeat Management (UK)
Park Promotions (UK)
Position Music (US)
Purple Rhino Music (US)
Q Prime Management, Inc. (US)
Reaction Management (UK)
Red Grape Music (UK)
Red Light Management (RLM) (US)
Revolt Artist Management (UK)
Running Media Group Ltd (US)
Russell Carter Artist Management (US)
Sterling Artist Management (US)
Steven Scharf Entertainment (SSE) (US)
Stiefel Entertainment (US)
Stormcraft Music (UK)
TAC Music Management (US)
Vector Management (US)
Wright Entertainment Group (WEG) (US)
Ska
　Fat City Artists (US)
　Purple Rhino Music (US)
Soul
　Act 1 Entertainment (US)
　AprilSeven Music (UK)
　Bandzmedia (UK)
　Chaney Gig Affairs (CGA) (US)
　Concerted Efforts (US)
　The Lost Atlantis Records (UK)
　Lucky House Management (UK)

Major Bob Music, Inc. (*US*)
Max Bernard Management (*US*)
NSB Artist Management (*UK*)
Plus Music (*UK*)
Silverword Music Group (*UK*)
Soulful
Max Bernard Management (*US*)
Purple Rhino Music (*US*)
TAC Music Management (*US*)
Soundtracks
First Artists Management (*US*)
Kraft-Engel Management (*US*)
Max Bernard Management (*US*)
Purple Rhino Music (*US*)
Soundtrack Music Associates (SMA) (*US*)
Steven Scharf Entertainment (SSE) (*US*)
Spoken Word
Bitchin' Entertainment (*US*)
Purple Rhino Music (*US*)
Surf
Purple Rhino Music (*US*)
Revolt Artist Management (*UK*)
Swing
Act 1 Entertainment (*US*)
Big Bear Music (*UK*)
Cantaloupe Music Productions, Inc. (*US*)
Collin Artists (*US*)
Fat City Artists (*US*)
Harmony Artists (*US*)
Mascioli Entertainment (*US*)
Purple Rhino Music (*US*)
Synthpop
Purple Rhino Music (*US*)
Techno
Bitchin' Entertainment (*US*)
F&G Management (*UK*)
The Lost Atlantis Records (*UK*)
The Major Group (*US*)
Nexus Artist Management (*US*)
OnDaBeat Talent Management (*UK*)
Purple Rhino Music (*US*)
The Weird and the Wonderful (*UK*)
Thrash
Holier than Thou (HTT) Music (*UK*)
Offbeat Management (*UK*)
Purple Rhino Music (*US*)
Semaphore Mgmt & Consulting (*US*)
Singerman Entertainment (*US*)
Traditional
Dawn Elder Management (*US*)
Riot Artists (*US*)
TAC Music Management (*US*)
Trance
Bitchin' Entertainment (*US*)
Involved Management (*UK*)

Tribal
Purple Rhino Music (*US*)
Trip Hop
Purple Rhino Music (*US*)
Twisted
Purple Rhino Music (*US*)
Underground
In De Goot Entertainment (*US*)
Purple Rhino Music (*US*)
Semaphore Mgmt & Consulting (*US*)
This Is Music Ltd (*UK*)
Urban
2-Tone Entertainment (2TE) (*UK*)
Bitchin' Entertainment (*US*)
Black Dot Management (*US*)
Good Guy Entertainment (*US*)
HQ Familia (*UK*)
La Rock Entertainment (*UK*)
Lippman Entertainment (*US*)
Loggins Promotion (*US*)
Lokation (*UK*)
The Lost Atlantis Records (*UK*)
Lucky House Management (*UK*)
Lyricom (*UK*)
Magus Entertainment Inc. (*US*)
Max Bernard Management (*US*)
MBK Entertainment (*US*)
Music World Entertainment (*US*)
NSB Artist Management (*UK*)
Position Music (*US*)
Purple Rhino Music (*US*)
Pyramid Entertainment Group (*US*)
Red Entertainment Agency (*US*)
Silverword Music Group (*UK*)
Thirty Tigers (*US*)
Val's Artist Management (VAM) (*US*)
The Weird and the Wonderful (*UK*)
World
Bitchin' Entertainment (*US*)
Cantaloupe Music Productions, Inc. (*US*)
Collin Artists (*US*)
Concerted Efforts (*US*)
Dawn Elder Management (*US*)
DDB Productions (*US*)
Domo Music Group Management (*US*)
Fat City Artists (*US*)
From the Whitehouse (*UK*)
Front Room Songs (*UK*)
Gold Mountain Entertainment (*US*)
Hardin Entertainment (*US*)
IMG Artists (*US*)
Impact Artist Management (*US*)
Ina Dittke & Associates (*US*)
Line-Up pmc (*UK*)
Macklam Feldman Management (*Can*)

Managers Index

McGhee Entertainment (*US*)
Music + Art Management (*US*)
Nettwerk Management (*US*)
Once 11 Entertainment (*US*)
Position Music (*US*)
Progressive Global Agency (PGA) (*US*)
Purple Rhino Music (*US*)

Red Light Management (RLM) (*US*)
Richard Lipman (*UK*)
Riot Artists (*US*)
Serious (*UK*)
Steven Scharf Entertainment (SSE) (*US*)
Val's Artist Management (VAM) (*US*)
Worldsound, LLC (*US*)

Get Free Access to the MusicSocket Website

To claim your free access to the **MusicSocket** website simply go to https://www.musicsocket.com/subscribe and begin the subscription process as normal. When you are given the opportunity to enter a voucher / coupon enter the following code:

- MSC-DDK-818

You should then be able to take out a subscription for free, or a longer term subscription at a reduced price.

Please note that this code will only remain valid until the release of the next edition, and is only permitted for use in the creation of one account for the owner of this book.

If you need any assistance please email support@musicsocket.com.

If you have found this book useful, please consider leaving a review on the website where you bought it!

What you get

Once you have set up access to ths site you will be able to benefit from all the following features:

Databases

All our databases are updated almost every day, and include powerful search facilities to help you find exactly what you need. Searches that used to take you hours or even days in print books or on search engines can now be done in seconds, and produce more accurate and up-to-date information. You can try out any of our databases before you subscribe:

- Search **over 1,300 record labels**
- Search **over 500 managers**

PLUS advanced features to help you with your search:

- Save searches and save time – set up to 15 search parameters specific to your work, save them, and then access the search results with a single click whenever you log in. You can even save multiple different searches if you have different types of work you are looking to place.
- Add personal notes to listings, visible only to you and fully searchable – helping you to organise your actions.

- Set reminders on listings to notify you when to submit your work, when to follow up, when to expect a reply, or any other custom action.
- Track which listings you've viewed and when, to help you organise your search – any listings which have changed since you last viewed them will be highlighted for your attention!

Daily email updates

As a subscriber you will be able to take advantage of our email alert service, meaning you can specify your particular interests and we'll send you automatic email updates when we change or add a listing that matches them. So if you're interested in labels dealing in hard rock in the United States you can have us send you emails with the latest updates about them – keeping you up to date without even having to log in.

User feedback

Our databases all include a user feedback feature that allows our subscribers to leave feedback on each listing – giving you not only the chance to have your say about the markets you contact, but giving a unique artist's perspective on the listings.

Save on copyright protection fees

If you're sending your work away to record labels or managers, you should consider first protecting your copyright. As a subscriber to **MusicSocket** you can do this through our site and save 10% on the copyright registration fees normally payable for protecting your work internationally through the Intellectual Property Rights Office.

Terms and conditions

The promotional code contained in this publication may be used by the owner of the book only to create one subscription to MusicSocket at a reduced cost, or for free. It may not be used by or disseminated to third parties. Should the code be misused then the owner of the book will be liable for any costs incurred, including but not limited to payment in full at the standard rate for the subscription in question. The code may be used at any time until the end of the calendar year named in the title of the publication, after which time it will become invalid. The code may be redeemed against the creation of a new account only – it cannot be redeemed against the ongoing costs of keeping a subscription open. In order to create a subscription a method of payment must be provided, but there is no obligation to make any payment. Subscriptions may be cancelled at any time, and if an account is cancelled before any payment becomes due then no payment will be made. Once a subscription has been created, the normal schedule of payments will begin on a monthly, quarterly, or annual basis, unless a life Subscription is selected, or the subscription is cancelled prior to the first payment becoming due. Subscriptions may be cancelled at any time, but if they are left open beyond the date at which the first payment becomes due and is processed then payments will not be refundable.

Printed in Great Britain
by Amazon